Kiwis
Can Fly

Kiwis Can Fly

Flying to Save Lives in Papua New Guinea

A MEMOIR BY
Ted Crawford

Kiwis Can Fly
Published by Ted Crawford
with Castle Publishing Ltd
New Zealand

© 2024 Ted Crawford

ISBN 978-0-473-73219-6 (Softcover)
ISBN 978-0-473-73220-2 (ePUB)
ISBN 978-0-473-73221-9 (Kindle)

Editing:
Andrea Candy

Production & Typesetting:
Andrew Killick
Castle Publishing Services
www.castlepublishing.co.nz

Cover Design:
Paul Smith

All scripture quotations, unless otherwise indicated,
are taken from the Holy Bible, New International Version®, NIV®.
Copyright ©1973, 1978, 1984, 2011 by Biblica, Inc.™
Used by permission of Zondervan.

ALL RIGHTS RESERVED

No part of this publication may be reproduced,
stored in a retrieval system, or transmitted
in any form or by any means, electronic, mechanical,
photocopying, recording or otherwise,
without prior written permission from the publisher.

Front cover: Ted with a DH89 Dominie in Queenstown.
Back cover, clockwise from top left: Ted with an MAF plane at Ardmore;
the Crawford family, 1969; the Crawford family, 2023;
Tom Hoey and Ted with a group of Biamis, PNG.

*This book is dedicated to the few pilots who have lost their lives
while flying in missionary service.*

*It is also dedicated to the thousands of MAF staff,
both national and expatriate,
who have in the past and currently serve as
'A servant of missions, flying for life.'*

Foreword

Do people read the foreword of a book these days? Perhaps sometimes. Most want to get into the main course of the book rather than have a nibble at the entrée.

My dictionary says that the word entrée means 'the act or manner of entering'. Therefore, it is not insignificant for someone else to write an entry commentary that may prepare the reader's mind to see Ted Crawford's amazing life in its unique reality. It may help them see beyond the stories that mark Ted's life as different; to see the reason and purpose of this life, the invisible thread, the power of such a well-lived life.

I haven't asked Ted whether that was his fundamental motivation for writing this book; I haven't needed to. I know my friend. I know his heart. I know he wants to point you to a higher plane, to the God he loves and serves.

In this book I see Ted living out the truth of the words written by a royal monarch centuries ago. They made sense in that day. They also make sense in Ted Crawford's day. In them, King David is speaking to God:

> One generation shall praise thy works to another
> and shall declare thy mighty acts.
> I will speak of the glorious honour of thy majesty
> and of thy wondrous works. (Psalm 145)

'Hang on,' you might say, 'This man was simply a young New

Zealander who took up flying as a career.' Is this book any more than that?

Yes, it is. He was a young follower of Jesus who chose to present his gifts, his very significant ability, all that he had, to God, to be used in a remarkable and special way in building the eternal, mysterious, wonderful kingdom of God.

I knew Ted as a pilot. He was good! Proficient, disciplined, dependable, professional, careful, consistent … and safe! It would require a large book to tell the whole story. Every flight had meaning, and there were thousands of flights. They are all classified as 'God's mighty acts, His wondrous works.' Yes, it was flying, but it was also helping build God's kingdom.

But my memory of those years is not of Ted Crawford as an individual person. It was always Ted and Elsie and Ann and Gwen. The Crawfords! This is their story. From the beginning, as you read, may the eyes of your heart be opened to see how God makes use of all kinds of gifts, even flying an aeroplane.

May you see how the use of somewhat unusual gifts has blessed the needy, but may you also see the deeper value of God at work – using people like Ted and his family to further establish and strengthen God's kingdom. These are ordinary New Zealanders with extraordinary value.

Max Meyers
Melbourne 2024

Contents

Acknowledgements   11

1. Growing Up at Kumeū   13
2. Family and Friends   30
3. High School Days   46
4. Starting Work   54
5. Receiving God's Call   63
6. Mission Aviation Fellowship   68
7. Southern Scenic Air Services   82
8. Flying Various Land Planes   92
9. The Cessna Floatplane   109
10. The Little 'Sally Lassie'   120
11. Ballarat Days   128
12. Heading for PNG   131
13. Operational Flights   146
14. New Experiences   156
15. Next Stop Mt Hagen   168
16. To Wasua on the Fly River   173
17. Moving to Kawito   182
18. Our First Furlough and Second Term   205
19. I Thank God for a Praying Wife   221
20. To Wapenamanda   254
21. Our Second Furlough   284
22. Our Third Term at Mt Hagen   290
23. To the Solomon Islands   315

24.	Back to PNG	327
25.	Returning to New Zealand for an Operation	342
26.	To Wewak for the Second Time	346
27.	Home to New Zealand	356
28.	Into MAF Again	364
29.	Retirement	377

Glossary	381
Comments	386

Acknowledgements

I had never thought of writing an autobiography, but it all started when Gwen, our younger daughter, sent through to me a series of probing questions about my youth and upbringing. As more questions were answered, I realised that there were the makings of a book within them.

As has been the case for the last 57 years Elsie, my wife, has been a constant encourager and, at times, a helpful critic.

Ann, our elder daughter, contributed digital photos.

Max Meyers, my first MAF Chief Pilot, wrote the foreword.

Marilyn Gleadall, who attends the Heart Club that I am a member of, read through the draft and made useful suggestions, as did Willy Fraser and Rod Peek, both of whom are ex-teachers who I knew in Papua New Guinea. The final proofreading was done by fellow church members – also both ex-teachers – Graeme and Lis Rix.

All of this fulfils a challenge given to me by Malcolm Sproull after I preached at a Hunua service some years ago.

And finally, Andrew Killick and the team at Castle Publishing, who with great patience brought everything together to make a book from what I provided them with.

Thank you to everybody.

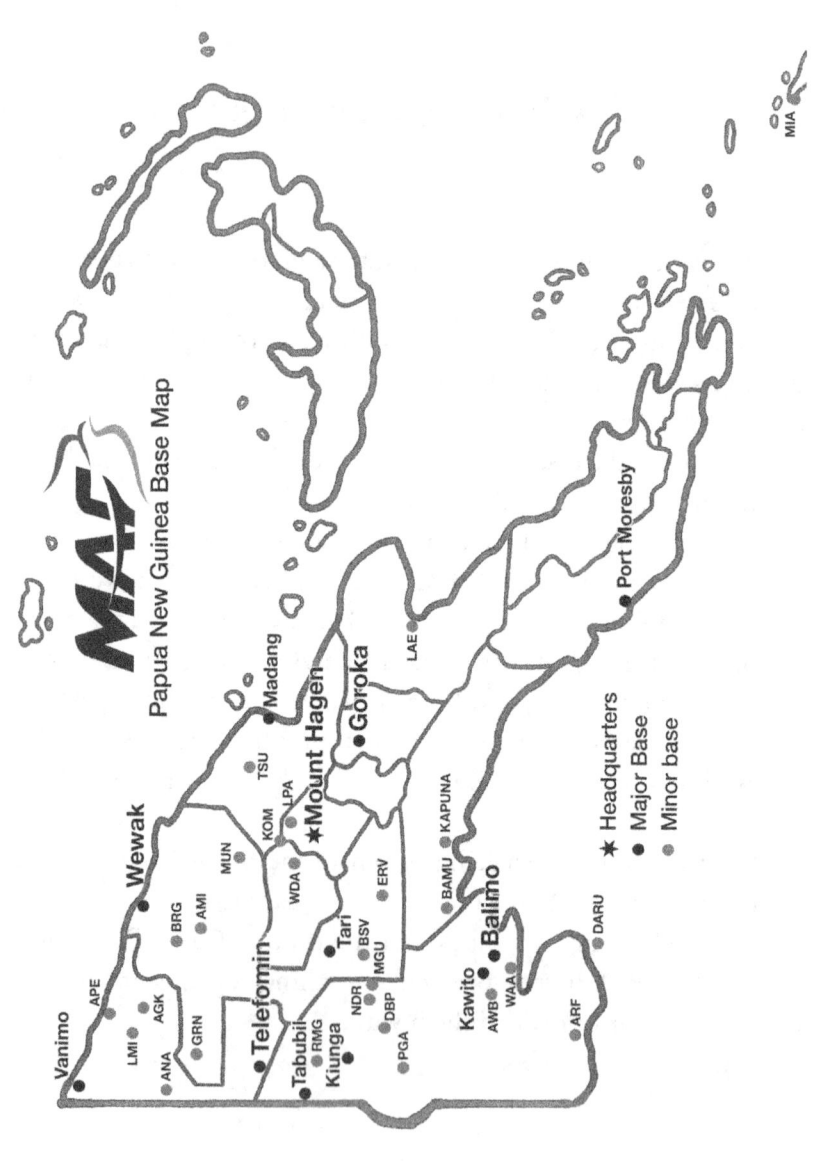

Chapter 1

Growing Up at Kumeū

I can remember it as if it happened just yesterday. It was in the early part of the year, when I was in Standard 6 (Year 4). I had just cycled home on the bike that I had been given as a hand-me-down from my only brother who was four years older than me. I rounded the corner of the large shed that trebled as Dad's workshop, a honey house where we extracted honey from the combs off the more than 60 hives Dad had, and a pumphouse for a deep well bore. There was also an extension to this building where we stored baled hay with just enough room for my bike to go inside the door.

As I rode around the corner, Dad came out of the workshop door and asked a question of me, which I had never given any thought to. 'What do you want to become when you leave school?' Obviously, Dad had been thinking ahead, and planning things out as he worked away at his woodwork bench. My brother was already doing really well academically at Helensville District High School (now Kaipara College) and was destined to become the male dux in his 5th Form (Year 11) year.

I'm not sure now whether it had already been determined that he was going to go to Massey Agricultural College in Palmerston North (as Massey University was then known) to study farming, but I think both of us, having been brought up on a small farm, assumed that we'd become farmers, so my answer to Dad's question was, 'Oh, either a farmer or a preacher.' A *what*? What did I just say? I can remember quite clearly thinking about my answer as I pushed my bike into the hay shed. Where on earth did that latter idea come from? Okay, both of my parents were Christians; my Dad was an elder in the Presbyterian Church and my Mum had been one of the first (if not the first) New Zealand-trained Presbyterian deaconesses. She was also active in Christian things, being the pianist for the afternoon Sunday school that my brother and I went to with her. But – *preacher*? That hadn't been given any thought, let alone talked about, even though my maternal grandfather had been one! The thing is, I now don't think it came from anything on earth. I feel sure it was the Holy Spirit giving me a nudge in a particular direction that I had never ever considered.

God knew what he had in mind for me, even though I wasn't even aware of it at that time! In hindsight, it reminds me of Jeremiah 1:5, 'Before I formed you in the womb I knew you, before you were born I set you apart.'

I was born at home in a rented house at 74 Orakei Road, Remuera, Auckland, on 6 August 1936, in the days before that area had become an upmarket suburb. Dad had been trained in Whangārei as a cabinet maker by a German craftsman and had worked in a number of cities, including Christchurch, on the majestically curved stair cases in some of the elegant old houses there. He had even owned his own business in Matamata at one stage, but sadly had become such a perfectionist/purist that when the 1932 Depression struck, he refused to make wooden farm gates (for which there was a market) as that sort of work was 'too rough' and not exacting enough for him. So at the time of my birth, he was working at a firm that was making the now near obsolete Auckland electric trams. These are now not running except for the limited line between the two Museums of Transport and Technology (MOTAT) in Auckland. The trams were replaced by diesel buses; many of the early ones I remember rudely belched their smelly exhaust onto the pedestrian footpath.

My mum had been brought up on a farm on Karaka North Road in Karaka and, after having been a chauffeur for someone in Auckland at one stage, she became a New Zealand Presbyterian deaconess. A posting to the Kamo area meant that Mum and Dad's paths crossed there, which led to their marriage later. Mum had many adventures up north as she used to ride everywhere on horseback and now when I drive through that area and see the place names I remember her mentioning, I realise she covered a really wide area!

She also had some different experiences! One wet windy day she was riding along a ridge top when suddenly a gust of wind caught under her raincoat, which went up around her head like a funnel so she couldn't really see anything. The net affect spooked the horse, and it took off with Mum not really knowing where she was going for a short while, which would have been rather scary! Once again, the Lord preserved her.

I was born at home under the watchful eye and help of the well-known Brethren Christian doctor, Dr W. H. Pettit who, in the days of the Rev Lloyd Geering's 'Christ didn't rise' controversy, wrote a strong, well-worded exposition in the personal column of the *New Zealand Herald* every Saturday for probably two years.

About six months after I was born, we moved from Orakei Road to a small farmlet on Koroha Road, Kumeū, which was where I grew up, so my first memories of 'home' were of that place. It was set well back from the road, down a long driveway, which was in fact a water drainage easement. The house was a weatherboard home with an outside toilet (down a bit of a track), the contributions of which had to be buried deep in the garden area at regular stinky intervals.

The house was essentially a two-bedroom home but when I was about eight, a third bedroom, inside flush toilet, and inside laundry were added, which made it a much more convenient place, with my brother Robert (Rob) and I having separate bedrooms. The place had quite a large lawn area virtually all around it. Mum and Dad gave my brother or me pocket money to push the hand mower around and around and around until we were finished!

After these renovations, a storage shed which had originally been attached to the house by a long covered passage, was now detached as a standalone shed. In it, Dad had stored his very large mobile tool chest. I clearly remember the day Dad took my brother and me into that shed and opened the tool chest to reveal a phial of strychnine which was stored in it. I have no idea why it was there, or what use he had it for, unless it was to try and kill off some of the rabbits that were very numerous on the farm. Anyway, he told us both *never, ever* to pick it up and investigate it as it was a deadly poison.

Now, we are all born with the traits of the 'original sin' that Adam and Eve gave to us, so what did young Edward do? Contrary to Dad's forbidding, I reached in with my left hand (I am right-handed) and picked it up to have a better look at it! Well, I am really proud of my dear Dad's reaction. He calmly said, 'Put it back and wash your hands,' which I duly did. But it was when I came back that Dad roared me up and told me off with so much energy, vigour and effectiveness that I clearly remember the whole incident 80 years later! Why the telling off? Because he loved me enough to want to protect me, as he well knew the biblical principle that disobedience has its consequences. In retrospect, Dad being the sort of person he was, I am pretty sure he wouldn't have left the phial there after that incident anyway!

The farmlet was a drained peat swamp that had previously been a citrus orchard. I also remember Mr Arnold Smith with a couple of his big draught horses pulling some of the lemon trees out while Dad dug around them and cut the roots. With the area having originally been swamp, it also had a lot of buried kauri logs embedded in it, and I remember Mr Smith coming again with a team of horses, dragging these logs out after Dad had done a lot of digging around them. We still have a bookcase and a couple of kitchen chairs Dad made from timber milled from one of these logs.

I enjoyed my upbringing on that little farm but things were tight financially for Dad and Mum, and everything was pretty simple. We had electricity but no running hot water or inside toilet for many years, and certainly no refrigerator. We had an outside meat safe with fine gauze flywire on all sides to allow as much breeze as possible through it to keep all within it cool. Meat, milk and much of what we would now keep in a refrigerator today was kept in it for a much shorter time. Also, I remember some food products being put in a shallow pit with damp sacks over them to keep them all cool in the heat of summer.

These were the days before large poultry egg-factory farms. Eggs must have been more of a seasonal commodity which necessitated preserving them when they were plentiful or cheap for the times when they were scarce. This was done by smearing a product very much like the Vaseline of today all over the egg which kept the egg from 'breathing', and if they were stored in a rat-proof box in the cool under the house with gauze on top and bottom so air could circulate, they kept for a surprising time. Mum used the sink or float test to tell whether an egg had gone off, which they occasionally did. If an egg was incorrectly 'diagnosed' and one that had gone off got cracked open – Wow! What a stink! It meant a complete evacuation of the kitchen and leaving it to air out for quite a while!

Mum, (probably as a result of Rob and I pestering her) would make up an 'ice cream' mix, and we'd put it out on the tank stand trusting it would freeze into ice cream. The funny thing was that this would only work in the dead of winter when there were hard frosts! Not when ice cream would normally be appreciated the most! When it did freeze – and often it only went slushy – it was generally quite flaky by modern standards, but of course for us it was really marvellous as with Mum's help we'd made it ourselves!

You may well ask how we bathed when there was no running hot water. For small quantities of hot water, there was the wetback on the coal range on which Mum made the most incredible meals, but this had limited capacity. So, bath night meant that Dad had to carry the hot water in a couple of 18-litre kerosene tins from the cowshed, which was about 185 metres from the house. Plenty of hot water could be produced in the cowshed, as it was heated in a fuel-oil fired heater which was similar in principle to a 'Thermette'. These used to be a common sight on the side of the road at morning and afternoon tea times as the road workers heated water for their tea breaks. This was in the days before thermoses became common. Both the cowshed heater and a Thermette were made of two concentric cylinders with a hollow centre which was the fire box. The space between the cylinder walls was filled with water, which heated very quickly considering the simplicity of the unit.

As for the 'kerosene tin' – in the early days before bulk supply by tankers, most types of fuel were packed for transportation into these tall, square, tin containers which held 18 litres each. Frequently two of these tins were packed into an oblong wooden box for bulk shipping. Later of course the fuel oil (similar to diesel) for the cowshed burner came in 44-gallon (200-litre) drums.

When it came to bathing, you'll be glad to know that we didn't work on the same principle which brought about the saying, 'Don't throw out the baby with the bathwater.' The way this came into being I understand, was because well before our time it seems that it was common practice in the United Kingdom for dad to bathe first, then mum, then the children in order of age, meaning that by the time it came to the baby, the water was so murky that the baby could hardly be seen, so it could potentially be thrown out with the bathwater. Being somewhat more enlightened, Dad and Mum and my brother Rob and I bathed on different nights!

I first realised the difference between the speed of light and the speed of sound at a very young age, when a chap was shooting rabbits in a neighbour's property about 80 metres away. Firstly, I saw the puff of smoke come out of the shotgun barrel and then heard the sound of it just fractionally later. Of course, my enquiring mind asked how this could come about, and one of my family members enlightened me on the difference between the speed of light, compared with the speed of sound.

Ours was a really happy home, and the only time we ever heard some conflict was when Dad considered Rob and I were old enough to learn how to use firearms. Dad had always had an old 12-gauge shotgun, but he wanted to buy a .22 Winchester pump action rifle for us to learn on and later use. Mum apparently resisted it, as Rob overheard Dad saying, 'Well if they were a couple of girls, you would be wanting to buy them a sewing machine or something so they could learn those skills, but these are boys and they will be wanting to do boys' things.' The net outcome was that he bought the rifle, and after a lot of very strict training and going with us on many shooting trips on the farm, we were able to use the rifle. When climbing through a fence or similar, the firearms had to be laid on the ground first and picked up from the other side, with other similar techniques for keeping us all safe.

With the rifle, you had to be much more accurate with your aim and if you were good enough, you could hit something much farther away, but after my first use of the shotgun, I could well understand why Dad wanted to purchase the rifle for us to learn on, as the old shotgun gave your shoulder a real thump – even if you were holding it tight into your shoulder. Woe betide if you forgot, and held it lightly, as the thumping recoil really gave you something to remember! Whether it was the practice of using the rifle on the farm, or just good natural ability I don't know, but my brother Rob was in the team of representative shooters at high school and was considered a very good marksman.

The Kumeū farmlet was my home for the first 16 years of my life. The original part of the farm was a mere seven hectares – but we had to make a living from of it as a family. It was a real privilege being brought up in the country (one which I didn't realise the full value of at the time), as many of the things I probably counted as chores then, I suspect many a town kid would love to do today. One of the most regular was helping get the cows in for milking in the afternoon, and then helping clean up the cowshed, milking equipment and stockyard afterwards; and of course taking the cows back to a specific paddock for the night.

We had friendly Russian neighbours, who had a very small holding adjoining ours which Dad leased and grazed. There was also a water well there with an old-style wing pump which was used to fill up the adjacent trough for drinking water for our cows whenever they were in that paddock. I was always amazed at how much water a cow could drink! Pumping was not an easy job when I was young, and it often seemed an endless and rather fruitless task. It meant pushing the handle backwards and forwards for a seeming eternity and was quite hard work for a kid even though it was probably for only half an hour. It was probably the thought of doing this when I was young that encouraged me later when I was in Papua New Guinea to seek out a rotary pump for filling aircraft with fuel from a drum. Initially this area was leased from the Droojinins, but after a time, Dad and Mum purchased two hectares from them.

Mr Smith was a wonderful cattleman and knew how stock would react in certain situations. When a cow has recently had a calf, they are quite naturally very protective of their young, and dogs are seen to be enemies as they would be in the wild. There is a certain bellow that a cow can make which calls all the other stock to rally with her when chasing the dog. Normally when that happens, the dog makes a hurried exit to get through the closest fence; or, if you happen to be in the paddock at the same time, it can sometimes run to you, and you then also make an equally hurried exit to the closest place of safety! I had to do this on a couple of occasions when I was in my late teens and once when much younger, when I was trying to get a calf out from under a hedge. Fortunately, on that occasion a flimsy two-wire fence was enough protection!

But on another occasion, Mr Smith was with Dad and Rob who were looking at stock over near the Whenuapai airfield. I would have been about eight years old, but hadn't kept up with the rest of those looking at the stock. One cow let out the protective bellow, and the whole mob of about 40 head of stock were after the dog which was running away to my right. Many of the stock were coming from my left. I well remember Mr Smith calling out to me, 'Stand absolutely still Edward – stand still.' Because cows charge with their eyes open (bulls charge with their eyes closed), they could see me standing there just like a fence post and they all went around me and while it must have been pretty scary at the time for me to remember the details so vividly, it was all over in probably 20 seconds! But it was his great cattle knowledge, and my respect and trust in him and his authoritative yet kindly voice that saved my skin on that occasion.

Of course, driving cattle from one place to another was commonplace back then rather than trucking them as is normal today. There were people called drovers which was a respected occupation. A drover would normally have a few dogs in much the same way as high country shepherds do today. The dogs were intelligent and better at times than another human, as they could jump through a fence and move along to the head off a mob with ease, to either redirect, or block a driveway or similar.

Along the road edge of the block of land we bought from Droojinons there was a line of quite tall pine trees, with clear approaches on both sides. Being only about a few kilometres as the crow (or aircraft) flies from the military airport of Whenuapai, this line of trees was often used by pilots to train for 'hedge-hopping'. This was a tactic of flying below the height of the trees and then 'zoom climbing' over the top and diving down to surprise the 'enemy' on the other side. This was obviously only a tactic that could be used by the slower aircraft that were being used at the very beginning of WW2. However, it would have given the pilot a real adrenalin rush flying so low to start with, and was also a good exercise in aircraft handling. On one occasion I saw a Tiger Moth trainer flying at about 30 feet above the ground, and then when he opened the throttle for the zoom climb, there was a bit of a cough and splutter before the engine really picked up. That would have given an adrenalin rush of a completely different kind! Did seeing this sort of thing as a kid have some influence on being willing to fly for God later? Possibly!

I can remember when the concrete runway at the Whenuapai Air Base was being built, starting in 1937 but still continuing for some years, as I must have been about four when I saw the trucks that I am referring to. As it was being made from concrete, the cement came by rail from Whangārei's Portland cement works, and a seemingly continuous stream of orange trucks went back and forth to Whenuapai from the Kumeū rail station seven days a week for quite some time. They were the little old British Bedfords which I imagine took about three or four tonnes maximum at a time! The Whenuapai runway was made in hexagonal sections butted together. When the first commercial passenger jet, a BOAC De Havilland Comet, came to New Zealand, they had to ask the pilots to modify their takeoff, for when the aircraft 'rotated' as they would for a normal takeoff, the blast from the jet engines would blow all the dust etc. out from between the joins in the runway slabs which started to make the runway unstable and uneven.

As it was wartime, we were all supposed to black out our houses by putting up heavy curtains over our windows in the evening so that no light would get out. The idea of this was so that if any enemy aircraft came over, they wouldn't see ours was a populated area because of all the lights. Sadly a neighbour across the road from us never ever bothered to do this. Perhaps they didn't feel that any enemy aircraft would ever class us as a target, but with a military airport so close, it did cause a bit of angst that they didn't do as they were asked.

During the war there were two organisations set up to help with the security of the population in mind. One was the Home Guard. The other went under the initials of EPS (Emergency Precautions Scheme) which did similar things as the Home Guard. I remember that Dad, being a woodworker, made a number of stretchers for the EPS for carrying any sick or injured people. Thankfully, none of what was learnt at these two organisations ever had to be used as a result of an invasion.

Our home was just over three kilometres from Huapai Primary School, where both Rob and I went, though of course with him being four years older than me, he was well established by the time I started. I can remember that at first, Dad would come in the afternoon, and double me home on his bicycle, with me sitting on an especially made seat on the 'doubling bar'.

As this was during the war years, the school had to do regular air raid drills. This meant that the whole school had to get out of the classrooms, line up two or three abreast under the acacia and pine branches overhanging a lane bordering the school, and on the word 'Go' run as fast as we could for about 90 metres while keeping roughly together to the trenches that our parents had dug in scrubby tea-tree beyond the horse paddock. The trenches had boards laid on the bottom of them to keep us out of the wet, sticky, yellow clay on the bottom. I'm sure glad that we never had to do it because of enemy aircraft overhead, as few, if any would have survived the run between the school and the trenches as we weren't under cover most of the way! However, full marks to those who were doing their best to prepare us should the worst happen.

The horse paddock had big blackberry clumps in it which made it a wonderful area to play 'cops and robbers' and other games. Later, a friend who was in the New Zealand Air Force reserves told me that when looking down from above at night at a row of people looking up, the whites of the eyes could be easily seen as they showed up quite well!

Now back to the farm. Another of the cowshed chores was to help carry the skim milk down to the pigs and feed the milk to them. For some reason the traditional pig trough was built in the shape of a long 'V' and it was very difficult pouring the skim milk into the trough when you had eight to ten pigs all scrambling and pushing to get all they could by being first with their heads into the trough. Normally this meant that the bucket was pushed aside and some milk even went down into some ears! Because of this difficulty, Dad came up with a very useful and simple idea that overcame the problem. He built a sort of chimney at one end of the trough, and we poured the milk down it which completely overcame the problem of the bucket being pushed around and made things much easier for both man and beast!

Later, when we got rid of the pigs at Kumeū, it was either Rob's or my job to make sure that the skim milk which was then being pumped into 200-litre drums to be picked up by a neighbour (our Sunday school superintendent – Mr Ralph Cates) didn't overflow, yet got as full as possible! If you filled the drums really full and the milk was left for a few days, a relatively hard crust of curd would develop on top with the whey underneath. Birds used to love it when this happened, as it became a veritable feast for them, especially sparrows, blackbirds and starlings. I can't remember the specific reason, but one of my teachers was interested in getting a bird captured and I said I felt sure I could get a sparrow, so I set a cage trap and had success! I remember Mum saying to me as I set off for school holding the cage in one hand on the handlebars, 'Be careful the trap doesn't catch on anything!' Fortunately it didn't, but I can still see that sparrow sitting in the trap with its wings spread out as if to start flying, as we sped our way down the hill past Mr Smith's farm.

We were told later that Mr. Smith was concerned at the speed with which both Rob and I went down this particular stretch of road, and perhaps this following incident bears testimony to his concern. Rob and I were, as usual, heading off to School on our bikes, as by this time we had a bike each, and on this occasion I happened to be in the lead. At the bottom of this incline there was a curve, a very short straight and a bridge crossing the Kumeū River. In those days, there were no trucks with flashing lights and cones spread out for a staggering distance before you get to where anything is happening. We both came around the curve to see a guy on the bridge laying out planks *across* the width of the bridge at about 0.75 metre intervals! I have no idea what the purpose was, unless they were going to renew some of the wooden bridge planking. What do you do? Clearly, Rob and I took a different approach to this. Rob being slightly behind me, tried to stop, did a broadside, came off, and skinned his knee. I just went straight ahead and bumped my way across the planks until about halfway across the bridge before finally stopping unscathed! Fortunate, or foolish? Who knows!

There was another thing we did as kids that we really thought was a bit of a chore at the time. Being on a dairy farm during World War 2 years did have some advantages! Butter was rationed as it was being exported to 'the mother country' as England was known then. But of course butter is made from cream, which was a source of income from our very small dairying operation. Even so, we made our own butter quite frequently. I remember we had a proper wooden butter churn but to use this, one needed to use quite a lot of cream, which was of course reducing the value of our farm's produce output. I don't know where Mum got the idea from, but she found out a way to make a smaller amount of butter from a much smaller amount of cream. The answer? A humble preserving jar and a heck of a lot of boy energy. You half fill the preserving jar with cream, (with the lid on!) and then shake or roll it backwards and forwards for a seeming eternity and eventually it thickens and then after about as much time again, it becomes butter and buttermilk!

I was to find the same principle worked equally well many years later, while in Papua New Guinea. I was taking a lady from Orokana to Balimo, and as they had cows at Orokana, she was taking the treat of a small bottle of cream in the cargo pod of the aircraft to the nurses at Balimo. Unfortunately for us both, we ran into a cloud buildup along the Woolley Hills with some related severe turbulence. I tried to outrun it by trying to skirt around the end of the storm-line. But because I couldn't fly around the end of the line as it went out into the Gulf of Papua, we landed at Baimuru and I found we had one bottle of butter and buttermilk instead of cream, because it had been shaken up so much!

At Kumeū we had quite a reasonable garden next to the cowshed which had been planted mainly by Mum and it was often our task to water the garden during the dry periods and in the right season pick its fruits. One thing that I learned while doing this was that with the peat soil we had there, if you let it dry out too much, it almost became oily and took an awful lot of water to really get it wet again. We had old-style scarlet runner beans which we used to pick by the bucketful and which were often given away to friends.

In this garden we also had a trellis with a passion fruit vine on it. Being right next to the cow yard, it was easy to shovel up the cow manure off the yard and throw it over the top rail to the base of the passion fruit vines. Wow, did they like it! They grew strongly and yielded buckets full of fruit, as apparently passion fruit are very hungry feeders.

We also had quite a number of fruit trees in three different locations on the small farm. I remember the Christmas plum which was in the area close to the bee apiary. This had to be picked late in the evening, as there was too much bee activity if picked earlier. The Burbank plum was in another location and it was always heavily laden. A delicious white peach was close by and always needed our tallest (wooden) extension ladder to get the top fruit as it was so tall – at least it was to a small boy! This brings to mind the pipping of jam melons which seemed to be a never-ending task! It was a bit like taking all of the seeds out of a full-sized watermelon. But as it was the base ingredient for many a jar of delightful jam, this task was endured with a certain amount of looking to the future!

We had an American tent camp based in a paddock across the road from the front of our place in Kumeū. They really had a can-do attitude when it came to some things. A lay preacher friend was working in the Kumeū Post Office at the time, and the camp commandant came in and requested the use of the Post Office safe. Our friend, playing it by the book, said that there would need to be an application request made out and approval from higher up, to which the American replied, 'Let's just use it, and we'll do the paperwork afterwards.' We got to see some rather different driving from these marines too, especially in the little old original four-wheel drive Jeeps, so unlike the modern versions! (Think of the ones used in *M*A*S*H*.) Coming home from school one afternoon was the only time I can ever remember seeing a vehicle come around a curve literally on two wheels with the other side off the ground and it didn't roll over! The two occupants were laughing their heads off!

To supplement our very small dairy operation, Dad also had about 60 hives of bees on our farmlet which I think bought us many things, like our bicycles, rifle and similar 'luxuries'. While Mum never, to the best of my knowledge, took part in taking honey off from the hives, she was a key processor in the honey house which was a large lined room off the corner of the aforementioned garage/workshop. Uncapping was done with a large specially shaped knife, (which in some bigger operations is heated) that shaved the little wax caps off the honeycomb cells the honey was stored in. Because a lot of our honey was manuka honey, it needed a special extra operation after the uncapping before being put into the hand-operated extractor. The bees harvested this nectar from red tea-tree long before its wonderful healing properties were known and fully understood, although I do know honey was used in WW1 as an antiseptic dressing for wounds.

There was also a lot of background work to be done for the honey operation – making new frames and embedding reinforcing wires into the new foundation, or reconditioning frames and also cleaning off propolis and extra wax from the supers and dry comb at the end of the honey season and helping put the wet comb into and dry comb out of the hives, etc. According to our age and ability, both Rob and I took part in all of these activities, including, when in Standard 6 (Year 8) getting up early enough before school to help take off the honey from the hives before breakfast and then leave for school. At the particular time of the year when the extracting of the honey was being done, Mum would frequently do the evening milking with help from one of us boys while the other helped Dad with some part of the honey operation. Another interesting observation relative to beekeeping was that we noticed that when our large purple wisteria vine was in full flower, one could almost guarantee there would be some swarming of the bees. This is a function of the bees establishing a new colony which occurs when a hive has a greater number of worker bees than the hive can comfortably contain and there is a new queen to lead the new colony and so it swarms to establish it.

As it was during WW2, a number of possible export products were being nationalised or put under some form of governmental control. Dad heard on the radio a government announcement that, 'Honey is not going to be controlled.' Whether by observation or inbuilt intuition I don't know, but Dad's reasoning with regards to this was that they had already thought about it, and knowing how politicians are sadly so often liars, it would only be a matter of time before it actually did happen for honey. So he rang all of our regular customers and told them to come and get their honey before some form of regulation was brought in, which would inevitably make getting the honey more difficult and dearer for them. I can remember that for the next week there was a constant stream of vehicles coming in and getting our still unregulated honey! Within about a month of the Government's previous announcement, all honey production had to go through the newly-formed Honey Marketing Authority, but due to Dad's instinct and action, we were free of those restrictions – at least for that year!

Chapter 2

Family and Friends

Mum was a great cook. She used the old coal range, until it was upgraded to an electric stove and she used to make really great cakes which she iced. I must have had a real love for cake icing (what little boy doesn't?) as the following incident may confirm. We had friends at Riverhead by the name of Shaw. They used to go to a church over there that we went to as well at times. On this particular occasion, the Shaw family was at our place, and I was sitting alongside their little girl about my own age – about four or five years old. We had got through the 'savoury biscuit' stage and were now onto the 'cake with icing' stage. My little friend must have also liked icing, because she had peeled off her icing and placed it on the side of her plate. I too, was looking forward to my icing, but I thought that I would help her by scoffing some of hers before I started on mine, so I took some (if not all) of hers and ate it and then started on mine. This of course brought forth an understandable teary protest from her, and my mum had to calm the waters by producing some more icing off the rest of the cake, with no doubt a stern telling off for me! I do remember Mum smacking my behind with a wooden spoon once but I can't remember exactly what it was for. Perhaps the fact that I remember these two things concurrently may have some significance?

Mum was also a very talented musician although she said she couldn't actually read music. However, she used to put the music book up in front of her and at times this caused her some embarrassment, especially when someone asked her to play something and she'd say, 'I can't read music, I just play by ear.' They would then say, 'But you always have a music book in front of you when you are playing!' She would then 'fess up and tell them that it was to get an idea of timing and key more than anything else. I know that on a number of occasions, Mrs Cates, our Sunday school superintendent's wife, would ring Mum up on a Sunday morning and sing to her a new chorus three or four times that she had just heard. Mum would then go and practise it on her old organ, and that afternoon we would be singing the new chorus at Sunday school with full piano accompaniment!

Both Mum and Dad were good examples for us boys in each and every way. They gave a united example in all the important moral and spiritual things. There was never any alcohol in our home so we never personally saw the down side of all the problems it can cause. When in my late teens I read a book which said that if you don't drink alcohol there are 12 diseases that you'll never get, so that sealed it as far as I was concerned! I have never knowingly drunk any.

In her quiet but strong way, Mum was a real example of humility, strength, and spiritual guidance. With the pain from one hip that she endured for so long, being housebound for about 20 years. She rarely complained, and while we knew that a hip operation would probably have solved the problem, she said she would rather have the money go into a bigger farm so we boys could have a better start in life. Even when I had to bathe her feet and cut her toenails, which must have been most humiliating for her, she was forever grateful for my most unprofessional attempts at podiatry. She exuded love, grace, and self-effacing self-control.

Dad was practical, inventive and hardworking. After having been involved in a very precise type of cabinet making, becoming a farmer was a huge change in occupation but one that he embraced for the sake of us all, to the extent that he became willing to make wooden farm gates! He was multi-talented and had a very strong sense of working out his Christian faith by helping others, as well as being astute and deep-thinking. After we had matured a bit ourselves, both Rob and I realised just how much both our parents had worked hard for our ultimate benefit.

From a very young age, I can remember having Bible readings on a Sunday morning and also on occasions at night. From as soon as I could walk the 1.5 kilometres to the Kumeū Sunday school, I was doing so, and put my hand up at the age of four in answer to the question, 'Who wants to go to heaven?' Of course at that stage I didn't fully understand what the New Testament covenant relationship meant, but I knew enough to know that it was a good deal! The Sunday school that I went to with my mother and brother was very focused on learning a scripture verse each week. I don't remember any prizes, but there were always a number of us who had learnt that week's verse. I can recollect our superintendent at least once lifting me up onto the table at the front so the others could see me while I recited my verse, because I was so small!

One that everybody learnt was John 3:16 'For God so loved the world, that he gave his one and only Son, that whoever believes in him shall not perish but have everlasting life.' This verse gives the invitation and reason for becoming a Christian, and also the promise of the sure hope for every Christian – everlasting life. Probably the other verse that was very meaningful to me as a child (and still is) was also from John 14:6 where Jesus said, 'I am the way, and the truth and the life. No one comes to the Father except through me' and John 14:2, 'I am going there to prepare a place for you.' These I think gave even more credibility to the one above. Sadly, we don't hear these spoken about in some churches very much these days the way they used to be.

Our Sunday school superintendent was Mr Ralph Cates who

was very overseas mission orientated. He was in touch with at least two missionaries who would often come and speak to us all at Sunday school and on at least one occasion one spoke at our anniversary. Both Hayden Mellsop of China Inland Mission (now Overseas Missionary Fellowship) and Rev Bennett Williams of Africa Inland Mission were regulars at the Sunday school and quite often at our home for a meal. While Hayden Mellsop was working in China, Rev Bennett Williams was amongst the pigmy tribe in what was then the Belgian Congo (now the Democratic Republic of the Congo or DRC). What with Sunday school and having these missionaries in our home, overseas mission was a quite natural and normal topic for us.

On the down side, I can also clearly remember an evening when I was probably about nine or ten years old in the Kumeū Hall, when a Youth For Christ (YFC) group came there on a mission. Afterwards, a guy came and spoke to me and really rattled my cage. I must have thought I was a pretty good guy and was really keen to point him to some others there that I was sure were in much more need of his attention than me! But no, I was in his sights and he wasn't letting me go, and my evasive answers only encouraged him to keep going and dig deeper! While he didn't get me to a point of admitting I didn't know as much as I reckoned I did, I'm sure that God was in it, and it must have got me thinking. A saying of Mum's that I well remember is so true: 'God has no grandchildren, only sons and daughters.'

It was at a Crusader Camp (later called Inter-School Christian Fellowship or ISCF) on Ponui Island when in the 3rd Form (Year 9) at college, that I fully understood what it meant to be a Christian and gave my life to Jesus by accepting him as my personal Saviour. Ted Meads, a high school teacher from Hamilton Boys' High School, took the session at Ponui when I made my life commitment to Jesus Christ. I am ever grateful for the Ponui Island camps, and the ministry of so many in the leadership of them. Since then, it has been a time of continual growth, with a number of setbacks and down times, but really, I have been wonderfully privileged to have known about the Christian faith for as long as I can remember.

Dad was an example of hard work and showed a willingness in his later years to work outside his comfort zone. As mentioned, he trained in Whangārei under a very skilled German cabinetmaker and so became skilled and a bit of a perfectionist himself in that trade. He made many of the now old and much sought-after (and copied) wooden cabinets for the wireless radios of yesteryear. He also worked on billiard tables in Auckland and fine staircases in Christchurch, but when it came to a crunch in later years, he became willing to do some boat building, coachwork, and even made wooden farm gates.

Dad was also deeply interested in the Scriptures and the background to scriptural events. I can remember him often quoting from Josephus who was an ancient Jewish/Roman historian, born a little after the time of Jesus Christ, a little later than the time of Paul (around 80-90 AD) and expounding some point from this non-Christian historian's point of view about events and the culture of the time. That aside, Dad was good to my brother and me, and with Mum they both set us an example of truth, honesty, hard work, integrity, and spiritual understanding – all of which I am truly grateful for.

Dad was a person who worked with his hands and was very good at it. I also liked making things and, in that sense, I think we shared those same interests. Rob made things too, but I think I was a bit more of a tinkerer, pulling things apart to see how they worked and just sometimes managing to get them together again! I remember that, quite regularly, I used to pull my bicycle hubs apart and grease the ball bearings, etc., and I think this stood me in good stead in later years. Dad was helpful in that he showed me how to do these things and then left me to it, to be just a backup if I got into any sort of trouble.

I don't know that Dad and I were good mates as some children seem to be with their parents. Because we had similar natures when it came to being inventive, we would often spar to see if we could improve each other's ideas! I had a much closer and more loving relationship with my mother, which I guess is more or less natural, as this is frequently the case. However Dad was one who had worked hard and in many ways made big changes to his lifestyle so that Rob and I could be brought up in the country and become farmers. It's quite a change from being a professional woodworking craftsman who was always indoors, to being a farmer.

I imagine that Mum's habit in her later years of reading the Scriptures during the day was probably fostered in her earlier years. A challenging thought she used to throw out to us was, 'You should read a page of Scripture for every page of any other book you read.' I'm sorry Mum, but I haven't been able to reach that goal – not yet anyway.

Everyday life wasn't quite 'be seen and not heard', but at times it came pretty close. Having said that, there was always a bit of wiggle-room, and there were certainly rewards and encouragement for doing things well – as they were expected to be! I remember 'toe the line' was a favourite saying of Dad's, and so long as you did that, life was jolly good. By today's quite liberal comparison, this kind of parenting would now be regarded as very authoritarian, but we always had clear boundaries and it was everybody's expectation that you kept within them. Both Mum and Dad had reasonable expectations and normally backed each other completely if ever one of us tried to play one off against the other.

I have memories of going to Riverhead with Dad when we were living at Kumeū. As I mentioned, Dad was a woodworker, and the local sawmiller (Mr MacMillan) was sufficiently forward-thinking to get a fairly large launch with which he was going to tow rafts of logs up the Waitematā Harbour from somewhere to a slip near the Riverhead bridge or hall, and it would be only a very short haul from there up to his sawmill. Dad was engaged as an assistant with a very experienced boat builder, and one day Dad invited me to bike over there with him and see the work he was doing. I don't remember much of the actual work Dad was involved in, but I do remember him inviting me to try and lift an ingot of what I learned later to be lead. It was to be used in the lower part of the launch as ballast. It was my first introduction to just how *heavy* lead is!

Getting firewood in for winter use could be a mixture of fun and hard work. Watching the use of gunpowder and its power in a log-splitting gun was *real* fun, until there was a misfire, and you didn't know when, or if, it was going to go off! However, over time Dad figured out the reason for the misfires and perfected a technique that made the process pretty well sure-fire. The log-splitting gun was like a cast piece of very heavy pipe, around 45 centimetres long, but solid for about 15 centimetres at one end. The other end was hollow and sharpened so that it could be driven into the end of a log with a maul hammer. Before driving it in, it was filled with gunpowder and approximately halfway along the hollow section of the pipe was a hole into which a slow-burning fuse was inserted. When the explosion took place, the results could be quite dramatic in splitting the log into many pieces, and one had to be well away as some of the wood could be thrown quite a distance. This was good grounding for our later use of 'jelly' (gelignite) explosives on the Silverdale farm, when we blew tree stumps out of the ground while clearing the land.

As for the probable cause for the misfires and how it was overcome, I explain it here. The type of delayed timing fuse that we were using was like a piece of spaghetti made out of a woven cloth-like material, with a fine core of gunpowder running through the centre. The concept was that when you lit one end of a piece of this, it would burn slowly down whatever length you had cut it to, and then when it got to the end, it would ignite the gunpowder in the log-splitter. However, Dad was initially chopping the fuse to length with an axe, which he later realised had the effect of compressing that end to the extent that the fire in the fuse fizzled out instead of igniting the gunpowder. When he thought about this, he still cut the fuse with the axe but he then worked both ends between his fingers to free it all up. This made lighting the end much easier, and virtually a sure fire every time from then on.

At Kumeū we had no tractor, no horses or any mechanical sort of motive power – apart from our legs! Dad had designed and built a handcart, about 1.2 metres long and 60 centimetres wide on two motorbike wheels. This was the primary means of transporting everything we did on that farm. Hay, bee supers (boxes) full of honey, firewood, etc. Rob and I must have been a little older, as Dad on this occasion, had attached enough rope not only to tie on the load of firewood, but also to provide for the two of us to pull the cart while he pushed and steered from behind. How often we did this I don't remember, but an old galvanised iron water tank on its side was our woodshed and we always managed to fill it up with very careful packing. We also helped to chop the firewood and kindling and wheelbarrow it from there to the house. I still have a scar on my left forefinger to prove that on one occasion I chopped more than just the kindling!

Because creams and salves were not common or easily obtained back in the 1940s in the country, we at times resorted to some age-old remedies which were a great help. On more than one occasion, the use of chewed-up plantain (rib grass) leaves to help heal a graze or cut was called for. Whether it was the rib grass or the saliva that was the most help, I truly don't know. Maybe the plantain did have some good qualities, as farmers are now (in 2023) being advised to plant it in their pasture to help with stock health and particularly to reduce stock flatulence.

Rob and I used to have to clean out the algae/slime from the water troughs where the cows drank. I think this came about from the cows dropping bits of grass into the trough as they drank, and it rotted and supported algae growth. In any case, it was an annual job to empty the troughs and scrub and wash them out before they were refilled.

I don't know whether something I got paid for could be called a chore, but as I said earlier, the Kumeū house had a large lawn around it, and someone had to mow it – with a hand mower! It used to take me about three hours to do it. I remember on one occasion being paid two shillings (20 cents, although it was certainly worth a lot more then than 20 cents today). The grass was fairly long and needed some going over again to clean up some bits and pieces. I think that must have been a lot of money for the job, since I remember it so vividly. But our lives weren't all chores or hard work. I remember bird nesting while milking was in progress. We would try and make up a collection of all the different sorts of birds' eggs and compare them with others at school. I think it was just something which was being done by youngsters in the country in those days, like collecting stamps or cigarette cards was.

Neither Rob nor I ever smoked a cigarette but my one and only attempt at ever trying to 'smoke' was to light a piece of cocksfoot grass seed stem on the way home from school once. There were plenty of these on the side of the road. Then I gave a tiny suck, and the flame shot straight through the hollow stem and burned the back of the roof of my mouth. That was it as far as I was concerned and I never ever tried anything like that again! Rob was a tad more sophisticated in that he rolled some lichen moss off a tree in some newspaper. Apparently the taste and smell was sufficient to put him off any type of smoking as well. Thank you Lord that these boyhood experiments kept us from taking up smoking!

My summer school holidays would often see me heading out to Aunty Pansy and Uncle Vic's place at Charles Road, Karaka. As we had no means of transport of our own, this meant catching an ABC (Auckland Bus Company) bus into the Auckland bus terminal, near the present site of the Britomart rail station, then catching an NZR (New Zealand Railways – now InterCity) Leyland Comet bus out to the Waiuku turn-off. When I was young, I'm sure Dad would have taken us into Auckland and put us on this bus, but I know that when I was still fairly young, I used to make the journey by myself from Auckland with someone being at the Karaka end to meet me. These were fun holidays with our cousins Ray and Colin Haliday.

Uncle Vic's farm was big by our standards and he ran beef cattle for fattening. Even when he was just a school boy, Colin had developed the skill to judge a beef steer's weight so well he could pick which ones were ready for sale, just about as well as the stock agents who came to sort them out. Uncle Vic also milked what was then for us a big herd of about 75 cows on his father's farm across the creek that was the boundary between the two properties. He had work horses, and it was a real treat being able to drive them when on the sledge going between the two farms before and after milking times. There was a small, narrow bridge over the boundary creek and Uncle Vic would take one horse out of the double harness and walk it over the bridge first and then the other horse would drag the sledge across. He then had to re-harness the free horse to make a double again. It was like VE Day when I was trusted enough to drive the horse with the sledge across the bridge!

I don't know whether it was done for our benefit or if it was just working with the seasons, but I seem to remember there was nearly always topdressing of fertiliser or lime to be done when we were there on holiday. This meant sledging the material out to the paddock and then using a wheeled horse-drawn top dresser (which would take about 325 kilograms of fertiliser or lime) going around and around the paddock, topdressing a mere 2.5-metre- to 3-metre-wide strip per circuit. But it was real fun for someone who didn't have and never drove horses at home!

Uncle Vic was a WW1 cavalry veteran and of an evening told many stories about his experiences with the horses that were used in that war. One wet afternoon he also took all of us youngsters out into their detached garage and gave us a very rudimentary lesson about internal combustion engines with the engine cover sides up on the faithful old Essex car they had. It was my first introduction to engines and their various components. On a Sunday when we were there, we always used to go to the Karaka church close to the Karaka school, which is sadly now closed and used as a gift shop. This church was one where I preached while I was doing my compulsory military training (CMT) at Papakura in 1955. Actually CMT was a time that crystallised one's faith, as there weren't any grey areas; you were either a believer or you weren't!

Something I remember about summer holidays when at home was the joy of haymaking. When I was very young, a couple of times we made hay using a sweep to get the hay close to a place where it could be stacked manually. There was apparently a real art in being able to build a stack of hay which would keep its shape, not slip sideways, but which also shed any rain. Few men could do it well, even though until about 1943 it would have been the primary method of making and keeping hay. One needed the grass to be really dried out because if it had too much sap moisture in it, it would heat up to such a point that it could start burning by spontaneous combustion up to a week after stacking. Rain moisture of the same amount wouldn't make it burn; it just made it musty or mouldy!

Hay bailers were introduced in about the early 1940s. First, there were stationary types when all the hay was brought by sweep to the bailer, and men with pitchforks loaded it into the bailer's pickup. Then came the revolutionary method of having a tractor tow the hay bailer around the paddock to bale the hay into long rectangular bales while on the move. Initially, two men used to ride around about midships on either side of the bailer (with a very small boy running alongside!) and somehow, by shoving a partition in at a certain place with perfect timing, they separated the hay in the square rear tube of the bailer and so made the bale. At that time, the hay bale was tied up using very light gauge ungalvanised wire. A little later, the bales were made in the same shape, but twine and automatic knitters completed the job. Even though I later operated such a baler for a period, I never could figure out how the knotters worked, nor did I try and dismantle one to find out!

But in the 1940s it was wartime and wire was scarce, so new hay bailing wire was very hard to come by – if at all. The local bailing contractor was Mr Arnold Smith. He was a good friend of us all. Dad did a deal with him for Rob and me. If Mr Smith could get all his clients to keep the wire off the previous season's bales of hay and bring them to us, we would straighten the wires for his men to re-use.

I think that I must have been destined from a very young age to be a driver of some sort. Probably the thing that I remember most from my earliest days at Kumeū was a tricycle, for which Dad had made a mini trailer that was attached onto the frame at the rear. I can also remember that even before I went to school, I was able to reverse my tricycle and trailer. I had many happy hours playing with it.

While the family was at Kumeū, we didn't have a car. It wasn't until after we had been at Silverdale for about four years that we made our first car purchase. At Kumeū, we either walked, biked or caught a bus to wherever we wanted to go. We were about 1.5 kilometres from a main road, where we could get a bus to either Auckland or Helensville, and a similar distance to the train station in Kumeū where you could also get passenger services going north or south. We only used the train if we were going a reasonably long distance, like Whangārei to see Dad's mum and his brother there.

Talking of trains, they didn't run to the tight schedule that our Auckland Transport electric trains do today, or for that matter the London or Singapore underground trains. I remember when on our one and only time in London, a voice came over the loud speaker apologising for the train being one and a half minutes late! A chap on the Kumeū platform when I was a kid would have been glad to hear that. I well remember once, when the train was late, his comment was, 'It's not a timetable you want, but a ***** calendar is what you need!'

We walked to Kumeū for Sunday school in the public hall, which at various times was the venue for a picture theatre, dance hall, church and Sunday school. In these early days, Mum's hip hadn't stiffened up, and she was able to walk to Sunday school over a swing bridge strung on steel cables over the Kumeū River which was capable of flooding almost up to bridge height.

But to this day I remember something that Mum said to me once. It was well known that I wanted to be a train driver, or similar – which was every young boy's dream in those days. On this occasion, I must have shown the rather short fuse (quick temper) which I had before I became a Christian. Mum said to me, 'If you can't control yourself, you'll never be able to control anything else.' That remark really struck a sensitive nerve. As I really did want to be a good driver, I tried from that time on to start controlling my temper. But it was accepting Jesus as my Saviour that made the difference in this area, helping me to be more level-headed, though at times I fear the 'old self' and quick response is still inclined to come through.

As Dad was 'handy', he made for us both a small aluminium toy truck, about 40 centimetres long. But this was no ordinary toy truck for its time because it had a wooden chassis, and mounted on that was a spring from a mouse trap which, when you moved a lever at the back of the cab, allowed the metal tray to tip up. Its front mudguards were cut out of the bottom of a small cooking pot. We didn't have a sandpit, but there were many happy years playing with that truck.

In my late primary to early high school years we had a number of homing pigeons and on a couple of occasions we flew them back home by sending them on the train to some distant point – Te Awamutu as I recall. We would put them on a train with a note to the guard asking him to please release them when the train got to the given destination. The birds always came home, which I still consider to be so wonderfully remarkable! We had blue bar homing pigeons and also a pair of white and speckled tumblers which, when released from the coop, would fly for about half a minute and then tumble backwards. The more tumbles they did, the better they were considered to be. I seem to remember that ours used to consistently do two or three, which was considered about average.

In fact, my hobbies tended more towards mechanical things. In hindsight, not all my pulling apart of things was 100 percent successful! I remember one pocket watch that wasn't working; I decided that I would try and fix it, but I ended up with a lot of parts which were ultimately thrown away. However, I am glad that I did that sort of exploring into the unknown when I was young, because much later in Papua New Guinea I had to try and fix things and had no idea whether they would be successful or not, such as the sewing machine at Kawito, a tape recorder at Wewak.

People who had a great influence on my life include Ralph Cates, the Sunday school superintendent of the Kumeū interdenominational Sunday school when I was a child, and for whom

I later worked during most school holidays. As I have said, it was wartime, and part of the American marine occupation force was located close by. Mr Cates had the idea of planting many hectares in watermelons and selling them to the Americans, who really loved them. After they left he got into producing pumpkins in a big way. Initially I was doing the most backbreaking work you'd ever want, hoeing metres and metres of pumpkin plants. Later, he taught me to drive his Massey Ferguson 28 tractor, and I rotary-hoed most of the weeds, just leaving a very narrow strip between the individual plants to be manually hoed. What a wonderful difference that made! Because he was cropping the same land over and again with pumpkins there was the need to give the rows copious amounts of fertiliser, lime, and also potash which made the pumpkins dry and tasty.

I enjoyed school and did quite well at most things, though there were some things that I didn't enjoy too much. I went through a phase after the age of seven of being quite fat, so much so that I had the nickname 'Ten Tonner' for a few years and because of this, I didn't take my shirt off to get a tan. You can imagine my embarrassment when Mr Brewer our headmaster at the time who was taking my class for physical education one day made a comment that focused everyone's attention on me as we had to have our shirts off for that particular exercise. Despite this, I was in our relatively small school's only football team and also the only cricket team when I was in the upper primary classes.

The Huapai school playing field had been constructed in the 1930s Depression, with dole labour and wheel arrows! There was a general transverse slope along the length of the area the rugby field was carved out from, and what was dug out from one side was barrowed over to the other side to make a level playing field. This had the effect that there was a great viewing bank on one side that was pure clay, but the far side was reasonably fertile. As a result, the far side grew grass quite profusely (enough to have a horse mower cut it occasionally), while the side near the bank was still almost bare. On occasions, the Waimauku school would come and play us at Huapai, and of course there was sometimes a less than friendly rivalry.

But there were fun times at school too – not that OSH would allow them today! There was a Lawson cypress tree shaped like the typical Christmas fir tree on the boundary edge of one playing field. We used to climb up the trunk to near the top and then leap out onto the ends of the branches and slide down them. Wow, what great fun!

It is amazing the insights that teachers have of their pupils at an early age. I remember Mr Simpson a later headmaster who taught me in Years 7 and 8 writing a remark on my Year 8 school report that confused but also encouraged me. He said, 'Edward has an inventive mind.' It was only much later that I became aware of the accuracy of his remark. Sadly for him, it was while I was in Standard 6 (Year 8) that his wife died from cancer, and being in the school's highest class, I helped to form a guard of honour for the coffin to the hearse as it left the school grounds. It was my first real encounter with the death of a person I knew.

Chapter 3

High School Days

As I mentioned earlier, my brother went to high school in Helensville but four years later when I started secondary schooling, transport options had changed. I wanted to do a technical course which Helensville High School (now Kaipara College) wasn't offering, so I went in the other direction from Kumeū towards Auckland to Avondale College. To get there I used a special pass on public transport. This meant being at the Kumeū bus stop at 7:15am, having ridden my bike for about 15 minutes to get to the back of the local chemist's shop where I parked it for the day. The bus didn't get back to Kumeū until about 4:30pm, having taken a circuitous route home.

One portion of the bus route was along Lincoln Road, a section of which was made of concrete from near the current Waitakere Hospital to the bridge just before the town. The concrete slabs were joined with a bitumen join which was sufficiently proud to be a bit like the old clickety-clack train lines as you went over them. It has only been in recent years that I have realised how forward-thinking the engineers actually were who laid portions of the road in concrete. A section of the Albany highway which had been made from extremely crudely mixed concrete back in the 1980s outlasted the bitumen at either end which needed either replacement or repair seven times during the concrete's life up to that time!

It was while coming home on the bus one afternoon that I witnessed a terrible accident between a car and an express train. It was of course in the days of the old steam trains, and our bus often seemed to get to the Taupaki level crossing at around the time the express from Whangārei to Auckland came through. Even before the accident, all of us high-schoolers were aware of the terror of the level crossing, and would keep our eyes open at certain points for the plume of white smoke away up the line, which would indicate that the train was on its way. When we saw it, we would call out to the driver, 'The train is coming!' just in case he hadn't seen it for himself.

Back then, on the northern side of the Taupaki crossing, there was the local store and a small shed which obscured the train coming from the north when close to the crossing. On this occasion, the bus had stopped well short of the crossing, as we had seen the train in the distance. A local woman came out of the store, jumped into her car and took off, obviously thinking about something else. Our bus driver sounded his horn a number of times to try and alert her, and just before the crossing she must have seen the train as there was a little wiggle as if not knowing where to go or what to do. The train engine clipped the front of her car which spun off to the left, rolling many times and demolishing some railway signs on the way. Of course this was in the days before seat belts, so she died instantly. The train driver obviously threw on his emergency braking, but it took probably 300 to 400 metres to stop. It has left a lasting impression on me as to the dangers of railway level crossings!

Avondale College which I attended was an old American wartime hospital that had been converted into a school, with a long row of classrooms that had previously been the different wards. There were some real benefits, as we had a fantastic gymnasium, assembly hall and plenty of tennis courts. One thing that was a surprise was there was no swimming pool! However in my second year of being at college, a sunken pool was built and I thought that would be my opportunity to learn to swim. I can't quite fathom the reasoning, except perhaps that they had no swimming instructors available, but the ruling came out that only those who could swim already were allowed to use the pool.

One of the underlying problems we have today (2024) with a lack of trades people started back in the late 1940s. Obviously, all the new students going to the College had to sit an entrance exam and those who were in the top band academically were encouraged to go into a special course. This didn't sit well with me, as the special course didn't include any technical subjects and when I told Dad about it, he was very supportive of me continuing with the technical course. But you can see how the education system was already not recognising the value of those who wanted to use their hands and take trade subjects, and wanted to divert them instead into an academic course to learn French and the like. To be fair, perhaps our 3A English master did get it, as I can well remember him giving us all a pep talk about how we needed to be good with our English, because he said, 'You chaps have the potential of being foremen and leaders and as such you will need to be able to explain lucidly and accurately what you want done!' I don't know whether our Year 10 English master would get away today with the remark he made to me after the final exam. 'Crawford, I'm blowed if I know how you did it, but somehow you managed to come out top of the class for the year!' All of us had a real good laugh at the comment, as others were quite well aware that English was not my best subject.

I enjoyed my time at Avondale College and have fond memories of a few things. Academically, I managed to do reasonably well, considering I had been a big fish in a small 150-child pond at Huapai, to become a real sprat in a school of over 1,200 at Avondale. I enjoyed some aspects of sport, holding the school record for the light discus throw for a total of nine months before another guy beat it, but never really got the art of the 'Western roll' technique for the high jump. Of course those were the days when all schools had some periods dedicated to some sort of military exercise for the boys as we were still under the shadow of WW2, which had ended only a few years previously. Fortunately, the air force came as well as the army, and just as fortunately we could choose which branch of the forces we would go with. I chose the air force, and while we did do some parade ground exercises where I became a flight sergeant, it was really minimal compared to the boys who went with the army where they seemed to foot-slog around the tennis courts almost the whole time. The air force instructors took us into a classroom and actually taught us things like aerodynamics and about engines. I was glad I chose to go with them as we actually learnt something, so it didn't seem so much like wasted time.

I enjoyed doing the practical engineering. I was one of the few who was allowed to use the big geared-head Colchester lathe and the milling machine. We had a furnace to melt down old aircraft pistons which were made into various cast objects. The power of steam was demonstrated forcibly to us all one day when some other chaps were pouring surplus molten aluminium into metal ingot moulds. Because we were using sand to make the casting moulds, the area where the furnace and the forges were had a very high roof (about five metres I would think) so any sand that was walked out on our feet into the areas where the lathes and work benches were would be drawn back into the lower pressure area.

On this particular occasion, the chaps were pouring the surplus molten material from a casting session into the ingot moulds. However, there must have been a drop of perspiration in one of the moulds which can't have been heated as they were supposed to be. When the molten aluminium hit the drop of moisture, it turned instantly into steam and expanded to about 1,600 times its original size and blew the aluminium material up onto the underside of the very high roof. Neither of the fellows doing the pouring was hurt, but it was mighty close for one who had a bit of his front hair burnt off as the molten metal flew past.

It's interesting isn't it, that kids will always come up with nicknames for their teachers? Our 3A English teacher was 'Froggy' Martin, Maths was 'Donkey' Adams and our Engineering instructor was 'Curly' Ball. I have no idea where Mr Martin got 'Froggy' from, but I am sure Mr Adams had an inkling of his nickname. He was very keen on cricket, and the guys would try and get him going on a cricketing theme, but once when they must have tried to push him too far, he said, 'There are times I can kick like a mule.' Mr Ball was as bald as anybody could be, hence the 'Curly' presumably. I well remember one remark Mr. Ball made that I have had occasion to console myself with a number of times over the years. He said, 'A good engineer is not so much one who gets it right every time, but one who has the skills to make it right when they have initially got it wrong.'

After three years at college I sat my School Certificate in the technical subjects that I had been taking and enjoying. Of course the two compulsory ones were English and Mathematics, and the other three electives I took were Electricity and Magnetism, Technical Drawing and Engineering; and you guessed it, my lowest mark (though a pass) was in English, confirming my Year 10 master's thinking!

In Year 8 my cousin Colin Haliday invited me to go with him to a Crusader Camp on Ponui Island in the Hauraki Gulf. At that time, this was a boys-only Christian camp run by Scripture Union. It was a totally new experience for me where you camped in tents, ate and had meetings in a big marquee and used uncovered toilets in the open air under large white tea-trees. The first night at the first camp was certainly a new experience for me as well as the others in my tent.

Neither the advance party who put up all the tents nor our tent leader can have had much experience of camping in the rain. With none of us taking note of our surroundings, we hadn't dug even a small trench around the tent on the uphill side. Sadly this tent, one of about nine old conical military-type tents, had been placed directly in the line of all the runoff from a farm track! That first night, it rained and water flowed freely through the tent. One lives, learns, and remembers!

Camping on Ponui has dramatically changed today though. The Chamberlin family who farm part of the island have built a large cargo and fertiliser shed which acts as a mess hall for campers; and separate, covered toilets enable mixed gender camps. Those camps were a wonderful combination of fun, fellowship, rough and tumble, and extremely good spiritual teaching and I enjoyed going there for four years running, being a tent leader at the last one. At my second camp, during a morning session taken by a secondary school master from Hamilton Boys' High called Ted Meads, I came to realise that my idea as a four-year-old of wanting to go to heaven was just a young child's understanding of Christian commitment. From that time, I had only been coasting along in my spiritual life. On that morning on Ponui Island, I accepted Jesus Christ as my Saviour from sin and made a full commitment to Jesus Christ and his way of living.

A new experience for me was sleeping under the stars for at least one night each camp. The leaders chose what they thought would be a fine night. We would go out to a more remote bay and cook over an open fire and then prepare to sleep under the stars. A number of us used tea-tree brush to try and make the ground a bit softer before laying our groundsheets over it. The success of that was, as I remember it, about four out of ten! On one of those trips, when we were not down by the seaside, I chose a place where I could put my feet against a tea-tree bush to ensure I didn't slide down the slope while I slept! On another occasion, we needed to get some drinking water and we found some coming from a spring in a cave which was so cold it almost took my breath away when I drank it. All good experiences for a young chap from a small Kumeū farm.

Another time, quite a group of us (if not the whole camp) went to what was thought to be a secluded bay, and for the sake of everyone feeling okay with their own bodies, we all went for a skinny dip. All went well, until the Chamberlins' launch rounded the corner. There was no time to make a dash for it, so we all had to stay put and this included Peter Chamberlin whose fiancée was on the boat!

The camp was (and still is) situated in Motunau Bay on Ponui Island. In earlier times the Island was called Chamberlins' Island as at one stage the whole island was owned by a member of the larger Chamberlin family.

After leaving college, I went back to Ponui Island and really enjoyed working with the Chamberlins (primarily Peter) for about four weeks. Peter's dad Fred, his wife Gertrude and Peter's sister Joan were fantastically hospitable and made me feel part of the family quite quickly. Having come from a dairy farm and a very small holding, it was a wonderful experience to work with a totally different set of parameters on a sheep farm on an island, where the timing of almost everything and life in general, revolved around the tides. My earlier short experience of trying to learn how to ride a horse came in really handy too, as we would often use a horse to ride well away from the homestead to muster sheep or do other jobs in more remote locations.

Once when we must have been reckoning on a big day, Peter and I rode towards the east quite early and, coming up over a ridge, were almost deafened by the sound of thousands of cicadas which had been awakened a little earlier with the first rays of the sun. Of course, shearing and dealing with quantities of wool was new to me too and Peter got me to consolidate the wool in the wool press. In ignorance, I must have done it a little too effectively, as he reckoned that particular bale was the heaviest he'd ever had to deal with!

On another occasion, having finished what we were doing and heading home on our horses, we came across one of the feral donkeys that live on the island. It was a jack (male donkey) on one of the many open tracks on top of a long ridge. Peter spurred his horse on and they took off, the jack going flat out while hee-hawing all the while. I didn't need to encourage my horse to follow suit, and the pursuit didn't end until the jack took to the tea-tree scrub where the horses couldn't follow. It was the fastest horse ride I have ever done in my life! Taken all in all, the time spent on the island was very enjoyable and a great experience. About 60 years later I went to the island again for a one-day Scripture Union celebration with folk from our church, and it was wonderful to see a number of great additions and modifications compared with when I had been there as a camper.

Chapter 4

Starting Work

My brother, who had spent some years working on other dairy farms, came home to work even though our family had not yet bought a larger farm, and he got a job at the local Kumeū garage. Sadly for him, he went down with a bug of some sort and I went to fill in for him as I had recently come back from working on Ponui Island. That garage job soon became a job for me for a short time, rather than for him. I was put to work as a 'grease monkey', changing oil and greasing all the various grease nipples (numerous in those days) on the cars that came in. Taken all around, I think things worked out reasonably well for one so inexperienced.

Battling with heavy truck tyres and wheels and having my bike mischievously chained up by my boss are the things I remember most about my short time there. Knowing who had chained my bike up, I switched the sparkplug leads on his car, but it didn't take him long to sort that out! A little later, when I wanted to make an attachment for our new tractor, I went back and used their lathe. After doing the work needed, I cleaned it all up as we had been taught to do at college, much to the admiration and delight of the shop foreman.

As both Rob and I had now finished our formal schooling, it was time to look for a larger property so we could all live off it as a family. We looked at farms as far south as Rangiriri and beyond Warkworth in the north, but none of them really seemed to suit our idea of what we wanted; or else they were more than we could afford.

Finally, we were taken to a place halfway between Silverdale and Kaukapakapa (which means 'a shag flapping its wings'). The farm was a total of 97 hectares, half of which was in standing native bush. It was owned at that time by a single ex-serviceman who wanted out, and as he was by himself, gorse was taking over much of the property. Actually he wasn't even scratching the surface of the potential of the property with milking fewer than 30 cows. Yes, we decided, this was the farm for us, and we made the purchase, officially taking possession on 1 April 1953. And no, it didn't turn out to be an April fool's choice!

We bought a new 1953 Fordson Major tractor and as there was a block of about three hectares that had been partially prepared for sowing in grass that autumn, Rob immediately went over from Kumeū with the new tractor to finish the preparation for sowing the new grass seed. In the meantime, the rest of us were frantically packing up at the Kumeū farm what we wanted to take with us, ready for transporting to Silverdale.

With the farm bought and the Kumeū farm packed up, we engaged our local carrier to cart all our Kumeū gear over to the new farm, together with a number of tractor and trailer loads. Our good friends Mr and Mrs Cates very generously provided the transport for Mum, whose hip joint by this time had started to really stiffen up. They had a 1948 Ford Super Deluxe car which we thought would be quite spacious and give a good ride – which it did for those without hip problems.

The homestead on the new Silverdale farm was built to a 1905 UK architect's winning design and had three small bedrooms, and two very large bedrooms, a lounge, a dining room, an extremely small kitchen, and a relatively small bathroom. There were six fireplaces and a verandah around three sides of the house. The previous owner, who lived by himself, really only used a couple of the eight rooms available, and had three or four dogs tied up to some of the verandah posts, with the net result that the place was heavily infested with fleas and cockroaches. One of the first priorities was to shake flea powder around all the skirting boards throughout the house in an effort to make it somewhat more liveable.

While this helped somewhat, it was decided to do a total fumigation job of the house, as there were also bees in the walls at one corner, and goodness knows what other sort of bugs lurking elsewhere! The contractors who came to do this enveloped and sealed the whole house in plastic sheeting (we all left the property for about three hours) and then released cyanide into the sealed plastic bubble. This was most effective and, once safe, we were able to go in again. As all the bees were dead, we opened up the wall where they had been and got a nice lot of meadow comb honey as a result!

Our telephone line when we first went there was just a single wire of various sorts joined together and connected at the boundary of the farm to a party line for about six farms The party line was owned by the Post and Telegraph Department (P&T). Our section was known as an earth return system which only necessitated one line, but it really had its problems. The first interesting thing about this line was that the various pieces of wire were joined together in a number of different ways. Some were the figure of eight join (like reef knot) and others were like two interlocking loops. Quite often the line would be almost inoperative because of the resistance in some of the joints, and we found that invariably it was the figure of eight ones that were the trouble. After a while, we realised that when the wind caused the line to sway, it made the two-loop joins keep themselves in good electrical contact, while the others with no movement between them soon corroded as there was nothing to keep them electrically clean.

I happen to be extremely sensitive to electricity and it was while we were fixing one of the joins one afternoon, that I was holding the two ends of the wires while Dad started to join them. Someone rang us and the resultant electrical surge went in one arm and out the other! I was tempted to let go, but didn't. We later realised that the call was probably from my brother Rob, who was at that time doing his stint in the army because of the compulsory military training scheme that was in vogue at that time. As Mum was disabled and also had a heart condition, paying for a proper two-line system joined into the P&T telecommunications network was a high priority and we managed to get it done within the first year.

While the farm was located in the Silverdale area, we actually had closer ties to the villages to the west. Whitehills Road which was the top boundary of the farm was the watershed between east and west at that point of the North Island, but we generally had more to do with Waitoki and Kaukapakapa over the hill to the west than with Silverdale to the east. Waitoki was where Rob and I taught Sunday school on a Sunday morning and where there was a regular evening Methodist service. As in the early days, we had no car, so it meant walking about two kilometres to meet up with Beryl Roberton who was our Sunday school superintendent and getting a ride with her for the extra five kilometres to Waitoki for Sunday school. We enjoyed being able to tell of Jesus' love to the young people of the area, and trust and pray that many of them, if not all, have by now trusted Jesus as their personal Saviour.

I must pay tribute here to those many people who selflessly ran up quite a few kilometres just for the sake of getting us either to a Christian service, or a midweek Bible study at Kaukapakapa. The mode of transport varied from one Presbyterian minister's Model T Ford to the Methodist minister's original VW Beetle to a little narrow-gauge Ford Prefect, and for me, a motorbike pillion ride, but any of these was far better than walking!

Our first car was purchased out of royalties from serpentine that was quarried from the farm, and it was a 1952 Belgium-assembled Plymouth Cranbrook. It was a lovely soft-riding car with big doors, which we had bought in the hope that it would enable Mum to get out and about a bit. Unfortunately, although of a reasonably high seating style, it wasn't comfortable enough for Mum and I think the only agonising ride she had in it was to cast a vote in a general election. She must have really wanted to vote someone in, or out! Having the car gave us more independence and meant that we could go to the various Christian meetings in Orewa, Silverdale and Whangaparāoa to the east, as well as Waitoki, Wainui and Kaukapakapa to the west. It became a necessary item later when I was on the Methodist circuit preaching roster, which meant I was ranging over an even wider area.

With fences being almost non-existent and gorse encroaching on what pasture land there was, a high priority was to try and establish some paddocks with electric fences and to push back the encroaching gorse from the pasture land. This of course meant a lot of grubbing of the gorse which was in the most part quite successful because by cutting deeply under the gorse and taking it out by the roots as much as possible, we successfully killed about 80 percent of it the first time.

Another priority was to start clearing and putting into pasture the areas where gorse re-growth or scrubby tea-tree had taken over. I designed and fitted a pipe crush bar to the front of the new Fordson Major tractor and with a set of 24-inch giant discs spent many hours crushing and discing the two-metre high lighter gorse and tea-tree growth. This basically just laid it down and killed a proportion of it ready for burning before further cultivation.

There were a number of areas that had been growing gorse for a lot longer and for those places, we hired Hopper Brothers of Whangaparāoa to come with their D4 Caterpillar tractor to crush and sweep the bigger stuff into rows for burning. The biggest gorse stem that we found was 100 millimetres in diameter.

There were also quite a number of areas where the tea-tree was smaller though still about two metres high. In fact we called one little flat of about two hectares 'Pea Stake Flat' because that is what the trunks of the tea-tree reminded us of. After crushing any area, we made and disced up a decent firebreak all around it, then we would burn it when the weather was right and it had wilted sufficiently. But that often left a lot of burnt sticks lying on the ground, so I designed and had the local garage build an easily coupled front-mounted bulldozer blade for the tractor which was lifted by means of the built-in rear-mounted hydraulics through steel wire ropes and pulleys. It was very successful for what it was designed to do, and a good number of hours were spent sweeping the sticks into rows for further burning on all blocks. These areas were then initially disced over again and left to fallow before further cultivation and sowing with grass seed.

My brother Rob, following the agricultural side of things, had seen advertised (probably in the *Power Farming* magazine) a particular type of tiller designed and made in Australia which was very successful when following the approximate contour of the ground by moving water from the damper areas out onto the dryer ridges. So we imported one as they weren't available in New Zealand at that time.

We had thought of doing this on our property until we realised the place had once been totally overrun with gorse, and breaking up the grass surface would mean we'd have to contend with a staggering amount of gorse re-growth. However, it was a wonderful tiller, and on one particular block of higher tea-tree that the D4 had crushed, after being burnt and swept and burnt again, there was little more than about 20 millimetres of topsoil. We agreed to not rush into grassing this block and used the tiller about every two months for a year, lifting and mixing the subsoil. At the end of the year we had about 120 millimetres of good rich soil to plant an initial crop of swedes into before more cultivation for planting the grass-seed.

On this block I remember using the strength of the tiller to lift out some old pine stumps that had obviously been milled 15 to 20 years previously. I would put the tractor in low gear, get a tine well hooked under the old stump and allow the tractor to rear up because it couldn't move forward. I was using steel lugged wheels, as rubber tyres wouldn't have had the traction for this to happen. When the tractor had reared to about 45 degrees, I would dip the clutch, and the weight of the front of the tractor rotating around the rear axle as a fulcrum would lift the tree stump out of the ground as trees aren't built to resist a vertical lift! It was on this block also that we extended our use of explosives on tree stumps that were too new and hence unable to be extracted by the above method.

Back in the 1950s we were able to go and buy whatever we wanted in the way of gelignite, fuse and detonators from the local metal quarry. How things have changed – for the better I guess! To get the greatest effect, we used to drill three holes around the stump, angled towards the centre. We then placed a stick of gelignite (about 180 millimetres long and 35 millimetres in diameter as I remember them) down each hole, after placing the detonator (and a slow-burning fuse) in one of them. We then used cordite which is an instantaneous fuse to connect all three charges. The final simple touch never ceased to amaze me as to how effective it was, and that was what is known as water-tamping. This means that each hole was filled with water, and the expansion of gasses from the explosion was so instantaneous that the water stopped the gasses escaping out of the top of the hole. The net effect was to have the stump blown completely out of the ground – if you had judged the holes and amount of 'jelly' right, that is! I used this same method later at Peter Dye's place to clear some unwanted New Zealand cabbage trees. The root under a cabbage tree is like a giant carrot but by drilling into the centre of it well down, the gelignite effectively cut the carrot tap root, making the tree much easier to pull over and out.

Taken all around, our farming operation was improving and we were doing things that even a farm advisor who came to a chap lower down the valley would ask, 'What new thing are the boys at the head of the valley up to now?' Initially we were supplying the Kaipara Dairy Company at Helensville with cream which was taken to the roadside and placed in a stand at almost truck tray level. Of course supplying cream meant getting rid of the skim milk. The traditional way of doing so was to have sufficient pigs to feed the skim milk to. But the fact that Rob and I were getting frequent boils (whether the pigs were to blame or not, who knows?) meant that we ceased keeping pigs.

So then – what do you do with the skim milk? We decided that it was, in fact, a good fertiliser which encouraged soil microbe activity, so we started to pump it into a square tank that could be picked up hydraulically with a rear tray I had made for the tractor and we put it out onto the poorer patches of the farm with wonderful results. Not long after this, the Kaipara Dairy Company moved to making dried milk powder as its main focus and we started to supply them with whole milk.

On wet, miserable days while I was on the farm, I did a correspondence course in automotive engineering, or plain automotive mechanics with the Sydney Technical College as there wasn't anything comparable here in New Zealand in the 1950s. I guess it did help me understand more of what goes on in a vehicle, and was probably one of the factors that encouraged me to tackle a number of sometimes rather complex mechanical problems. I wonder now at my arrogance when on the farm in my early twenties, how I went about replacing a camshaft in our 1953 Fordson Major tractor. I realise now all the snags I could have got myself into, but mercifully

I managed to pull it off and it was a real success. It also gave me confidence to do all sorts of repairs later when in Papua New Guinea – like very carefully pulling the sewing machine completely apart and getting it to go again at Kawito.

Chapter 5

Receiving God's Call

Taken all around, things were going pretty sweetly on the farm after about eight years. Much of the farm was now broken in and productive. Many improvements had been made, a new cowshed and large implement shed had been built and because we had culled the cows very heavily for both production and temperament, we had a good herd that we didn't need to leg-rope or chain in our internal race cowshed. This took eight cows at a time which is, of course, very small by today's standards! The only drawback to not chaining the cows into their bails was if an aircraft flew low overhead, or if there was a heavy shower with hail and the cows got spooked; it then became a case of sorting out cows and teat cups, as they were free to back out of the bails. Fortunately, this only happened a couple of times that I remember.

As mentioned, I was involved in the Waitoki Sunday school and Bible class and a home group in Kaukapakapa. This weekly home group was held in the home of Alan Osborne who was another person who was an encourager spiritually, though he didn't always lead the study. I took a number of sessions but once, giving a few facts about alcohol brought about quite a reaction from one person. I will always remember Alan's consoling remark to me when I told him about it. He said, 'If you throw a stone into a group of dogs, it's the one who was hit that yelps.' In other words, it must have really struck a chord with that person. The local Methodist minister, a former wheat farmer from Canterbury, had also taken a real interest in a number of us in the Kaukapakapa Bible class. He taught us something of how to preach and let us loose on various small local congregations. (Remember what I had said to Dad?)

It was after I had been preaching out on the Whangaparāoa Peninsula one Sunday afternoon that I met for the first time a Salvation Army officer who was home on furlough from working in Colombo in what was then known as Ceylon (now Sri Lanka). The Salvation Army officer was staying with Miss North from whom Dad had learnt all of his beekeeping knowledge. They invited Dad and me back to the bach where they were staying for afternoon tea and it was while we were walking to their place that the SA officer said, 'I covet you for the mission field and will be praying to that end.' My internal response was not very spiritual I must confess, because I could sense she was a real prayer warrior, and I mentally thought, 'Oh, drat you.' I also remember one time when I had been reading in Isaiah about his call to service, and Isaiah said, 'Here I am Lord, send me.' I am ashamed to say I closed my Bible and thought, 'It might have been okay for him, but not me.' Yes, I still had a way to go to be willing to do whatever God wanted of me, but then things began to change.

Although the farm was going well, I gradually felt that there was something else that God wanted me to be involved in. As many of my Bible class peers were going to New Zealand Bible College, I wondered whether that was what I should do too. This of course was an extremely poor motive, as I honestly didn't have a spiritual call to do anything in particular, so I decided to go to the next Bible College graduation in the Auckland Town Hall to seek some guidance. The person who gave the valedictory address was a South African by the name of Campbell McAlpine and the main thrust of his message was, 'Be absolutely sure of your call before you move out.' In other words, don't move out in missionary service or any other fulltime service in God's name unless you are sure that is what

God wants you to do. So I thought, okay God, that was a clear red light and a resounding 'No' about going anywhere at this stage; I'd better just go back to the farm and wait. I looked up in my mum's concordance the word 'wait', which occurs a staggering number of times in Scripture, so I thought that wait was what I had to do.

I actually didn't have to wait too long. Our Waitoki Sunday school superintendent who had wanted to go to the mission field, sadly died of hepatitis when relatively young. Her husband was in the RNZAF reserve, and had tried to get me involved in it too, but hadn't really taken too much notice of her faith. Suddenly, after her death he wanted to go to the mission field 'and dig the straightest post-hole that anyone could dig.' As a result of this, he sold his farm to Lew and Billy Shepherd. Lew had also trained as a pilot in the New Zealand Air Force without becoming operational but as he was a Christian, he had linked up with Mission Aviation Fellowship, and was an MAF council member. As it was still in the days when neighbouring farmers shared equipment and helped each other, we became really good friends, helping each other on many occasions in different ways.

Being a council member, Lew was in the know about when our very first New Zealand pilot family was almost ready to leave the country and a meeting at his house was organised. Doug Hunt came to tell the Kaukapakapa home group what he would be doing in the future. As the meeting progressed, it was as if a still, small voice said to me, 'This is something you could do.' Doug was going to hold a field day at Ardmore Airport a couple of weekends later when people could take a joyride. I believe that the God we worship today is the same God Gideon worshipped centuries ago, and so I asked God to give me a sign that when I took the joyride, I would either be thrilled with the flight or I'd be sick. I knew the latter would be most embarrassing for me, but it could give a very clear indication of the way ahead!

In the late 1950s when coming from the north of Auckland to Ardmore, one had to meander one's way through Auckland streets to get onto the southern motorway and so we arrived a little later than many others. When I enquired about a flight, the answer was, 'Sorry, all the seats have been taken.' I must admit I was a tad confused by this but was prepared to think it may have been God showing me a shut door. You can imagine my delight and surprise when Trevor Strong, the chairman of MAF (and a WW2 Lancaster pilot) came and told me that he had heard of my desire to fly and had asked someone whom he knew who had flown a number of times if he would give up his seat so I could have a flight! So thank you Lord for undertaking in this and opening up the way for me to get to know what you want me to do! I must confess I was so excited at the way things had worked out that I forgot to ask who it was that had given up their seat for me and to thank them for it, so I trust that they might just read this.

Doug kindly seated me in the front right-hand seat of the four-seater Cessna 180 (ZK-BUF) so I could observe what he did, and to say I was thrilled with the experience would be a gross understatement, even though, sadly, it wasn't for one of the other passengers. It may have been a lack of faith, but when I got home, I can remember kneeling by my bed for a number of nights asking God if I had got the message correctly, as it was going to mean breaking up the family farming partnership. Even though I tried to dismiss the thought, I can still remember what I saw in my mind's eye – the curvature of the engine cowl and the propeller arc as I saw it from the front right-hand seat.

The next obvious thing to do was for me to go back to Ardmore later and take a test flight with an instructor to see whether they thought I would be capable of becoming a commercial pilot, which I would need to be if I was to fly for MAF. I explained this to the instructor Ken Windsor who took me up and asked me to do a number of things and then he took me through a few manoeuvres which I since realise could have scared the pants off many people. After we landed, I asked him what he thought and he said, 'You'll make it okay.' Wow, as far as I was concerned, this meant that what I felt God wanted me to do with my life had just been confirmed!

Chapter 6

Mission Aviation Fellowship

So then, what exactly was this Mission Aviation Fellowship, how did it originate, and what was its aim and purpose?

What is known today as Mission Aviation Fellowship (MAF or 'Maf' for short) had its beginnings in a Holy Spirit prompt in the mind of a young itinerant Kiwi Christian evangelist some time before WW2 began. Murray Kendon was in a King Country town and went to hear a missionary from Papua New Guinea tell of his experiences. From my research, it's more than likely this was Len Twyman (an Australian married to a Kiwi, hence the New Zealand deputation) who was a very early missionary to the Huli people in the Tari Valley of the Southern Highlands of PNG.

Before the war, Qantas Airways was using amphibious Catalina flying boats into a number of the remote areas of PNG – especially those that had no airstrip but a suitable water landing area. For Len to get to Tari meant taking the Catalina from Port Moresby to Lake Kutubu in the Southern Highlands, followed by three days of hard uphill trekking to get to Tari. Murray listened as Len related what he had to do in order to get into the Tari Valley area where the Huli tribe lived and remembers thinking at the time, 'Why can't they just use light aircraft to save time and effort?' In those days, it would probably have been Tiger Moths that he was thinking of.

Not long afterwards, WW2 started and although Murray had no real desire to become a pilot, he was drafted into the RNZAF and started training in Christchurch. Doing well, he went to Canada and then to the UK for further training before being posted to 179 Squadron Coastal Command. There he was destined to co-pilot Wellingtons on depth-charge missions as part of the Battle of the Atlantic, which was WW2's longest continuous military campaign. Their aim was to reduce the number of enemy submarines that were playing havoc with the convoys of ships bringing troops, food and supplies to the European theatre of war.

Meanwhile, a Helensville grocer's assistant named Trevor Strong entered the RNZAF. Trevor had always wanted to fly, and after his training was completed in New Zealand and he had done further training in the UK, he was posted to No. 7 Pathfinder Squadron of Bomber Command. Trevor initially flew Wellingtons, then Stirlings, and finally Avro Lancasters, flying 44 bombing sorties before being shot down. He was a prisoner of war for nine months, escaped and was recaptured, then finally freed and later decorated with a Distinguished Flying Cross. The measure of the man was that when he gave orders to abandon the aircraft as they went down, he went all the way back to his rear gunner's position to make sure he knew to bail out, but sadly the gunner had been shot and was dead already. Only after he knew that all his crew were accounted for did Trevor bail out himself!

When I was still at Kaukapakapa, going to a home group there, Trevor came to share some of his experiences. We were blithely singing that great old chorus, 'Anywhere with Jesus I can safely go' and Trevor in his typical slow dry manner said, 'For sure that is true, but those words take on a whole new meaning when you hear bloodhounds barking and you know they are on your trail!'

A couple of years before the war's end, Murray wrote an article which was published on 5 July 1945 in *A Christian Weekly*, a UK Christian newspaper. There he outlined how he felt that light aircraft could be used to aid people instead of pilots using their skills as they currently were, which was essentially for destruction. After

Trevor had been released from being a POW and was flown back to England, he joined Murray in his vision to use aircraft to help in mission and charitable work. Murray had written his article in bold faith, and it struck a chord with a number of Christian pilots from various countries who also supported the vision.

Separate incidents in each of their lives had helped cement both Murray and Trevor's belief in this vision. For Murray, it had been while he was flying out over the North Atlantic. From the air he spotted a young chap about the same age as himself, speedily retreating into a submarine that was temporarily on the surface before it dived below. Murray thought that this young guy was probably in much the same position as himself, drafted to do a job that he hadn't really desired and all because others had caused an antagonistic situation. From then on, the concept of using light aircraft to help rather than destroy became even more of a focus for him.

A key moment for Trevor, who had flown many sorties over enemy territory, came at a time when he was flying towards his target area. As he flew over the Bay of Biscay, tracer bullets were coming up all around him and the others in the squadron and in the midst of this, Trevor gave a promise to God; that if he got out of all this alive, he would use his influence in some form of Christian mission work.

After the pair were de-mobbed at war's end, they set about promoting the concept of using light aircraft to help in humanitarian work. While many thought the idea was a good one, the two men struck a brick wall when it came time for others to put their money where their mouths were! Perhaps they had not explained well enough what they meant by 'light aircraft', as almost everyone – businessmen, church leaders and even most mission leaders felt the whole idea would be far too expensive. In fairness to those who didn't grasp the idea, it has to be remembered that this was immediately after the end of the war, and the whole country was in full recovery mode. But even about 25 years later in the then British Solomon Islands, the British administration had the idea that a DC3 was a 'light aircraft' when MAF was negotiating to work there!

All this negativity changed however, when Murray and Trevor met Dr Cochrane of Mildmay Mission. Not only did Dr Cochrane encourage them to follow the vision they felt God had given them, but he gave them space in his Mildmay Mission offices in London to begin operating from. He later gave Murray and his new wife Minnie a very small flat in those offices to live in. As Murray was a true evangelist at heart, he would travel around preaching and evangelising when he was on his weekend leave. Minnie his wife was in the WAAF (Woman's Auxiliary Air Force) and had come to the Lord as a result of the Holy Spirit working through Murray's speaking.

Murray and Trevor spent about a year travelling around the UK making the cause of MAF known, and other English Christian airmen became very interested. Together they all managed to purchase a Miles Gemini aircraft which, after dedication, was used to make an initial survey flight into Africa. This was flown by a couple of British airmen while Murray and his new wife Minnie stayed in England to continue promotion. For a full account of the survey trip to Africa and the beginnings of MAF from a UK perspective, Stuart King's book *Hope has Wings* is well worth a read. In it you can read about how the poor little Gemini didn't make it over a ridge in Africa due to not having enough power to out-climb a downdraft, possibly because the ex-wartime pilot was used to a much more powerful aircraft. The Gemini finished up crashing into a banana plantation! I have no doubt that this is the reason why MAF now trains its pilots in the 'acute angle' method of ridge crossing.

Meanwhile, Trevor returned to New Zealand and got married

and also began raising awareness of the fledgling MAF here. It took some time to formalise things, but in 1958 Missionary Aviation Fellowship was formed as an incorporated society with Trevor as the first chairman of the council, a role he held for many years. The name was later changed to Mission Aviation Fellowship. After remaining in the UK for a couple of years, Murray and Minnie came to New Zealand to help in the establishment of MAF here. Whether due to a misunderstanding or whatever, Murray was under the impression that after their time here, he and Minnie would go back to the UK and help with the work there. When the time came for that to happen, MAF-UK said they couldn't afford the boat fares for them to go back to the UK, so the Kendons were effectively stuck here in New Zealand. While disappointed at first, they remained and helped establish MAF-NZ, and they were always most supportive in every way.

Kiwis have been in critically useful places throughout MAF's history. On the survey flight into Africa when the Gemini landed at Khartoum, Sudan, they contacted a mission based there (SUM – Sudan United Mission, now part of Pioneers) to see if they would be interested in the crew coming and explaining what this new entity called MAF was all about. Fortunately, or providentially, they had contacted a mission that was holding an executive council meeting at the time. The Kiwi chairman, the late Ken Nobbs, immediately grasped the possibilities, cancelled the council meetings and invited the crew to come and explain the whole concept. He immediately saw the benefits of air travel, especially in Sudan's wet season when roads became bog-holes. He encouraged Stuart King to consider Sudan as a possible field of service and it was, in fact, the first field of operation for MAF-UK.

Even though that first African survey flight sadly finished in a banana plantation, many people by then had caught the vision of the fantastic possibilities of using light aircraft as an aid to this humanitarian and Christian mission operation. This first MAF-UK programme operating in Sudan used a De Havilland DH 89 Dominie which had been purchased from the Israeli Air Force. This initial Dominie was joined by two others a little later as the work expanded.

Space precludes listing the senior roles Kiwis have held in Papua New Guinea, Sudan, Arnhem Land (North Australia), Indonesian Timor, Tanzania, Kenya, UK, Ache (Indonesia) and now in the Asia-Pacific office of MAF International at Cairns. On the critical engineering side, MAF Kiwis have also excelled, firstly in the Ballarat (Australia) training centre, and many of the locations mentioned above. The old RAAF airbase at Ballarat became possible to purchase due to a King Country farmer being led by the Lord to give the value of the sale of his farming property to MAF in New Zealand. MAF-NZ was then able to donate half of it to Australia (and loan the other half) for the establishment of MAF-AIR at Ballarat. The first manager of MAF-AIR, was also a Kiwi/Englishman (Alex and Molly Jardine) who was an aircraft design engineer working for TEAL (Tasman Empire Airways Ltd., which has become Air New Zealand) prior to moving to Ballarat. MAF-NZ wrote off the loan portion when Australia later gave a very substantial donation towards the hangar MAF-NZ built at Ardmore.

So despite the seemingly negative start with the survey in Africa, MAF has now grown into an international organisation, operating 130 mainly light single-engine aircraft to the remote rural areas of around 32 countries worldwide, with an MAF aircraft taking off or landing somewhere in the world every five minutes.

God has literally given Murray and Trevor's vision wings, which daily fulfils the MAF purpose of 'Flying for Life'.

With the Lord's clear calling on my life, I had to now make the preparations needed. I also realised that at that stage the requirements for MAF were: a commercial pilot's licence, an aircraft engineering licence and a minimum of a year at Bible College, so the flying was only part of the whole. The idea of having a flying as well as an engineering licence was because initially, most MAF bases were usually manned by just one couple out in the bush, so an engineering licence was obviously needed there to maintain the aircraft.

The crunch came for me one morning when Rob and Dad were discussing the idea of buying a nearby farm as a runoff so the whole farming operation could be expanded. I had been having what I call 'holy discontent' for some time and had to tell them that my heart really wasn't in expanding the operation and told them why. I was surprised and gratified to experience Dad's acceptance of what I felt God wanted me to do, even though he hadn't allowed me to go into the air force for my compulsory military training. As I relayed my thoughts about God's guidance to the rest of the family, they too accepted how I felt, and the farm actually paid for all my private pilot training, which I did while I was still at home on the farm.

One Saturday afternoon, I went over to Kaukapakapa to see one of the home group chaps who owned quite a big farm and runoff to see if he knew of any opportunities for employment. I realised that I needed to leave our farm and take what work opportunities I could, to be free to further my flying training. Peter (Dye) was going to his runoff to feed out some hay, so while the chap he had currently working for him drove the tractor, Peter and I rode on the tray at the back. Peter knew my situation in needing to have space and time to gain extra flying experience and as we went along, he said to me, 'I don't suppose you want work do you? The young chap (pointing to the tractor driver) is leaving me, and I need to get another worker.' Once again the Lord had gone before me, and I was able to leave the home farm and go and work for Peter who, until I bought a car for myself, loaned me his to drive to Ardmore so I could spend time flying. My co-workers at the Waitoki Bible class (Neville and Beryl Bradley) were also always most encouraging by asking, 'How many hours have you got up now?' I think they thought that it was a pretty slow process, which in fact it was to begin with.

Peter not only had a reasonable-sized farm on the Kaukapakapa flats, but also a runoff on much higher ground. The flats were inclined to flood and had a liberal number of New Zealand cabbage trees dotted over them. I was able to help Peter remove some of them by using the explosive skills I had learned on the home farm.

After gaining my private pilot's licence, I dallied for almost a year. The farm had been my material security and I knew that I needed to gain my commercial pilot's licence (CPL), but to do this, it would be best for me to take a ground course with the Auckland Aero Club which were the only ones providing such a course at that time. I realised when taking the CPL course, just how little I and my fellow private pilots actually knew and how potentially dangerous we were! Very fortunately for me, I had Aunty Pansy and Uncle Vic at Karaka (where I often used to holiday when younger) who were very happy to have me stay with them while I did the CPL ground course. But Charles Road in Karaka is a long way from Ardmore Airport! Well, the Lord had this sorted out for me too, in that it was an easy walking or biking distance from a Ministry of Works chap who went to Ardmore every day and was willing to take me with him. Praise the Lord!

After the course, I went back to the home farm for a short period but I realised that now was the time to finally break my ties with the farm and the family agreed to change the partnership details and pay me my share. It had become obvious to me that it would be best to see if I could gain employment closer to Ardmore so I could pursue my CPL flying training. Somehow I heard that Rex Hillary (brother of Sir Ed) was looking for a worker for their beekeeping business in Papakura. A lot of people are understandably a bit scared of bees but having helped Dad with his at Kumeū, they didn't hold quite the same dread for me, though I still had a healthy respect for any bee's tail end! I think it may have been from Rex Hillary that I heard about the MacKays exactly opposite his home and business were looking for a boarder. An added bonus to this was that the MacKays also went to Papakura's First Presbyterian Church. And so it was, I was able to work a few days of the week and do flying training on the others. Once again, the Lord had gone before and paved the way.

Most of my initial flying training was done with the Auckland Aero Club in PA18 Piper Cub aircraft, a faithful, light tail-wheel type that was pretty forgiving. I had a number of instructors and I have to give the women top marks for being the most empathetic and understanding. An experience that I vividly remember relates to how light the Cub was. On one occasion, I was on the coast just north of the mouth of the Clevedon Valley doing some manoeuvring exercises and there was a reasonably strong easterly wind blowing against the rising ground there. I suddenly realised I was rather dramatically gaining altitude even though I wasn't trying to climb. When it became more noticeable, I moved the stick forward to put the nose down and we were still going up! I then opened the throttle more for extra power and with the stick forward I dived myself out of the very strong updraft.

Yes, it was a relatively slow process building up the hours of experience needed, firstly for my private pilot's licence and then many more flying hours (and hence experience) for my commercial pilot's licence. Because I had heard from a missionary from Papua New Guinea about the airstrips that MAF used there, I spent quite a high proportion of my time practising short field landings. Not everyone did this. Many I knew who were also heading for MAF used to spend quite a lot of time (and money) getting new ratings on various sorts of aircraft, but I couldn't see the point of doing that, knowing I would most likely never usefully fly those aircraft. (Ratings in this context are like different classes on a driver's licence.) Rather, I endeavoured to get quite proficient in short field landings which actually was going to pay big dividends for me personally in a year or two and for MAF very much later in my flying career.

After quite a few months of this part-time flying training, when I had been up with Jim Bergman doing some advanced training one morning, he asked me if I would be interested in acting as an office worker and coordinator for a new venture he was about to start – Auckland Flying School. Jim knew I needed to build up hours, and said he would pay me with flying hours. That suited me fine. It also meant that I was to fly the training aircraft over to the Whenuapai airbase for their maintenance. These flying hours were on top of those I was paid with. Jim was good to me, and we worked well together with the flying school really taking off (excuse the pun!) It expanded rapidly and became quite a significant player in the flying training work done at Ardmore for a period. The Lord again had opened the way for me to progress, without me even having to ask.

As well as office work and flying to Whenuapai, Jim got me to do some other commercial flying once I got my CPL. He had the use of a clipped wing Auster J5F (ZK-BBZ) which, because of its shortened wing could easily flip into a spin if you mishandled it. Because of this, one of the exercises that had to be undertaken to gain a rating on it was to deliberately put the aircraft into a spin and then recover from it. I must confess that this was something I endured more than enjoyed! But the reward was being able to do aerial photography in that aircraft which it was quite well suited for. One of the companies that we used to fly for was White's Aerial Photography. Mr White himself was brilliant in that he could tell you exactly what was needed to get the shot he wanted and then it was just a case of positioning the aircraft accordingly.

After a period doing administration work for Jim, a commercial operator who flew from Whenuapai to almost all points north in a Cessna C180 crashed into a mountain in poor weather on his return to Auckland after having maintenance done in New Plymouth. Jim saw the opening and asked me to develop Northland Airways using a Mooney Super 21 (ZK-CFV). It was quite a fast four-seat aircraft which was rather critical when it came to weight and balance and getting the centre of gravity into the safe operating envelope. It was so clean aerodynamically that one had to really reduce power when on any sort of descent to keep the airspeed out of the so-called 'yellow arc'. (Most aircrafts' air speed indicators have a green arc which means the aircraft is built to withstand normal turbulence within that speed range and a higher speed yellow arc in which the aircraft should only be flown in smooth air, up to the red line above which it should never be flown.) On flights from the north, I frequently had to start my descent away up beyond Warkworth to get down to circuit height at Whenuapai because it was so clean.

I remember on my first commercial Northland Airways flight into Whenuapai to pick up a reporter and a couple of others who could promote the service, I forgot that Whenuapai was a military airfield. One of the first people to meet me was the air force commander, telling me where I should park and pick up from in future! We did operate this service for a period but with me (and the aircraft) not being instrument certified, it didn't come up to a number of expectations and so the service ceased.

When this service ended, I saw the possibility in collaboration with Jim of operating a training facility for prospective MAF pilots and talked with Rev Graham Miller about the idea. In his reply he quoted to me 2 Timothy 2:4 which says, 'No one serving as a soldier gets entangled in civilian affairs, but rather tries to please his commanding officer.' Isn't it wonderful, how God's Word seems to have an appropriate answer to so many of life's situations? It was to be about 24 years later, before I was to have a small part in MAF's Flight Training Centre at Ardmore!

A recent programme on Prime television about aircraft mishaps reminded me of an incident that I had when still based in Auckland. It was when doing a skydiving/parachute drop on the Thames airfield from around 10,000 feet. There were three skydivers – one Australian and two Kiwis. All the preparation went well but the Cessna C172 was struggling somewhat to climb to that height with four people on board. The marker run went well, with the senior skydiver saying that the winds below were almost at the maximum that they should try, a factor that became much more evident later. All the divers evacuated the aircraft, and I commenced a left-hand spiral descent, keeping an eye on the three of them as they rocketed towards the earth below at terminal velocity in a freefall.

And then it happened – just *one* parachute opened! Had two parachutes not opened and was I the reason for two people falling to their deaths? Then – wow – the other two parachutes opened, and my heart stilled and I thanked the Lord that at least all were going to land safely. Those two were almost spot-on with their landing but the other who had opened his chute first was about 500 metres away close to some stockyards. The reason? The Australian had been briefed that in New Zealand (at that time at least) the standard height for opening one's parachute was 1,000 feet, whereas in Australia it was 1,500 feet. His years of training took over and hence he had opened 500 feet earlier than the Kiwis and because of the rather strong winds closer to the surface, he had drifted well away from the proposed landing spot.

Knowing that one of the three requirements for being able to fly for or join MAF was an engineering licence, I tried a number of places on the airfield to get the experience. I honestly can't remember exactly in what sequence these events occurred but I worked for a time assisting the engineering team at the Auckland Aero Club and also for Airwork, assembling imported aircraft.

It was during the time at the Auckland Aero Club that I had the unnerving experience of an engine starting on me when I was doing the morning pull through – and no! – it wasn't because I had left any switches on. It was in fact a fault in the ignition system. It was particularly unnerving because it happened with the rear engine of a push-pull Cessna C336 and I was positioned between the rear tail booms. This aircraft had been developed by Cessna as a centre-line thrust aircraft so those pilots with less, or no experience in asymmetric (normal multi-engine) flight could handle it should one of the engines quit for any reason. At another stage I worked for Airwork with a Canadian engineer helping to reassemble imported four-seater Piper Cherokee aircraft and then had the honour of doing the initial New Zealand flight test of these aircraft. Thankfully, they all performed flawlessly, as I had no problems on any of those flights.

All this time, while boarding in Papakura, I attended Papakura's First Presbyterian Church where Rev Dr Graham Miller was the minister. He encouraged me to do private biblical studies which I did several nights each week in the church vestry. Also during this time, I was friendly with a young woman who was training to be a doctor, inspired by the work of the Leprosy Mission. Having gained my CPL and realising that another of MAF's requirements was at least one year's Bible training, and that Jean was going to be studying for another year or so before graduating, I thought that I could wait for her while doing the Bible training. So I registered at the Bible College of New Zealand (BCNZ, now Laidlaw College) in Henderson, took the entry test, and was accepted. More about Bible College later.

From the time I first started flying, I kept in contact with MAF through the MAYF (Mission Aviation Youth Fellowship) which was then meeting monthly in the home of Mr and Mrs Ken Nobbs. The Nobbs had previously been missionaries in Sudan for many years.

The Sunday afternoon MAYF meetings were not only mutually encouraging but we often had missionaries home on furlough visit us, which gave us valuable insights. One such was Brian Tucker to whom I will ever be grateful for telling us that from a missionary's point of view, there are three types of pilots. The ones who were super-efficient, never forgot anything, knew exactly where anything for the missionary was in the plane and then just shot through after unloading the stuff. At the other end of the spectrum there were those who were so relaxed that they frequently forgot some stuff, but had all the time in the world to talk with folk. And then there were those in between who normally remembered everything, did their job well, usually arrived when they said they would, and still made time for a little chat. This type was so encouraging for missionaries and I tried my best to be like them when on the field.

I am aware that there was one pilot who was so willing to talk with folk that he didn't get all the work done which he had been asked to do. Not at all helpful when the airstrip is quite a long way away from the missionary's home and the aircraft doesn't turn up at the end of the day because 'he didn't have time'. Not to mention the hoopla for the poor flight programmer trying to fit everything that was missed into the next day's programme if it was a multi-plane base!

Chapter 7

Southern Scenic Air Services

I'm not sure how Mrs Nobbs got to hear of it, but she rang me and told me that Southern Scenic Air Services (SSA) was looking for a pilot and suggested that I phone them. I was well aware of the limited experience and flying hours I had, which would most probably not be up to the parameters SSA would be wanting, but I phoned them anyway. After a good talk with Tex Smith, the chief pilot, I was asked to put my details in writing and send them in – which I did.

Thinking that it was only the right thing to do, I went to Bible Collrge one afternoon and told the secretary that there was a remote possibility that I could get a flying job in the South Island to gain further flying experience. He said, 'Well, if that is the case, you obviously don't want to come to college, so I'll take your name off our list.' I tried to explain it wasn't like that; there was only a possibility, but he was having none of it. You can imagine my feelings as I drove back to Papakura, now not able to go to Bible College and by then not having heard anything from SSA. But you can imagine my elation when I looked in the mail box on getting back to the MacKays' to find a letter there from SSA asking me to be in Queenstown as soon as possible! Thank you Lord!

As soon as possible? I had just traded my first little car, a Fiat Bambina, for a Morris 1000 which I wanted to take with me. Once again the way opened up for me, as there was a newly married couple from First Church who were going to Dunedin to attend the Presbyterian Knox College there. When I asked if they would consider driving my car south because I needed to fly down to get there as soon as possible, they jumped at the opportunity. They had been wondering how they could possibly take all their possessions with them. Having the car was a wonderful answer to prayer for them – and for me!

It's amazing what excitement, nervousness and a bit of apprehension can do to one. At Whenuapai, I boarded a SPANZ (South Pacific Airlines of New Zealand) DC3. It was the first time I had flown in a much larger aircraft and as others boarded it at the terminal, it was amazing how much it rocked on its undercarriage as various people came aboard. But the most surprising thing for me was that for the first time in my life, I felt motion sickness! What? Going to take up a flying job and I felt sick with just this sort of movement? Fortunately though, as soon as we were airborne I felt fine. Again, thank you Lord!

For someone who had lived at home on the farm all my life (except for the 18 months with Peter and Joan Dye), making the move to Queenstown and 'the big wide world' was a bit scary to start with. The first thing to do on arrival was of course to find somewhere to stay and I chose one of the many tourist guest houses to start with. Arriving just before the weekend gave me the opportunity to go to church on the Sunday morning. Having been given approved membership of the Presbyterian Church back home, I went to the local Presy church. It wasn't hard to find, as that church, the Salvation Army hall, and the Anglican church are all in central Queenstown and all on the same road, about 250 metres apart. Back in 1965 the Anglican church was covered in autumn with stunningly coloured Virginia creeper and was most picturesque. The Salvation Army (at that time) also had another venue in Queenstown – a guest house which I was directed to by Trevor Cheetham, the office worker at Southern Scenic Airways.

Tutuila House had been gifted to the Salvation Army by someone who had a close association with Tutuila Island in American Samoa. Tutuila was a magnificent old home with a number of large bedrooms, dining area, kitchen and lounge, but also with an annex out the back that had more single bedrooms as well as a laundry. There were also a couple of cabins which were used mainly to accommodate some of the transient staff (normally from overseas) as well as any of 'the family' who wished to have a little more freedom of movement. Being part of the family had both privileges and some responsibilities.

On the very rare occasions when there were no guests, the family would all sit around the very large table in the equally large kitchen and have our meals there. When the place was full (it could accommodate about 40) the family pitched in with a few of the mundane chores that needed to be done with a full house. The mid-1960s was a time when the *Scripture in Song* choruses were well known and being sung in Christian circles; there was a record player in the dining room often playing them as well as other Christian songs during meal times, which was really wonderful!

Initially, I went to the Presbyterian Church whenever I was free on a Sunday. It wasn't long however, before I realised that the minister there, sadly, had been greatly influenced by Dr Lloyd Geering and his radical departure from many of the scriptural truths that I had known from years of Bible studies and my own private study of the Scriptures. As I was living in a Salvation Army guest house, it was logical for me to try the Sallies to see whether their theology was more like what I understood to be the truth. It was, and so I stayed worshipping there with a great beneficial spin-off later on.

Southern Scenic Airways (SSA) was in those days owned by two individuals, who both worked daily in the company. One was an office person (Bill) who managed the accounts and all kinds of paperwork while the other owner (Barry) was an aircraft engineer who worked on the aircraft as well as repairing the old high-frequency valve radios that were being used for airborne communications mainly with home base and Air Radio. As there were two 'Bills' on staff, the office Bill was known as 'Inky' Bill, while the other, being an engineer, was known as 'Greasy' Bill. All the employees were really decent guys.

On 9 February 1965 Dave Cowan, a former American Air Force jet jockey, checked me out on a Cessna C185 which was the first of many I was to fly. However, I was not rated on any twin-engine aircraft, which was the type SSA used on the Milford scenic and timetabled route. Because of this, SSA sent me to Nelson to gain a twin-engine rating and I started that flying just 14 days later.

I flew commercially to Nelson on 23 February, arriving there about midday and immediately got into studying the details and procedures for the Piper PA23 Apache that I was training in the next day. The initial training the next day was pretty normal stuff – doing circuits, etc. – but the second day we got to do the upper-air manoeuvres and exercises. As I knew that the whole purpose of getting this rating was with regards to the twin-engine aspect, I had really studied up on that, so when the instructor called out that we had a fire in the starboard engine, I immediately went through the drill. In a rather confused voice, he said, 'Hey what is happening?' as the propeller had started to 'feather'. I replied, 'You said we had a fire in the starboard engine, so I am shutting it down.' He said, 'Start it again! We never completely shut down an engine when in training as it can chill the cylinders. We normally just pull the power back to idle.' Communication! That procedure was never, ever mentioned in any briefing or in the manual. Despite this episode, I still got the twin rating, thankfully!

When back in Queenstown, I started doing some local scenic flying in a C205 (the passenger forerunner of the Utility U206) and it wasn't long before I was in the air being checked out on the route to Milford Sound. Back then, there was a limited list of pilots who were allowed to fly into the Milford grass and gravel airstrip and it was a privilege to have made that grade. My first solo trip in the C205 on the SSA scenic route to Milford was a bit memorable. Quite differently to the Aussie system I worked with later of being checked out over any particular route a number of times, I was only checked a couple of times. Much of the route was quite easy to remember, but at Glade House at the top end of Lake Te Anau, my sense of direction took over. I headed more north, which in fact was about a direct line from that point to the Milford airfield rather than northwest. But it was not the right valley, so we came to a dead end and I needed to turn around and go back to the point where I went wrong and pick up the correct valley. At the Milford Hotel, when rounding up my passengers to head back to Queenstown, one guy was certain I needed some alcoholic fortification for the trip home – something he'd obviously convinced himself he needed! I thanked him for the offer, but declined.

After several successful trips to Milford, our chief pilot thought it was about time I was checked out on the DH89 Dominie twin which was at that time the mainstay of the scenic and regular service trips to Milford. To say that the Dominie was a beautiful aircraft to fly is an understatement. While basically being underpowered by the two 210hp six-cylinder de Havilland Gipsy Queen engines, the saving factor was that they were wonderfully reliable. As a DC3 pilot had earlier said to me as I flew with him 'The one saving factor for both the Dominie and the DC3 is that they are both powered by extremely reliable engines.' But if one engine does fail, you need to start looking for somewhere to land as just one engine only prolongs the glide!

On 23 March 1965, Tex Smith the chief pilot took me out in Dominie ZK-AKT and showed me how it handled. But the interesting thing with them is that there are no dual controls as there is only room for one person sitting in the pointy cockpit up front, so when being checked out, the trainee sits in the right-hand front passenger seat. Likewise for the instructor when the trainee is flying, the checker has to sit in that seat hoping to goodness that the new chum up front does everything correctly! After a short while with Tex flying, it was my turn. As everyone who has flown a tail-wheeled aircraft knows, for a number of reasons there is always a tendency for the aircraft to swerve to one side as power is applied. This is commonly referred to as 'swing on takeoff'.

With a tail-wheeled twin it is no different; however, instead of leading with full rudder in one direction, you can advance one throttle earlier than the other to overcome the swing on takeoff. Thankfully all went really well, and after the first landing which was quite good, Tex said, 'Okay, one more circuit to make sure that one wasn't a fluke.' As it wasn't, Tex got out and I continued on for a while getting the feel of the aircraft. However, I have to be honest here, and say that the Dominie had the softest, most forgiving undercarriage of any aircraft I have ever flown. In fact, it is possible when landing to fly them on (or wheel them on) and not actually know if you are in contact with the ground until you pull the power off. Now it didn't happen every time for sure, but the more time I spent in the Dominies the more frequently it did happen.

The Milford Sound airstrip is positioned very close to the junction of two main valleys and one small side valley (Ada and Cleddau and a branch thrown in) with sheer ex-glacial cliffs forming the sides of both main valleys. The SSA scenic flight to Milford came down the Ada Valley which positioned us at right angles to the line of the airstrip. Whether it was the way my checker had been shown, or whether he had formed the habit himself, I don't know, but I was checked out to turn right into the bottom of Cleddau Valley, circle to the left, and then turn right to line up on the Milford strip doing a sort of 'dumbbell' turn. This was okay (but in my opinion not ideal) in the morning as the sunlight was behind you so it showed up the cliff face of the mountain that you were turning towards while circling left. However, in the afternoon, if it was sunny, you were circling out of sunshine into the shadow towards a black face and you lost all depth perception as to how far you were away from the valley wall.

After a couple of afternoon flights under the above conditions, I changed my approach to flying alongside the black face, *out* of the shadow and circled right into the sunshine which, when the circle was about two-thirds done, gave you a straight approach to the airstrip. In my opinion, this was a very much safer direction flying-wise, as well as better on the nerves.

However, because it was at the confluence of three valley systems, the winds at the Milford airstrip could at times be very strong, turbulent and gusty. I well remember on one afternoon coming into land and having to move the throttles from full power to power right off to full power again a few times while stabilising some rocking motion with the ailerons because of the turbulence due to the whirling winds on approach. Upon safely landing and letting the passengers off, a young American chap about my age came up to me and said, 'I am a navy pilot based on an aircraft carrier and how you handled the aircraft on that approach was done really well considering the conditions you were contending with. Congratulations.' I thanked him for the encouragement and reverently thanked God too for the enablement!

Southern Scenic had a range of aircraft: C180, C185, C205, DH89 Dominie and a C180 floatplane. Having been checked out on the first four types, I only had to be checked out on the Cessna 180 floatplane. This is basically just a Cessna C180 mounted on a pair of floats and was used primarily for sightseeing off Queenstown Bay, but at later times we took hunters into various lakes and also recovered venison from lakes and rivers, before helicopters were available at an affordable price. Taking off on floats is not dissimilar to a land plane once you have it up on the step, but landing can be quite different! Probably the most surprising thing for me, was just how hard and unforgiving water can be! Yes, you can bounce a floatplane when landing (as I did a couple of times) because a C180 floatplane doesn't have any springy legs like its land-based sister! By the same token, once you are a bit more familiar with it, it is relatively easy to execute quite a smooth landing, especially when there is a slight ripple on the water surface to give you depth perception.

But, new pilots beware! Very smooth water is entirely different. If there is no breeze and the water is what is called 'glassy', it is like a mirror and just like a bathroom mirror, you can't tell how far away you are from it. A completely different technique was used in those situations. On my check-out with Tex, we headed for Moke Lake and it was glassy. I hadn't been briefed about the dangers of landing on glassy water, so was making a reasonably normal approach to land on the surface when Tex grabbed the controls and pulled the nose up as he considered I didn't know how close I was to the water. It was my introduction to the absolute need for the right approach in those conditions. Back then, our speed was calibrated in miles per hour rather than knots as it is today. For glassy water we would get well back from the landing point, set up a relatively high nose attitude with normal approach flap at 80 miles per hour and a 200 feet per minute descent rate, wait for the touchdown contact, then pull the power off immediately. This of course took quite a lot of space, so you had to start this landing procedure quite a distance back from where you wanted to touch down and pull up.

Another Christian pilot couple (Sam and Rosina Sands) had arrived a week or so before me and we naturally chummed up quite quickly. One thing that wasn't in place at SSA when I arrived was any sort of a duty roster. For some of the pilots, it was as if they didn't have anything else to do and so they just turned up every day.

I naturally wanted to be free to go to church and even do a bit of exploring on land, so asked if I could draw up a duty roster. The general response was quite negative initially, but while old Tex said they had tried rosters previously that hadn't worked, he said, 'Okay, have a go and we'll see if it works.' This was my opportunity to introduce a three-stage roster:

1. On duty
2. On call by the telephone (no mobile phones back then!)
3. Off work.

I worked out a rotation of all the pilots and, praise the Lord, it worked really well and even those who were initially negative were happy to use it.

But it wasn't without one of them saying that they thought it was so Sam and I could be off every Sunday to go to church; to which I replied, 'No, we will take our turn on any Sunday we are rostered on.' So it was very interesting to have a particular reaction one Sunday when I was on duty and Inky Bill was in charge. It was a day when flying to Milford was out of the question because the Alps were socked in with cloud, the winds were strong, and nothing was happening. Bill said to me, 'Ted you may as well go to church; there doesn't seem as if anything will be happening today and we know where to find you if we need you.' That was a thrill to me, realising that Bill recognised my desire to have Christian fellowship and was prepared to honour that fact in those circumstances.

On another occasion, shortly after I had got my floatplane rating and needed to build the necessary solo hours before taking passengers, the same pilot who had indicated we wanted our Sundays off said I ought to do it on the Sunday afternoon. It was nice to hear another say, 'No, he can do it whenever he wants to.' As an aside to this, for anyone who has heard the sound of a floatplane's engine and propeller under full power during takeoff reverberating around the nearby mountains of the Frankton Arm or Queenstown, the locals would be most grateful for me choosing not to practise take-offs there on a Sunday afternoon!

Having been checked out on all the aircraft types that SSA were using, I could now be called upon to fly any type at any time, though we always tried to keep it to one type per day. SSA was operating on what was then called a remote area licence from the Civil Aviation Authority. I never saw what the expected limitations of it were and although to the best of my knowledge we were never hauled over the coals, I feel sure that our interpretation of what could be done on a remote area licence was probably somewhat different to what CAA had in mind.

We interpreted the licence to mean that, 'If you reckon you can take off from it again then it was okay to land on it!' In reality, we were doing with fixed-wing aircraft much of what is being done today with a helicopter. But please remember that helicopters at that time were very pricey and there were not many of them around. The most available helicopter of the time was the old 'Bubble' Bell 47G which most people will know as the helicopter used in the programme *M*A*S*H*. It could only carry two passengers, or 33 percent of what we could in a Cessna C180, travelled at half the speed and was much more costly per hour; all significant factors when the hirer is paying by the hour! However, helicopter design has changed vastly over the years, which makes them a more economical option today for much of the work we were doing.

As can be expected in any bush type of operation, there were the highs and at times the very deep lows and I had a share of both.

Chapter 8

Flying Various Land Planes

I had been rated on the De Havilland Dominie as already noted. I will always remember my Dominie check-out to Milford, as I resolved never to do something with any aircraft that was done on that ride, even though it was done by both operators using Dominies on scenic flights to Milford at that time (SSA from Queenstown and Ritchies Air Services from Te Anau). The Sutherland Falls are one of the highest waterfalls in the world, dropping 580 metres in three steps and fed from a relatively small lake. Lake Quill is surrounded by high, steeply sloping, solid rock walls with a limited entrance which also served as the exit point. My check pilot, in showing me what is done on the scenic flight, flew into this physically restricted area at about 100 feet above the surface of the lake, which necessitated a continuous medium-to-steep circular turn to come out of it again.

I observed the tourists who were with me and there was an understandable and definite air of disquiet amongst them – and not only them, as I felt the same! Apart from the fact that all you could see was water on the left side (it would have been ice in winter), and a high rock wall on the other, I realised if either of the engines decided to quit while in that space (especially the inboard engine), there would have been absolutely no opportunity for a safe escape. I decided there and then that I would never fly in there by myself or with passengers. I told the folk back at base that Lake Quill was one place they would never, ever need to look for me if I went missing! After all, the main attraction at that point of the flight was the Sutherland Falls themselves, and doing what my check pilot did gave little to no opportunity to observe or photograph them. Once I was flying the route by myself, I would fly past with the falls on the left, do a relatively steep turn in the head of a little valley and fly back the other way with the falls on our right, giving the passengers on both sides of the aircraft an equal opportunity for a decent look, and photo opportunity at the falls.

On our scenic flights to Milford, we followed the same route as the world famous Milford Track up the Clinton Canyon, over the McKinnon Pass, past the Sutherland falls and down the Arthur River past Lake Ada which has a petrified forest in it and on down to Milford. I distinctly remember a few rather different incidents while flying this route. As so often happened, on one occasion I had on board a young newly married couple. All seemed to be going well until the young wife had had enough and decided it was time to get out! I'm not quite sure how she expected to survive this idea as we were flying up the Clinton Canyon at the time, probably 2,500 feet above the valley floor, but she apparently did manage to open the rear passenger door before her new husband was able to calm her down and convince her that getting out at that point wasn't a very good idea! The net result of all this was that, before someone got the door shut again, every speck of dust in the cabin was dislodged from its place and got swirled around – even up to me in the cockpit up front. For those not familiar with light aircraft doors, they are normally hinged at the front edge so if a door is opened in flight, the air pressure of the flight movement stops them being opened too far.

Of course the Dominie is built as a biplane, that is, it has two pairs of wings held together with struts and bracing wires. It was designed away back in 1934 to fly short distances from the UK to the Channel Islands, for which it would have been excellent. With the two wings, it was an extremely efficient aircraft which would today be classed as quite underpowered with the two engines only developing a combined 410 horsepower. But despite this it had a fantastic rate of climb of almost 1,000 feet per minute with a full load of eight passengers and pilot. This rate of climb served us well on the Milford scenic route, which was about an hour and a half round trip, as we would normally climb to 9,000 to 10,000 feet to cruise over the Southern Alps after leaving from Queenstown which is 1,017 feet (310 metres) above sea level.

But not all days were nice and sunny or calm, and I was to find out quite early on what it was like flying in strong winds across the Alps. I was asked quite early in my time there to take a Dominie over to Haast on the West Coast and bring the one that had been doing the Haast to Hokitika regular route back to Queenstown. The chief pilot, knowing I hadn't flown that route previously, told me to head just to the right of Mt Aspiring and keep going and I would come to Haast straight ahead. So I did what I was told. But this didn't account for the wind on that day. After a bumpy, rocky ride just before Mt Aspiring, I hit really heavy turbulence with a severe updraft followed by an equally severe downdraft! It was so bad that both my airways and the public address microphones leapt off their respective hooks and landed on the cockpit floor. Not only that, but a heavy set of platform scales that had been quietly standing in the aisle (unrestrained) had moved forward about 60 centimetres! Right then I decided to fly home with the other aircraft at low level via the Haast Pass – which I did.

On one nice fine day, there were enough passengers from Queenstown to send one Dominie DH89 and our new 300 horsepower Cessna C185 over to Milford at the same time. I was flying the Cessna and, because it cruised so much faster than the Dominie, I thought I would easily beat the Dominie to reach Milford. But it wasn't to be, because the DH89 climbed so much better than the fully loaded Cessna that it could take a more direct route while I had to take a longer route because the climb rate was nowhere near as good. I remember thinking when I came into Milford behind the Dominie, 'I didn't think I was such a poor pilot,' as I hadn't figured out what the real difference was at that stage. The delightful revelation came about four days later, when I was flying a DH89 and the same other pilot was flying the Cessna, and I beat him to Milford by a similar margin! On that route, the climb rate rather than the cruise speed was of the greater significance.

Of course, not every day was a nice fine day, but folk still wanted to go to Milford, so we often took another route where we picked up the Milford road not far from the Homer Tunnel and went across a pass into the head of the Cleddau Valley. This particular day was icy cold and as I lifted the aircraft to give a little extra clearance to cross the pass, everything in front of me went white. I had gone up high enough to encounter the freezing level and so what moisture there was on the windscreen turned to ice. Fortunately, there was enough vision out the side of the cockpit for me to see when I was safely over the pass and all the ice cleared in front of me when we descended about 50 feet. This also happened once when crossing the McKinnon Pass on the normal route, but thankfully with the same result!

On another trip, as so often happened back then, I had a group of American tourists on board and I remember one chap saying, 'I'll have to get a strut or something in every photo, as the folks back home won't believe I have flown in a biplane.' On yet another trip, I was again in the DH89 and one of the other chaps was flying one of the Cessna C180s. This had an even better power-to-weight ratio than either of the other aircraft, and so in the cruise, he was able to overtake me in the Dominie. Whether he drifted across in front of me, or I drifted into his slipstream I don't know, but I found out just how much of a corkscrew effect there was in another's aircraft's slipstream, as I had to apply full aileron for quite some time to keep the aircraft level to counter the twisted air I was flying in.

The Dominie was a good aircraft to do airdrops from. In 1965 there were still Department of Conservation (DOC) deer cullers positioned in various places in the Southern Alps with the specific purpose of reducing deer and tahr numbers as they were destroying a lot of the natural flora. Because the DOC staff would be in an area weeks at a time, we used to drop supplies to them when there was no airstrip close by. The supplies would be double-bagged, so that if the inner bag burst due to the impact, the second outer bag would hopefully contain the spill. We used a very simple parachute made of a metre square piece of calico tied to the bag. This broke the fall of an 18 kilogram bag of goods sufficiently so that not too much was wasted.

With all the seats out, the necessary goods loaded, and the aircraft fitted with a special chute installed right to left in the back with the luggage door off, all was set for an airdrop for the pilot and one secured assistant. I helped with a number of these airdrops as the assistant and the job was fairly simple. Place the bags in the chute restrained with a rope, thread a static line through the parachutes' rip cords and wait for the pilot to call 'Go'. Tex Smith our chief pilot was brilliant to work with. After the first drop when he gauged your reaction time, he could drop cleanly into a very confined space, sometimes no bigger than an average urban section with trees all around it.

I once flew a Dominie out of Benmore airstrip in the late autumn to drop rock salt well below the expected snowline to encourage the sheep down from the tops so as to avoid a lot of snow raking (i.e. getting the sheep down out of the snow by making tracks for them and encouraging them down). It was surprising just how effective this was, as within half an hour some sheep had started to make their way down the slopes towards the salt. They must have been recipients previously.

However, there was one time, on 15 June 1965, that an early dump of snow meant that an aircraft needed to go up and see where the sheep were so the owners could bring them down below the snowline. I was detailed to do the job, and initially we were to have been in a Cessna, but because four chaps turned up it was switched to a Dominie. All went well for a time, circling Mt Soho which is north of Arrowtown. As I passed over a ridge on the north-northwest side I noticed a slight downdraft, but not enough to worry about. Much further around on the north eastern side, there was quite a large valley with a big number of sheep in a few groups huddled together in the snow.

Here is where having been a farmer previously probably wasn't a good thing. Because I wanted the fellows to get a good look at where the sheep were and in what numbers, I turned in towards the mountain around the head of the large valley so they could see their location in relation to the general area. Unknown to me, there was a very severe smooth air downdraft in the head of the valley and also, because all ahead of me was white snow with no horizon, I didn't realise I was rapidly heading earthwards until I saw a small ridge appear before me. I realised that we were going to hit it, so I thought to myself, 'I will make sure the strongest part of the aircraft impacts first,' so I planted the aircraft on its main wheels on this ridge. We bounced, swerved uphill and then tail-slid back down the relatively steep slope for about 75 metres until the tail wheel jammed on one side of a gut (a very small valley/ravine within the main valley) and the nose of the aircraft swung to the right, resting on the far side of the snow filled gut.

We came to rest straddling the gut full of snow with the whole aircraft totally intact, apart from one plastic window which was broken by one guy who immediately dived out through it. I called for everyone to get out in case the aircraft caught on fire. We exited through the rear luggage door. So the five of us were safe but the old Dominie was not! For the next three hours we trekked towards the nearest road head through quite heavy snow. I have heard it said, that some people, faced with an inevitable disaster like this, say that their whole life flashes before them. This didn't happen for me, possibly because of a lack of time!

When the base realised I would have run out of fuel if we were still airborne, they sent Dave Cowan out in a Cessna to see what had happened. We had almost reached the road head when Dave came in very low and buzzed us and obviously counted us to see if we were all there. When I talked to Dave later, he said that in the area that I'd gone down, he had encountered a 2,000 feet-a-minute smooth air downdraft which was obviously a big factor in the accident. (If you are flying at 500 feet above the ground in these conditions, it only takes four seconds to lose it all.) At the time, one of the other directors was up from Invercargill (as SSA had just been bought out by Tourist Air Travel) who took a rather realistic view of the situation by saying, 'Well, we were going to get rid of one of the Dominies, and it looks as if Ted has determined for us which one it is to be!'

Not that it had anything to do with this accident, but in my opinion and with my then limited experience, if one of the Dominies was to be lost or sold, the one I crashed was the best one to go. Why? I reckon there must have been something wrong in the rigging of the wings, as several times before this, when doing a moderate turn in towards the Milford airstrip from the Sounds end, it gave a very unnerving buffet on the controls, something that didn't happen with any of the other Dominies doing the same manoeuvre at much the same rate of turn.

Once, because flying into Milford wasn't possible due to poor weather, I was taking a load of tourists through to Te Anau to be bussed into Milford from there. There is a quite a sizeable valley running from Mt Nicholas on Lake Wakatipu's south western shores through to Te Anau, and I was taking this route below the height of the peaks because of cloud cover. I became aware of a sinking feeling and looked at the altimeter and sure enough we were losing height. I applied climb power and speed and we were still losing height. Ah ha, so once again there was a smooth air downdraft (most often a downdraft is somewhat turbulent) so I edged my way across to the other side of the valley to gain the rising air there and carried on without any problems.

However after my crash on Mt Soho, I flew single-engine Cessnas for a while and I remember flying into Milford and seeing two distinct wheel marks on the raised sea barrier mound at the western, seaward end, signifying that someone (not me!) had been a bit too low, and had left their signature there. But I was going to get a surprise the next time I flew a Dominie into Milford. As it was my first DH89 flight after the accident, I forgot to adequately advance one throttle before the other to counter the takeoff swing, and had to rather hurriedly stop in the parking bay. I was so convinced that one wheel must have got moss or grass in front of it that I went back and looked at the tracks. But no, it was definitely the result of a swing due to me opening both throttles together. Taken all around though, the Dominie was a lovely aircraft to fly and could get into moderately short airstrips, or beaches like Big Bay at low tide.

Back in the 1960s there was a very successful rabbit board operating in Central Otago, and Southern Scenic had the contract to firstly drop fresh carrots for two or three days so the rabbits got a taste of the free lunch and then on the third or fourth day the carrots were soaked in the now very controversial 1080 poison. The effect was an extremely high kill rate, which it needed to be, as the area was being overrun with rabbits, as I understand it is again today. I never flew on any of these sorties, but as I had a heavy traffic licence, I became the loader driver for those who did. This was essentially the same work as a loader driver for a topdressing operation, moving the tractor fitted with the front end loader and bucket from one place to another and loading the aircraft when it came in each time for a new load. I enjoyed being back on a tractor seat, as it was quite a while since I had left the farm. For a period, my days consisted of doing the dual jobs of flying scenic flights in many different aircraft types and also working as a loader driver.

As I have mentioned before, there was another Christian couple working with SSA – Sam and Rosina Sands – and I used to pop in on them quite frequently and enjoy their company. One Monday morning soon after arriving at work, Tex said to me, 'Sam's wife has had a medical problem this morning and Sam is staying at home with her.' He added, 'I was going to check Sam out on a number of remote airstrips today, but as he can't do that, you jump into the Cessna 180, and follow me. Where I land, you land.' Wow, by this stage I hadn't fully mastered the Cessna's 'springy legs' but did manage (by God's grace) to hold everything together for this rather novel check-out system.

To explain the Cessna's 'springy legs': Every aircraft has some sort of 'give' in its undercarriage to help absorb runway irregularities as well as acting as a cushion for a not-so-good landing. On the C180 and C185, Cessna used a tapered piece of spring steel, firmly held in place on the aircraft, with the wheel at the thinner end. This steel 'leg' flexed to give the effect of the cushioning required. However, it not only absorbed a heavy landing, but was inclined to push the aircraft back into the air on the rebound, hence the idea of being 'springy'.

This was the very beginning of a whole new set of experiences, and I thanked God for the fact that I had spent so much time at

Ardmore when in training, trying to get really short strip takeoff and landings under control, because some of the strips were really quite short. In very general terms, the work that was being undertaken by Cessnas into these remote airstrips was either to service deerstalkers who made a living by shooting deer for venison off the valley floors or to take sports shooters seeking a trophy to take back home with them.

There was one exception to this – flying whitebait out of the Cascade Station airstrip. In those days, it was the most valuable cargo we ever carried, apart from people. The family who fished there used to come down from Christchurch each year and clean up the airstrip; we would go in and fly the whitebait out. If my memory serves me correctly, a Cessna load back then was worth about £5,000 (or around $240,000 today) when a scenic return flight from Queenstown to Milford was £12 and 10 shillings per person or £100 for a full load! The whitebait was packed into large, lidded 20-litre tins, so one could get quite a number into the aircraft at once.

There were also a lot of deer in all of the South Westland valleys causing much damage to the flora in our National Park; several shooters were exploiting this fact and shooting the deer for venison. This was flown out to Mussel Point and picked up by a large articulated refrigerated truck and taken to a specialty abattoir owned and operated by Tim Wallis of Warbirds over Wanaka fame. In the early days of this operation, the deer were hung in large meat safes and one had to do a fairly regular pickup, for obvious reasons. As time progressed some of the shooters invested in chillers which were generally placed *very* close to the airstrip. This meant the pickups could be farther apart. I well remember a couple of chillers were placed so that if you needed to approach from the chiller end of the airstrip due to the wind direction, you had to lift your wing over the chiller just before touchdown!

I guess it says something about me and my perception of these men that I was really surprised one morning when one shooter took me to his one-roomed shack for a cuppa, where I found he had a battery-operated record player, playing *classical* music! In hindsight, however, these operations were wonderful training for MAF; because for many, we were their only supply line for everything they needed to stay in the bush for a period. It was a special day for them when we arrived with their mail, groceries and fuel.

Later, when most of the deer had been shot out on the valley floors, many of these chaps became shooters on the helicopters that came in to exploit the fact that there were still many deer in the bush and above the bush line. At this stage, I would often go over to the West Coast and stay for several days, lifting the deer off established airstrips or river beds and transporting them out to the road head. There were still so many deer in these valleys, that for some time the helicopters and shooters would cover a valley per day for a week, working their way south from the Haast River, and they would repeat the same for weeks.

The airstrip at Mussel Point had one quite long runway running roughly parallel to the coast (another operator was later positioned here) and it also had a much shorter vector roughly NE/SW and this was where the group I was working with had their base.

Heading to the southwest, which was the most frequent wind direction, the approach was over scrubby bush, some telephone lines, a road width, a fence and then 140 metres of grass runway before a soft patch which one needed to avoid. One had to develop and use a different approach from a normal approach for this vector when landing with a full load. On almost all of the strips we were using, if the stall warning wasn't sounding on your short final, you were going too fast anyway, so there wasn't any change there, but having to allow for the fence on the threshold meant that one had to use a lot of power to maintain the slow speed until just past the fence, pull the power off and let the aircraft sink rapidly, and at the right time momentarily put power on again to arrest the rapid sink and then pull it off again, plant the aircraft on its main wheels, and brake quite heavily. Thankfully I never got stuck in the soft patch.

Once as I was going home to Queenstown late in the afternoon with the sun setting behind me, all the snow on the tops of the mountains of the Southern Alps was coloured pure gold. This would have made a stunningly glorious photo, but for some reason I didn't have either of my cameras with me which I have lived to regret as it was so beautiful. Because one was flying this same route fairly regularly, one was able to identify the various silhouettes of the mountains along the route; which was like coming home under today's equivalent of 'night visual flight rules' (VFR) happened occasionally when the weather allowed, apart from the fact that there was no lighting at the destination. Whether it was on this trip or another, I can't remember, but when approaching the unlit Queenstown airstrip in the late dusk, with only the aircraft's landing lights on, I noticed one of the windsocks out the corner of my eye. But – oops! – it was on my right and it should have been on my left, so a rather quick readjustment of my approach was needed for a safe landing!

Not all of the venison recovery came from valleys running out to the coast. We had one airstrip in a valley on the eastern side of the Haast road and also one in the Landsborough Valley tucked under Mt Cook, the water from which emptied into the Haast River. The Landsborough airstrip was set in an elbow of the valley and beside a river by the same name. It was a one-way strip, which was normally approached from over the river but at times the local wind dictated approaching from the other end, and then you felt as if you were sliding down the tops of the trees on the valley wall. The river here showed the effects of the grinding of at least one glacier high up on the Alps and – wow! – the colour of the water changed when that was happening in spring. Instead of being nice and clear as it was in late autumn and winter, it was a very distinctly grey colour, as in the spring thaw it carried so many microscopic rock particles.

I remember this airstrip for another reason too. Nearly all the shooters on these sorts of airstrips appeared to be single, or at least they didn't have any wife or partner with them there, but one shooter had managed to get his wife to come out to one very remote and isolated spot. You guessed it, she became pregnant, and as I kept flying in there, I realised that her time for giving birth was coming up before too long. I became increasingly uneasy about this, as they had no means of communication with us. They were tucked right in under Mt Cook on the western side, so there would be many days that we couldn't get in there even if they could get a message out. So after consulting with the bosses at base, I recruited Rosina Sands (a former nurse) to come with me and we went out there one sunny afternoon. Rosina persuaded the wife to come back to Queenstown with us. Fortunately there wasn't too much resistance to the idea. I don't ever remember taking her back again with the baby; that must have been the privilege of one of the other pilots.

We had a number of airstrips in the Southern Alps' eastern valleys which emptied into Lake Wanaka. Very few of these had any windsock or even a rag on a pole to give an idea of wind direction, so it was a case of getting down really low and flying over any pool of water that might be close to the airstrip to see if there was any air movement indicated on the pool. Knowing what sort of air movement there was on the surface was important, as some of these strips were of minimal length and we even used to factor in whether we were in a high or low-pressure atmospheric area at the time.

Tex checked me out into several of these airstrips and one has a particular memory. Back then, some of the more remote farms had just a single wire connecting them to the Post and Telegraph Department's network. On this occasion we had landed at an airstrip close to Mt Aspiring and Tex had sent me away to Wanaka for some reason. Returning, it seemed the obvious thing to do was to land straight in as that lined up perfectly. All went well until I saw a single wire (without any flags on it) strung across about seven or eight metres above the ground. Thankfully, a sudden zoom climb missed it. Tex said to me when I landed, 'That's why we land from the other end.' I thought, yeah okay, but it would have been helpful if the wire had been mentioned.

At least I never cut off the communication for the farm but further up the Makarora Valley there was another farm that wasn't so fortunate. They had a single copper wire strung across the Makarora River to their home from the P&T network on the Haast road. One of the few helicopters operating at the time went chugging down the valley at low level due to poor weather and chopped the wire. The next wire was some No. 8 fencing wire and surprisingly it suffered the same fate. Desperate to continue communications with the outside world, the farmer next used high-tensile wire. This time it was the helicopter that didn't come off so well, in that the wire got caught around its collective mechanism (just below the rotor) and as it tightened, caused the chopper to first shoot skywards before collapsing in a heap! Yes, unmarked wires can be a real hazard.

One sunny Sunday morning, it was my turn to go and pick up a load of venison that Tim Wallis's helicopter had dropped off in one of the valleys. The pilot said he had dropped them at the end of a good landing strip. It was the only task that day, so I got up fairly early, hoping to be able to do the job and get back in time for the morning church service.

I arrived over the strip and it did appear to be quite reasonable so I landed, but I hadn't factored in two things. As it was quite early in the day, there was still heavy dew on the grass which made it slippery. That might not have been so bad if the strip didn't have a couple of little humps in it that couldn't readily be seen from the air; both of which bounced me off the surface. The scrubby tea-tree at the end of the strip was looming up quite fast, so I initiated a ground loop. This was looking successful until the starboard (right) wheel went into the entrance of an old rabbit hole! The result was the aircraft leaned over just far enough to slightly bend the wing tip. Leaving the aircraft behind, I remember having to cross a freezing cold swollen river on the long walk out to Makarora to tell the sad news to the folk back at base.

As mentioned, we were doing with a fixed-wing aircraft the sort of transport that is being done by helicopters today. One of those things was taking trophy-hunting sportsmen into remote areas. Normally we would try and take them into an established airstrip used by the venison shooters. I remember on one occasion taking a New Zealand Air Force wing commander into the Waiatoto Valley. It was a nice clear morning and as I lined up on the Waiatoto airstrip which looked very much like a couple of Land Rover wheel tracks, the obviously uneasy wing commander said to me with a slight tremor in his voice, 'Is that what we are going to land on?'

I replied as casually as I could, 'Yes, this is the Waiatoto airstrip where you wanted to go.' In reality, he had some reason for being slightly worried though he wouldn't have been aware of it, because I wasn't!

Another time when I was in there, several kea (New Zealand's alpine parrot) were doing a bit of a dance away down on the approach to the strip. I had my camera, so went to see if I could get a shot of them, which I did, but it was what I saw on my return that gave me the shock. As the strip was built on a reclaimed portion of the old river bed, it wasn't exactly smooth and had some hollows in it. What the shooter had done to fill those depressions (thank you!) made me realise there really wasn't any margin for error when using that strip. The guy had dug holes for gravel to fill the hollows, but he had dug them about 60 centimetres or more deep about 70 centimetres on either side of the tracks. A wheel going into one of them would have not only ripped out the landing gear, but also flipped an aircraft on its back! Oh well, at least his intention was good.

Many trophy hunters wanted to be dropped off in a river valley that had no airstrip. What do you do then? Most of the South Westland rivers were quite wide and had beaches with various sized stones and sand within their width so it was a case of looking for a suitable landing area to let the hunters off. All our C185s had semicircular mudguards covering their main wheels and rear rubber flaps attached to them to help prevent damage to the plane's tail plane and elevators from stones being flicked up at them. But how did you know if the patch you are looking at is suitable? The process I went through was to make sure the approaches at either end were okay, then do a very low pass over what I thought would be a suitable beach to look at the size of the stones and any apparent soft patches. The next was to make sure there was sufficient length to land and take off safely and so I would set the aircraft up at 80 miles per hour and see if the selected beach area was at least 12 seconds (122 metres) long. Then I would make a slow approach and lightly put the main wheels on to feel if there were any soft patches that weren't visible by observation. If all of that was successful, I considered it was safe to land on.

Of course with the amount of rain that South Westland has, by the time we went back to pick up these people a few days later, the original beaches might not be there as the rivers frequently changed course overnight, and so the whole process happened again. Fairly exacting sort of stuff, which you couldn't get bored doing!

One of the Cessna 180s was set up to do special drops of various sorts of material from what were called 'bomb racks'. These were reasonably easily fitted and removed from the underside of the wing and consisted of a framework attached to the wing and a mechanism to attach and release material to them. The pilot had a press button switch on the control column and an overriding master switch on the instrument panel which was only activated when almost ready to do the drop. Two loads that I distinctly remember helping with were, firstly, a whole lot of waratah fencing posts and a number of coils of wire netting. These were dropped so the Department. of Conservation could erect a protective fence around the area in a valley on the western side of Lake Te Anau where NZ native Takahe birds (thought to be extinct) had recently been rediscovered. The second drop was also of waratah fencing posts, but this time it was to lift them from the valley floor to away up on a high ridgeline for a boundary fence. I only assisted and didn't fly on either of these drops.

Chapter 9

The Cessna Floatplane

As mentioned earlier, I had been checked out and rated on Southern Scenic's floatplane. It had originally been an amphibious model until a chap with aircraft carrier experience called to the base, 'Landing at Queenstown Bay, wheels up,' while he was actually putting them down! This is a totally unforgiving situation, as the wheels dig in and the plane immediately flips on its back without warning – or so I am told! Having the floats modified to pure floats did make it much easier to operate. But this made for quite an adventure getting the whole unit up for maintenance at the airfield hangar from its especially constructed wharf/anchorage pen at the airfield end of the Frankton Arm. Can you imagine the situation now, of getting the aircraft onto an especially built trailer at the boat ramp just off the Frankton-Queenstown road and then trundling the whole thing along that road and across the then golf course to the hangar on the airfield? It really just goes to show how few vehicles there were on that road back then, compared with today.

I was first assigned to fly the floatplane out of Queenstown Bay on scenic flights over the Queenstown area. This was quite fun and it was great having many different tourists to take up for the ride. One thing that took a little while to become skilled at was steering the aircraft *backwards* with the water rudders up, just using the two large doors in the breeze as a means of directing it. I am sure that those who have sailed yachts would adapt to working a floatplane on the water much more quickly than a landlubber like me!

The floatplane was always returned and moored in the previously mentioned pen. One morning I saw what I knew in theory, about how the colour black absorbs heat faster than white. When I went to fuel the floatplane, there was frost all over the top of the wing where it was white, but exactly where the black-painted registration letters were, the frost had melted completely away.

One evening I was near the Queenstown jetty and my first flight instructor Ken Windsor was there too, as he was then flying DC3s for Mt Cook Airways and he was aware that I had been checked out on the floatplane. In the approaching dusk, a couple of teal ducks came rocketing down from the skyline chalet area with their wings tucked in so that their speed must have been close to their terminal velocity. They curved towards the side of the jetty, opened their wings, put their two feet out forwards like water skis and perfectly kissed the surface of the water before sinking into it as though nothing had happened. Ken turned to me, and said, 'How would you like to be able to do a water landing like that, Ted?' This reminded me of a Christian 'Fact and Faith' film, called *Prior Claim* in which they showed how many human inventions copy what God has already created in nature. Just one example I remember from the film was that the same type of gyroscope used by the Nautilus submarine as it navigated beneath the northern ice cap is under every housefly's wings, and if plucked off, the poor fly doesn't have any control of its flight!

The floatplane was not only used to fly tourists, it was also used where water was available on the same sort of operations as the wheeled Cessnas. Sometimes, our load was carried externally. The pair of floats were kept apart and in line with a couple of spreader bars which were really strong, so when a hunter wanted to transport a small dinghy to Lake Alabaster, we turned the dinghy upside down and strapped it tightly to the spreader bars! So there was the dinghy upside down under the cabin.

As with the wheeled aircraft, hunters sometimes wanted to be taken to remote lakes. I will never forget one experience. Someone had taken a couple of hunters into Lake Lochnagar near the headwaters of the Shotover River much farther upstream from the Skippers Canyon. It then came time to lift them and their gear out of there. It was an almost cloudless sky on the eastern side of the Southern Alps, but there was a strong north westerly wind blowing. Flying over the lake, it was obvious by the 'cat's claws' (wind marks) on the surface, that there was not only a fairly strong wind blowing on the surface, but it was also very gusty; It was the worst possible combination in this situation as the lake is surrounded by high mountains almost all around, allowing only one broad entrance which was also the exit point. What to do? It was going to be a tricky takeoff, as the wind direction would mean taking off towards the mountain rim and turning downwind in a somewhat confined and possible downdraft area to get over the lip of the dam-like exit. I figured it was possible, but certainly not nice.

After loading, I used a factor that can be used on a waterborne aircraft that you can't use on a land-based aircraft – a curved (almost circular) takeoff. A floatplane can take quite a long time (and distance) to get 'up on the step', i.e. to the speed when the floats are planing. At this speed the aircraft can be steered much the same as a speedboat can be, but with the air rudder. The takeoff was successful, but now came the business of turning downwind in a moderately steep turn to get out of the situation in gusty winds. I can still remember holding onto the control column with my left hand while my right was adjusting the flaps depending on the wind gusts. I guess you can imagine my relief at being able to dive over the exit lip to gain good flying speed and finally, full control. Thank you Lord for your enabling in such a dicey situation!

Another part of the float operation often meant there was venison to be lifted out of remote areas to a pickup point. Sadly for

Ritchie Air Services, their C206 floatplane had a bad accident in Lake Gunn which is very close to the Te Anau to Milford road, so I was sent to fly out of Te Anau with the Southern Scenic floatplane. The floatplane was mostly used for venison recovery from lakes, taking 'liquid refreshments' to cray fishing boats, doing Ministry of Agriculture and Fisheries (as it was then) inspections of crayfish boats and transporting goods to Doubtful Sound to those who were at that stage building the Manapōuri power station.

One rather memorable day when I was temporarily based at Te Anau, I had a dual task. There was a local personality who had developed a tourist adventure by creating a walk down the Hollyford Valley to Lake McKerrow pretty well on the West Coast near the bottom of the valley but at this stage he hadn't finished the track the full distance to reach the bottom of the lake. My assignment was to lift a number of loads of venison out of Lake McKerrow to Lake Gunn and then shuttle quite a number of these track-walking tourists from the end of his track to the bottom of Lake McKerrow. It was quite an assignment, and I was going flat out with having to refuel at Lake Gunn with not the best equipment and then start the shuttling of the walkers and their gear to the bottom of the lake.

All of this went brilliantly, even though the afternoon was starting to get a little old. And then it happened! Because of all the short shuttles and having to shut down each time for safety's sake, the battery wouldn't turn the engine over for the final start to head home. One of the walker passengers was an NAC air hostess and she very kindly offered to swing the prop for me to start the motor. But this was far too dangerous for a couple of reasons. I would have to be facing the bank for her to do it and would have no way to back away from the bank, and what if she slipped on the bank edge after it started? The consequences of that just wouldn't bear thinking about. So I decided to get her to tie the rear of the aircraft to a small tea-tree bush and swing start it myself; a task that is very easy to say and write, but fraught with danger and excitement in reality!

An explanation here: A swing start is when there is one person in the cockpit or cabin and another person swings on the propeller by pulling it in the normal rotational direction. Because all piston aircraft have magnetos to create the spark for the ignition, this can be a successful way to start a piston engine. In fact, before electric starters were fitted to planes, all aircraft engines were started by this method. But it can be dangerous, as one chap in PNG found out when he got a massive cut in his upper leg.

With the aircraft duly anchored with the stern rope to the little tea-tree bush, I primed the engine, set the throttle, climbed out of the *passenger's* right-hand door, swung myself under the wing strut and, standing on the front of the starboard float, tried to swing the propeller from behind, which wasn't an easy task. After a number of swings and re-settings of the throttle, the engine finally started. This was the beginning of the fun, because I now had to go back under the wing strut while being blasted with prop wash, open the passenger door that was closing from the prop wash against it, scramble inside, and pull the throttle back to idle as I was now quite a way out into the lake. But hey, wasn't I supposed to be anchored to the bank with the stern rope? Actually, it was all my fault, as I had fallen into the novice's trap of just edging the throttle a little more open with each failed swing, which had resulted in the engine being at about 20 percent power when it finally caught. I was free of the bank, but with a small tea-tree bush in tow! Was this going to stop me going home? Not likely after that drama, so after a circle so I could wave thanks, I took off for my temporary home at Te Anau.

The elapsed time was a little longer than I had reckoned on, (probably because I was towing a small tea-tree bush like a drogue) and by the time I was flying down Lake Te Anau the evening tourist boat was heading up the lake to the glow worm caves. We both had our navigation lights on, so it was easy to keep our distance from each other as I was coming in for a long shallow landing in the near dark. If the captain thought that the pilot was mad coming back at that hour, I'm pretty sure he would have thought his suspicions were confirmed when he saw a small tea-tree bush in tow on the end of the stern rope! I can distinctly remember thinking, 'I hope there aren't any CAA blokes on that boat!' The landing was successful and thankfully the area where the aircraft was to be tied up was all floodlit.

Something that was quite unnerving for me happened on Lake McKerrow on another flight, and this was the way the front of the floats could 'bury' when you are taxiing with a strong tailwind, even when holding the control column back, which one would have thought would help in that situation. This happened as I was heading towards a beach to allow some people to get out, but in the meantime, the front of the floats went almost completely under water. And then all of a sudden, it happened – the flotation took over and the front popped out to a relatively normal level of flotation. Scary when you can't swim, but fortunately the disembarking point was close!

Another two venison recovery trips were quite memorable as well. Roughly halfway between Queenstown and Te Anau, (if you track from Mt Nicholas Station to Te Anau) are the Mavora Lakes. One assignment was to fly from Te Anau and pick up a load of venison from South Mavora Lake to take back to Te Anau. All went well in finding the pickup spot and the meat safe. This hunter hadn't yet progressed to having a chiller. Now, I understand that game should always be hung for a period before being cooked, but this was the first (and thankfully the last) time I picked up venison that had obviously been hung for quite a while. Picking up one animal carcass by the two rear legs, I was left with nothing but two handfuls of skin that just peeled off the legs. It was the first of three times in my life that I dry-retched before taking to the air again.

My second memory of venison recovery into Te Anau was a lot more pleasant, but quite a long way away from the base. Lake Poteriteri is a 30-kilometre-long, narrow lake at the very bottom of the South Island with the southern end of the lake barely 8 kilometres from the absolute south coast. I was to pick up a load of venison from the northern end of the lake. There was a strong south wind blowing right up the lake with the result that the water was quite rough even for landing. After loading, taking off in these conditions is hard on the aircraft and pilot, for while the head wind was useful, the roughness of the water was not! Finally I got airborne and headed back to Te Anau, but wasn't at all happy with the idea of doing a return trip. I told the folk I was working for that the water had got too heavy (rough) for a floatplane, and asked that they send the Te Anau-based Grumman Widgeon to get the second load. The Widgeon is a twin-engine amphibious mini flying boat and taking off in it is a vastly different experience from a floatplane. I was very fortunate to be able to go with the Widgeon and even happier when the chap who was flying it sat me in the left-hand (pilot's) seat for the return trip!

Firstly, instead of initially pulling back on the yoke during take-off, one has to push forward as it gets up onto the step extremely quickly, and the second thing that impressed me was that instead of going thump, thump, thump as one would in a floatplane it was more like zip, zip, zip as it cut through the tops of the now quite substantial waves. A truly exhilarating experience!

Another operation that we did from Te Anau was taking a fisheries inspector out to inspect the size of the crayfish being caught by the goodly number of crayfish boats operating in the Fiordland National Park's waters. At times, we would just start at the bottom of the South Island's west coast, and work our way up the coast fiord by fiord. Many of these inlets were so deep in from the coast, that what was happening in the Tasman Sea had no effect on the waters in the particular fiord. But this was not the case one time that I had to land close to the most south western inlet (Otago Retreat) of Preservation Inlet by Puysegur Point lighthouse. The surface of the water appeared to be relatively smooth and it was only when I got down to a few metres above the water that I realised there was quite a southwest swell rolling in from the Tasman Sea! It wasn't the smoothest of landings, but it was safe.

After the inspector had done what he needed to do with the boat that was operating there I had the fun job of taking off again to move up the coast. Fortunately the wind was very light (hence the water appearing to be relatively smooth when landing) but to take off again down the inlet over the long rolling swells wasn't an option because the swell, while not big for a floatplane (about 60 centimetres), was going to make a takeoff directly into it both very rough but also quite dangerous. Fortunately, in the mouth of the Inlet there is a reasonably large island, called Coal Island. This island was effectively forming a barrier from the swell, so I taxied into the lee of the island and commenced the takeoff run. Now a floatplane takes quite a long time to actually get up to 'step' (or planing) speed and then to takeoff speed and sadly the lee area of Coal Island wasn't long enough for all that to happen, so I ended up rocking across the rolling swell for the last stages of the takeoff run. Not the most pleasant sensation when going about 80 knots!

It was very interesting to see the reaction from the different boats' crews when the floatplane approached them. Some would happily throw a line and welcome you which made tying up to them quite easy, while others would rather sullenly stand on the boat, and you'd have to manoeuvre the aircraft to try and get a line across to tie up. Actually, if only they had realised it, their attitude was a complete giveaway as to whether they had undersized crays on board or not. The cooperative chaps rarely had anything to hide but the uncooperative ones almost always had undersized crayfish in their holds. Oh yes, there was always a 'good reason' for them being there! One reason I remember was that their crays were okay according to their measuring stick; the trouble was, their measuring stick was several centimetres too short! Sometimes one didn't have to actually tie up to the boat. I can remember once asking myself the wisdom of a person like me who couldn't swim, standing at the very front of the float with my left arm wrapped around the propeller with the other holding onto one of the boat's rails, while the boat rolled back and forth as it lay across the light swell. My arms were acting like the bellows of a concertina to keep the aircraft 'tied up' to the boat. Good fun, or just plain stupid?

Something that wasn't quite so funny was an experience the inspector and I had while well within a fiord. It had been a long afternoon; the last crayfish boat had been inspected and it was time to leave to go home, but we were both feeling the need to reduce our personal bladder pressure. Well, no problem really. There at the side of the fiord was a nice beach area with plenty of bush down to the water's edge, so I pulled in there and as we weren't going to be long, we both pulled the plane up the beach a very short way, just enough to make it safely 'secure'. Now up until this time, I had only been flying out of lakes and rivers where the water level remained basically static. I forgot that I was now in a tidal situation! Providentially the tide was going out, rather than coming in, or the story could have ended rather differently if the plane had floated off, but as it was, in the very few minutes we'd been in the bush, the tide had receded and the floatplane was quite firmly stuck on the sandy beach. However, there was just enough flotation with the inspector standing on the rear of the floats and me red-facedly heaving on the front end to get the plane back into the water again.

As we took off for home, both of us were quite relieved in more ways than one! Thank you Lord for undertaking for my forgetfulness and ignorance!

As mentioned earlier, what was happening on the coast could be quite different from well up a fiord. I clearly remember this point quite dramatically one afternoon when flying up the coast between sounds. There was a really strong northerly blowing down the coast almost parallel to it, creating some heavy white caps – not the sort of water to land a floatplane on. I wondered what the water surface would be like in the fiord/sound we were going to, as some sounds extend a long way inland. For instance Dagg Sound is at least 11 kilometres long running deep into Fiordland National Park. As we cruised up the sound, the water became calmer and calmer until we finally located the crayfish boat at the head of the sound on – would you believe it – glassy water, indicating absolutely NO wind. As a result, I had to head back down the sound for a few kilometres so I could set up the long shallow approach needed for the glassy water and then taxi to the boat which was to be inspected.

When the crayfish boats were having a good catch, they would often celebrate the fact by getting us to take to them a load of alcoholic 'refreshments'. While I would have preferred not to have been engaged in this activity, knowing how alcohol is so detrimental to individuals and families, I was employed to do it, so it had to be done. On this particular occasion, the boat was in one of the fiords west of Te Anau, and as I hadn't been there before, and as there was the weight availability, another more senior local pilot came with me who was familiar with the area. Our company had been in touch with the boat, which had given a cloud base of 'about 5,000 feet' which would have meant that there would normally be plenty of room to find a hole in the clouds through which to descend.

As we passed over the divide and were able to look down the length of the fiord, we saw a shelf of quite low cloud stretching ahead of us. The accompanying pilot passed a remark that I am unable to print, but it essentially meant, 'The sods, they have got us to come over on false pretences saying the cloud is far higher than it actually is.' It certainly seemed that way. Fortunately, closer to the mouth of the fiord, there was a good break enabling us to get down under the cloud shelf without any problems. The crayfish boat was anchored in an enclosed bay on a little Island, shaped like a horseshoe and as I taxied the aircraft through the opening of the very sheltered little bay, I looked up through the windshield and asked the other pilot what height he would say the cloud base was? After another expletive he said, 'You could mistake it for being much higher than it actually is couldn't you?' I learnt then, that unless an observer has a nearby point of reference of a known height, it can be very hard to give an accurate idea of the height of a solid cloud base. I had reason to remember this much later when flying in Papua New Guinea!

Chapter 10

The Little 'Sally Lassie'

Because I had grown up in a family with no sisters and had remained on the farm in that family bubble, I really didn't have much of an idea as to how to relate to females or how they ticked. A very high proportion of those helping at the guest house were folk from other countries but then a young Kiwi woman about my age came to work at Tutuila who was a Christian, a pilot, and a farmer's daughter. We had a lot in common and became good friends. I have to thank her for helping me understand quite a lot more about women, and the way a female thinks and reacts compared to a male! However, as I came from what I now recognise was a rather conservative spiritual background compared to where she was happiest in a Pentecostal fellowship, when she went away to Christchurch to go on a long course there, we drifted apart.

Meanwhile, things had changed at my accommodation at Tutuila. Instead of having two Salvation Army officers managing the guest house, a Christian couple came in and took up the reins. This meant that a new, young Salvation Army lieutenant was given the responsibility of running the corps (church side of things). Elsie Gray had been there previously when she came up from her prior appointment at Riverton to help some other officers with the door-to-door Red Shield Appeal in the Queenstown area. There had been no mutual attraction at that time. In fact, when those officers told her about my accident on Mt Soho and that I had been taken to Invercargill Hospital for a skull X-ray, apparently her only reaction was, 'Oh the poor guy,' and that was about it!

I have to say that the nurses in the little Queenstown hospital were wonderful. It was the first place the policeman who picked me up from the road head after the crash took me, and the head nurse was surprised that I was concerned about getting up on the bed, dirty work footwear and all! I would have been more than happy to take them off. After I was flying again, I took a couple of the nurses on a scenic flight around Queenstown in the floatplane.

Elsie, the 'Sally' officer, who was also a farmer's daughter (a background which has served us both well over the years), was in Queenstown full-time and living in Tutuila until the Salvation Army's own living quarters became available. During this time, we both helped keep the place running. I helped her do the many dishes that our guests created and later, when she was managing the place, I helped her with the corps' accounts and reconciliations which were all done manually in an extremely large ledger book. Seeing her in operation and benefitting from her ability as a cook (highly important!), not to mention her spiritual leadership in the corps, I felt attracted to her, and wonderfully for us both, Elsie felt the same towards me! She felt called to overseas mission service and already had one sister in India with her husband.

Elsie's family was well aware of our love for each other, and her young brother Alan came down to Queenstown from Foxton for a short stay. (He says he was sent down to check me out!) I had venison work to do in the Hollyford Valley with a Cessna 185 but had free seats to the location and back again, so it was a wonderful opportunity to take them both with me to show them a bit of the work that I did in moving the venison to a road head. All went really well until I swung the aircraft around at the top end of the airstrip to head home – SNAP! The tail spring broke, and there we were in a relatively remote place with no tail wheel. What to do? Well, what I did was to release the wires for the tail wheel steering and put the wheel into the aircraft. Then I thought that I would try something to see whether I could pull it off as I had not heard of it being done before, though I have no doubt it probably has been done a number of times.

As I was already lined up ready for takeoff, I got both Elsie and Alan to put their weight as far forward as possible in the cabin, foot brakes hard on, and full power and control column full forward, and hey presto, the tail lifted off the ground. Then came the really tricky bit – releasing the brakes just enough to move, but not so much that the tail would sink down again. With both Elsie and Alan with their weight forward, we got up to takeoff speed and under way. The landing back at Queenstown's old grass runway and taxiway was pretty much a reversal of the takeoff. I landed on the taxiway rather than the main runway and fortunately held it all together until at the hangar entrance. As I had called the base and told them the situation, the chief engineer was there to welcome us home with, 'Well done, Ted' as I powered off and the tail sank to the ground. Again, thank you Lord for helping in a very tricky situation!

After a time flying a floatplane at Te Anau, when I got back to Queenstown, I found the married couple who had been managing the guest house had left and the 'little Sally lassie', Elsie, was managing Tutuila as well as doing her 'church' duties. One afternoon when I was dressed in my white uniform shirt and shorts, I came back home during the day and happened to walk into the kitchen. Elsie was there and she told me later that on first glance, she thought I was her brother-in-law Dave Millar whom she really respected. That little episode gave our relationship a bit of a boost! Thanks Dave!

Our relationship deepened over time, as well as our respect for each other. But there was a slight problem and for a number of reasons getting to the point of an engagement wasn't altogether plain sailing. Elsie was a Salvation Army officer and couldn't get engaged to me without losing rank, although by that time I had become a Salvation Army 'soldier'. For good reason, the SA's rule for officers was that they had to marry another officer. There was another factor too, and this was that MAF was asking for two years' Bible training from their prospective staff. We talked this whole situation over with the very understanding and helpful Salvation Army area commander and he said that if MAF wanted me to get the Bible training, then I could train to become a SA officer, and the SA would second me to MAF. That was a real relief, and so was the answer from MAF, that for whatever reason, they wouldn't insist on me having to get the Bible training. Perhaps my referees and my preaching, etc. had helped, or Elsie having been a SA officer? Anyway, this opened up the way for us to become engaged, recognising that Elsie would ultimately forfeit her rank in doing so.

Elsie and I had made several trips to Invercargill for various good reasons and on one particular trip I had made up my mind to 'pop the question'. All went well, and we decided it would be fun to go to the southernmost tip of the South Island where there is an AA signpost pointing in different directions to various foreign cities. This was going to be the time! I took a photo of her there, but a little way away from us there was a group of young people keeping an eye on us, and I got the distinct inner feeling that they didn't have our best interests in mind, so we got in my car and started on our way back to Queenstown. I had in mind stopping at Kingston and asking the critical question there.

As we cruised along through Southland farmland Elsie had a question of her own for me! 'Were you going to discuss something at the southernmost signpost?' Okay, I got the idea, so I pulled up, backed into a farmer's roadside gateway, which we both felt was rather appropriate as we had been brought up on farms, and parked. Using God's terminology from Genesis 1, I asked Elsie if she would please be my 'helpmate' for the rest of our lives? Sorry, there was no getting down on my knee, or even handing over a ring at that point. But her answer made us both very happy and as I have said in so many deputation meetings since, I couldn't have done half the work that I did in PNG, or later, if it hadn't been for Elsie's faithful support, help and wisdom.

Things moved along steadily for the next few months and there were, of course, the farewells from the Christian community that we had been a part of. Elsie had been part of the ministers' fraternal in Queenstown with the Presbyterian and Anglican ministers. It was humorous but in some ways sad, that they would always ask Elsie to do the prayers at ANZAC dawn parades for fear that it would be too dark for them to read their prayers! Actually there was a good rapport between them all and they would take turns to share pulpits, especially at Easter and Christmas.

On one occasion, the Easter service was being held in the Anglican Church with a bit of pomp and much decorum. Elsie was to preach and had been seated in the front pew. The Anglican minister, who was quite tall, did the introductions. At the appropriate time, she was escorted to the pulpit where she found she could hardly see over the top, as it had been set to a convenient height for the regular minister. Her first reaction was to giggle but that would not have been appropriate on such an occasion, so with much self-control, she moved to the side and preached from there. All the ministers were at our farewell and one comment I remember was from Rev Bob Coates (Presbyterian) who congratulated Elsie for making a decent Sally out of a questionable Presbyterian (referring to me!) We all took it in good part, and it was a great evening.

In late February 1967 we packed all our earthly possessions into and on top of my Morris 1000 (with the rear axle permanently sitting on the overload buffers) and made our way north. The first overnight stop was in Timaru and with a little disquiet and some faith, we parked the car on the side of the road in front of the motel where we were staying, as there was no parking available elsewhere. We were both very relieved in the morning when we looked out of our separate rooms to see the top load was still there and intact. Those were the days when the population in general respected other people's property! The next overnight stay was in Picton, ready for the Cook Strait crossing the next day, which all went as planned. This was the first of a number of times that we crossed the strait with a vehicle.

Once we had made it to Elsie's parents' place at Foxton Beach, wedding preparations needed to get into full swing. All the necessary bookings had been made from a distance, but all the last minute bits and pieces still had to be done. Elsie's dad, Clarry Gray, had a mischievous fun streak in him and from the tales I have heard, Elsie in her younger days (and some of her older days too!) also manifested that part of the Gray gene. Both of us were going to reap the results of that later on our wedding day.

The day, 4 March 1967, dawned bright and sunny though very windy, as shown by Elsie's veil in one of the photographs we have. To keep the prescribed 'social distancing' protocol for a groom, my father and I stayed with Elsie's sister Nancy in Foxton, while Elsie was at Foxton Beach with her parents, Alan, and another sister, Alison. My brother Rob had stayed at home in Silverdale with Mum, who wasn't able to travel.

Our wedding service was in the little Salvation Army church at Foxton at 11:00am. Because both of us had been brought up on a farm and knew that a good number of our guests needed to get back to milk cows or travel reasonably long distances, we decided to break from the usual custom of having the photos taken immediately after the wedding service and went straight over to the nearby Foxton Community Hall for our wedding breakfast, which was a lunch. This worked well for the guests, but not quite so well for Elsie as she didn't have an opportunity to 'titivate up' before the wedding photos, although to me, she looked great as she was! After the photos, because her much loved and revered maternal grandfather was in hospital, we were taken there to see him and I am sure you can imagine the stir that it caused when a fully-dressed bride walked through the ward to see him!

After all this it was back to Foxton Beach to change and get under way – or so I naively thought! At an earlier time, we had packed our car and backed it hard up against the cypress hedge in front of Elsie's parents' place, thinking it was going to be safe there. How wrong can one be, when there are a number of relatives around! There was no car there at all, and that was just the beginning. Somehow they had gotten into the car, taken it across the road and parked it in the neighbour's garage, after writing in whitewash on the blue car many things including 'Me and my teddy'. But worse was to come; they had ripped open the boot from the inside (breaking a component in the process) and gotten into our suitcases. Yes, confetti in everything, right down to stuffing some in Elsie's hair shampoo bottle!

Fortunately, as a local, Elsie had a good relationship with her old band master Jack Brown, and we went there and washed the car and sorted a few things out so we could head off for our first night away together at a motel in Taihape. It was on our way back to the car after lunch at Taumarunui the next day that we got the full impact of just how thorough the confetti artists had been, for there on the reverse side of the central rear vision mirror was confetti glued to the back of the mirror! Because my mum hadn't been able to come to the wedding, Elsie in her loving graciousness had brought her wedding dress with us, so when we got back to the farm, she dressed up again so Mum and Rob could see us, and we had some photos taken of us all together there with Mum and Rob at the farm at Silverdale.

It was in these early days of our marriage that we established the habit of joining in a Bible reading and prayer time together, in which we committed the day's activity, our children (later) and others to the Lord for guidance and sustaining. We are privileged in the fact that we are still doing this 57 years later.

After a couple of days at the farm, we headed up to Paihia and Waitangi; then, for a reason that escapes me now, we went down to Gisborne. Prior to all of this, we had 'gone through the hoops' and been accepted by Mission Aviation Fellowship (MAF). It was while we were at Gisborne on our honeymoon that we got the call from MAF-NZ that we should move to Ballarat Australia as soon as possible to MAF Australasia's training and orientation base there. While not actually cutting our honeymoon short, we wasted no time in complying with the request. In those days there was a bus service from the downtown bus terminal (near today's Britomart Station) to the airport at Māngere, so the final farewells were done there in Auckland with my dad, Rob and some older church friends of the family.

Chapter 11

Ballarat Days

Quite early in my training phase, I had somehow (probably through MAF Youth Fellowship) got to know Gordon Chisholm and his wife Margaret. He had already moved to Ballarat as an engineer/pilot so he came down to Melbourne and picked us up to take us to the MAF-AIR base at Ballarat. On our way there, Gordon made a statement that I hadn't thought I'd hear and which caused me a little disquiet. He said, 'Just because we are all a bunch of Christians, don't think that there isn't friction and some relationship problems.' I guess up until that point, I had been a bit naive about the relationships amongst Christians working together, for my experience to that time had indicated otherwise.

We were taken to what was then called the 'guest house' which was going to be home for quite a while. A couple of days after getting there, we were settling down for a good night's rest when all of a sudden a bunch of the other staff surrounded the place with tin cans and all manner of things, making an unearthly din. Yes, it was our initiation of acceptance, led by Gordon! The evening went off well and we got to know some of our new neighbours over a cup of coffee. Something that was entirely new to me there was the hot water system that sat in the back porch and was fuelled by briquettes, something that I had never had any experience with previously. All went well until I needed to clean out the ash. What appeared to be cold ash actually wasn't and you can imagine my consternation when I went out early the next morning to see a small fire starting in the cardboard box I had put the ash into for disposal. Another ten minutes, and the back of the guest house would have been well alight! Phew, thank you Lord for undertaking for my ignorance regarding this!

The MAF-AIR base at Ballarat was an old RAAF base which had become redundant after WW2 with long runways and quite a few hangars, barracks and houses. Although classed as sitting atop the Central Highlands' Great Dividing Range, it had an elevation of less than 1,000 feet. However, it was a jolly cold spot (it snowed while we were there) and especially so if you were on the hangar floor working underneath an aircraft as the wind whistled through the gap of about 150 millimetres under the hangar doors!

During our time in Ballarat, I helped assemble three aircraft, one of which was the first turbocharged Cessna 206 that MAF Australia bought for the PNG operations. Its initial registration was VH-MFH. As I had a C206 rating, (and had converted my New Zealand commercial pilot's licence to an Australian one) I had the privilege of test flying this aircraft, all of which went very smoothly. The second was a Cessna 182 with modifications and the third was a Citabria, a light training aircraft that was fully aerobatic, hence its name (sort of) spelt backwards! This, along with helping on the local fertiliser-spreading aircraft helped to keep us all quite busy. There was also a paint shop which was in constant use, though I was never involved with it.

While Ballarat was the major engineering facility at that time, it was also a place where pilots were put through their paces, and the one who did that in my time was Ron Robertson who was himself an ex-PNG field pilot. MAF's first Cessna aircraft, a Cessna 170 'tail dragger', had been retired from MAF-PNG to MAF-AIR and its registration was VH-BUX. It was *extremely* light on the controls, and caused many a pilot some red-faced embarrassment. It took a little while to get the feel of its super-sensitive, light controls; and yes, when I first went up in it with an instructor, I too, 'ballooned' on my first landing!

Fortunately for me, when Ron Robby took me up first to 'see where I was at' we went in a Cessna 180, an aircraft I was familiar with and reasonably confident in, as I had flown the type while with SSA out of Queenstown. He asked me to land on one of the long tarseal runways, but he nominated the approach speed which for the weight of the aircraft was way too fast and we floated and floated as a consequence. I said to him, 'This is embarrassing, as the approach speed is far too high. Can I please do the next landing the way I am used to?' To his credit, he agreed. On the next approach, I used a speed approximately 15 knots slower, dropped over the fence, and put the aircraft down right on the end of the runway, to which Ron said, 'There aren't any strips in PNG that you will need to use that technique on,' and left it at that. All other checks were pretty well a breeze.

While at Ballarat we joined up with the Wendouree Salvation Army and, amongst other things, Elsie taught a number of teen-aged young women how to play a timbrel. After a time, we left the MAF guest house as one of the barracks closer to the hanger became available and we moved there for a time before boarding with the Seddons for the final few weeks. Apart from the cold weather, we both enjoyed our time at Ballarat and made lifelong friends of some folk who were there at the same time.

Chapter 12

Heading for PNG

After six months in Ballarat, it was time to move to the PNG field of service. As Elsie was pregnant by this time and not keeping in the best of health, MAF graciously allowed her to fly to PNG by commercial aircraft, while I was to fly a newly modified 300-horsepower Cessna A185 (designated 'A' because of the Australian modification of putting the 300-horsepower motor into the aircraft) up from Melbourne to PNG.

Vic Ambrose, the MAF Australia general secretary, himself an ex-MAF-PNG pilot, was going to be with me for the flight. As this route had been done several times previously, there were some well-used maps available which I had studied. On 23 October 1967 we left Melbourne early, and after 3 hours 44 minutes flying, we stopped at Bourke in western New South Wales for fuel and lunch. I must admit that I was pleasantly surprised with the accuracy of the maps – or my navigating! Such small things as a windmill were marked on the map, and it was most reassuring to see it appear on the left of track at the time expected, or when we crossed a railway line right on time. I noticed that Vic had also been keeping an eye on the map and how the navigating was going.

After taking off from Bourke and heading for the next stop which was Charters Towers (inland from Townsville) I was interested to see that Vic went to sleep. Did he feel he was in safe hands, or was it a very satisfying lunch? Who knows! All went well, and landing at Charters Towers after 4 hours and 42 minutes, we refuelled and got a motel for the night. I got my very first idea of what living closer to the tropics would be like. I couldn't get over the fact that it didn't start to cool down in the evening, at least not noticeably! Next morning we headed for Horn Island which is the Australian customs point when exiting the top of the Cape York peninsula, which is a very long strip of land. It doesn't look all that much on a map, but it took 4 hours and 38 minutes to fly it. After clearing customs at Horn Island and flying on to the PNG entry point of Daru, we headed directly for MAF's base at Wasua on the Fly River, with a combined time of 1 hour and 27 minutes. Crossing the Fly River, I noticed that there was a mud bank developing about midstream, especially when the tide was low. About 14 years later, I flew that route again and noticed to my surprise that the 'mud bank' was now an Island, with trees about four metres tall growing on it! Such is the growth rate in the tropics!

Back in the late 1960s, Wasua was the headquarters for Unevangelised Fields Mission (UFM) whose church arm later became the Evangelical Church of Papua (ECP). Even later, UFM became the Asia Pacific Christian Mission (APCM) in PNG, and has now joined with and become a part of Pioneers Mission. Before the introduction of aircraft, most of this mission's transportation was done with boats using rivers, and so many of the established mission stations were on a river, which was very handy if you had to fly IFR (I Follow Rivers) in less than perfect weather! It was at Wasua that first evening that I experienced dehydration and one of its consequences. As being in the tropics was a totally new experience for me, I hadn't kept up with my fluid intake, and was totally embarrassed when I polished off a two-litre jug of Ruth Charlesworth's 'muli' (PNG lemon) flavoured water, and had to ask for more! It didn't end there either, for when I walked, I could hear the slosh of fluid in my stomach! I learned later that an early sign of becoming dehydrated was the thickening of your saliva, and so I took the appropriate action of drinking something when I realised that was happening.

After a pleasant evening and a good night's sleep, we refuelled for the trip to Wewak on the north coast of PNG. As I hadn't flown this route previously and I knew we would be traversing the high mountain backbone of the country, I took on full fuel to the disgust from Jim Charlesworth who said we didn't need that much. To be fair, he was right, but for me it was a sort of insurance as I didn't know what sort of weather we might encounter over the highlands. Later, when we were based at Kawito, I realised that fuel at an outstation like Wasua was an extremely valuable commodity. With the full fuel load, we were pretty heavy, possibly even over AUW (All Up Weight) and I held the aircraft on the ground until a clean break into the air was available speed-wise. Vic said he had thought the aircraft would have performed better in that it had an extra 40 horsepower over a normal C185. However, once airborne we were up and away with, as it happened, a good clear run through to Wewak. It was quite different crossing mountains at over 10,000 feet, all covered with bush instead of bare rocks with a bit of snow here and there as it had been out of Queenstown in summer!

After meeting up again with Elsie and having lunch, Max Meyers (the chief pilot) took me up in a normal C185 for some circuits in the afternoon. All went fairly well until my first landing, for I was too much in awe of him to actually ask Max to clarify what he meant by: 'Land *by* the first marker cones.' Now, for someone who had been landing on a strip 122 metres long with a load of venison, there was actually plenty of space for me to land and pull up by the time I reached the first marker cones. Nah, I don't think he meant that, but what if he did? So I split the difference and touched down a bit before the first cones. Well, did I get a lecture (which was fair enough) as to the fact that we couldn't land 'short' on any of the PNG airstrips. Ah, so that is what he meant – land *abreast* of the first cones. From that time on, I did so and had no more problems. Now to be fair, back then before the shocking sports rivalry which has developed between New Zealand and Australia kicked in, we basically spoke the same language, but at times had a slightly different meaning for the same word, so that could quite easily have been the problem here.

Some days later, Max checked me out into the West Sepik airstrips including Amanab (ANA). On approach, it didn't appear to be overly long and it had a slight hump at the approach end then a shallow hollow before taking up a slight gradient which made the airstrip level overall. I felt we were floating too long, so 'pinned it onto its main wheels' so I could start braking and Max remarked, 'You surely know how to pin it on, don't you?' He wasn't quite so impressed later in the day after all the checks around the West Sepik had been done when time was starting to run out in the late afternoon and I did a curved 'fighter approach' into Anguganak. He didn't like that at all and was advocating the standard square circuit!

(For non-aviators, 'pinning it on' is a term used when flying a tail-wheel aircraft when the pilot will force the aircraft onto its main wheels for the sake of braking and extra control. Also, just to clarify what I mean by a 'fighter approach' – a standard, normal circuit for a light aircraft is an oblong centred around the runway or airstrip with the extended runway line forming the first leg. On the downwind leg, flying parallel to the runway but with a tailwind, you then turn onto a base leg with the runway ahead to the left. You descend on that leg from the 1,000-foot circuit height to 500 feet, then you turn onto final approach completing the two final parts of the four-part oblong. In a fighter approach, you do a curved, descending turn from the 1,000-foot point onto a short final point.)

Some time later, I became aware of an interesting story relative to the establishment of the Amanab airstrip, so I contacted Kay

Liddle, one of those involved in the story. With his permission, I'm using pieces of information he has written in his first book *Into the Heart of Papua New Guinea*. If you want the full, most informative account, you will find it in Chapter 14 of his book.

The Brethren mission or Christian Missions in Many Lands (CMML) had already established mission outposts at Lumi (LMI) and Green River (GRN), but there was quite a big area between the two without any airstrip that MAF could use. In the early days, MAF was the main means of getting absolutely anything and everything to a place to establish a mission outpost in the jungle. So in March 1955 Kay and Roy Austin went with MAF on an aerial survey of the area to see if they could find a suitable place for an airstrip which would allow them to make contact with the many native people in that area. They were elated to find a seemingly suitable bush clearing with a nearby landmark which they could use to identify it when on the ground.

A few days later, after farewelling their families, they set out with some carriers on what proved to be a difficult and at times quite terrifying trek until they eventually found the same spot. With the aid of some people who had a basic understanding of the Melanesian Pidgin trade language, they were able to get permission to use the clearing (as the locals reckoned it wouldn't grow anything!) and some bush land for an airstrip and a mission station. You can imagine the elation of the party as they went back home to loved ones with this fantastic news!

Five years later, Kay and family went to Amanab to enjoy a slightly cooler climate as it was about 1,000 feet higher than Green River where they were stationed at that time. This may not sound much of a difference, but every 500 feet makes for a temperature difference in the tropics! While there, they found out just how God had protected that first exploration party. I quote a portion from Kay's book:

> It soon became apparent that our carriers had been justifiably edgy, and that we had indeed been watched by armed warriors hidden from view. They intended to ambush and kill us and steal all our trade goods and remaining axes and bush knives. ... However, one old man reminded them of a legend that one day two of their ancestral spirits would return to this particular clearing and that would usher in 'a good time' for their people. He advised 'Don't attack and kill them but wait and see what happens.' His counsel prevailed. ... I still believe God used the timely remembrance of this legend to save our lives and initiate his plan of holistic salvation for the people of the Amanab area.

When I first heard about this, it reminded me of when I was learning to fly at Ardmore in 1963 and a woman missionary came to First Presbyterian Church in Papakura and asked us to pray that the Holy Spirit would go ahead and prepare the hearts and minds of the people in Nepal which at that time was a 'closed' country. This was so that when it opened up, they would be ready to receive the message that the missionaries would bring them. In 1960 there were 25 known Christians in Nepal but after just 30 years that number had grown to 50,000! To help this come about, one enterprising Christian mission took on contracts with the Nepalese Government and used Christian professional people with expertise to go in as 'workers'. Personally, I believe the same sort of thing happened in the above instance at Amanab, where prevailing prayer beforehand saved the day by using a local legend to save God's servants' lives! Does God use the opposition at times to fulfil his purposes? Yes, he certainly can and does! See Ezra 5 and 6.

As MAF developed from its beginnings, things stayed much the same for quite a long time. Initially, most MAF bases were a single pilot operation out in the bush, so the expectation of all early staff was that they were to be an engineer as well as a pilot, which made perfect sense so long as the bases were one family and there wasn't a centralised engineering base. It seemed to me that this dual requirement carried on a bit too long, and as a result, there were both positive and negative outcomes. When those who didn't have engineering experience went to another base that had a licensed engineer to officially cover all the work, the pilot was expected to help with the engineering phase which was fine.

I had no problem with this, though there was also a downside, for when a snag was found in the aircraft when the engineering was being done away from home, it was either a case of the pilot staying on for longer or taking a spare aircraft from that base and continuing with his programme. This idea worked well when there was a real understanding on the part of the engineer in charge who would let the pilot depart at a time that didn't put undue pressure on either him or the programme, considering the weather.

Not all of the new pilots who went to PNG had the privilege of the number of hours that I had. All the South Island flying meant that I went there with an excess of 1,400 hours of real flying experience. Many other 'newbies' had 500 or less, with a number of them having built up their hours with instructing. What is the problem with that, you may ask? When you are instructing a student, it is normal and legal for you to log that time as PIC (Pilot In Command), but in fact you aren't doing any actual handling of the aircraft, the student is, so while you might have say 1,000 hours PIC, you might have only had say 600 hours or less actually flying the aircraft.

Having worked for a commercial company that used the same types of aircraft as MAF had its pluses and minuses. The pluses were that I was familiar with the aircraft and was able to slot into things with little effort, but the minuses were mainly the fact that Kiwi and Australian cultures – at least back then – were somewhat different. Speaking quite broadly, something new for an Australian was to be analysed, thought about and hopefully tested by someone else before ever being implemented. We Kiwis thought more like Americans – if it looks as if it will work, give it a go, and if it works, you are so much ahead, and if it doesn't work, you've proved something. I hasten to add that this is a generalisation of both cultures! Despite these differences, there was a real ANZAC spirit between us and we still have some really great Australian friends whom we still cherish. A couple of examples of these attitudes follow.

For a reason best known to Cessna, they had the handle on the handbrake for parking positioned at the bottom of the instrument panel and basically centrally between a pilot's legs, with the handle pointing *down*. You may ask, 'What's the problem with that?' In fact, it gave the pilot greater ease as well as more purchase when pulling the hand parking brake on. The problem was that because of its position, it was extremely easy to hit the handle with your right knee or leg when getting out of the aircraft, so releasing the handbrake, which could be a significant problem if you were parked on a downhill-sloping airstrip! Southern Scenic (or perhaps Cessna itself) had also obviously had the same problem and had come up with a 10- to 15-minute fix which I told the engineering staff about quite soon after our arrival. It just involved knocking out a roll pin, turning the handle 180 degrees and putting the roll pin back in again. However, it took about six weeks after telling them that before one aircraft was changed!

As mentioned, I had also flown floatplanes while at SSA and to his credit, Max Meyers the chief pilot did at times ask me for an opinion relative to flying floats, as initially, I had more experience on floats than he had. However, with the brand of floats that MAF were then operating, the manufacturers didn't make any provision for protecting the propeller from damage from the spray the floats create in the early stages of getting up onto the step for taking off. When it is hit by the aluminium propeller travelling at almost the speed of sound, water may as well be a small pebble, as it is so hard and it can open up the leading edge of the prop. Once again, SSA had either caught up with a modification or devised one on their own, which I passed on to the field leader. Nothing happened for months until a MAF-US chap came across from Irian Jaya. The field leader had seen the modification I had spoken about in a magazine, and while I happened to be in the office doing accounts work one day, he asked the American pilot if he thought it would be any use. The reply? 'I don't fly floats at all, but it looks as if it would work okay.' The modification was then done. Perhaps, as the new boy on the block, I had too many new ideas?

The chief engineer at SSA had a saying when something needed doing on an aircraft: 'Throw the cat another goldfish,' meaning it will cost, but it needs to be done, as an aircraft sitting on the ground isn't making any money. One afternoon a C185 had been loaded up and was ready to go out on the West Sepik run. I was rostered to do it, but when I went to start the engine, the battery just didn't have the power to turn the motor over. I asked for another battery but got the response that the dead battery would be taken out and recharged. I'm afraid it was the only time I can remember that I almost lost my cool. I responded, 'Don't be so jolly stupid, if you have another battery, put it in so I can get going and do the work. You can charge the dead battery at your pleasure while I am away.' To be fair, it might have been the only time someone had been quite so bolshie, but it worked. I got a new battery fitted and my afternoon's work got done! I was told later that few, if any, had ever spoken to the chief engineer like that and the cooperative response I got was somewhat out of the ordinary.

You will have undoubtedly heard the old saying, 'It was the last straw that broke the camel's back.' I was involved in an incident that proves that saying. In the early days at Wewak, we used to have a siesta as it was so hot and, during this time, the cargo handlers would make up a load for a run to be done in the afternoon. On this particular day, I was rostered to do the West Sepik run again and the aircraft was all loaded up with the cargo well tied down except for the bags of freezer goods which I got from the big deep freeze (incidentally, made in and sent up from New Zealand). I took the freezer bags out and just put them on the top of the load, and 'Crack!'. The three to five kilos of freezer goods had caused the C185 tail spring to snap! I thanked the Lord that it was on the concrete in front of the hangar rather than at my first landing!

The Church of Christ mission was based about half an hour away to the east of Wewak on the Ramu River where we used to go regularly for many movements of personnel and goods. They had a good river to use for transport, but there were stations in the Ramu Basin well away from the river that needed to be serviced by air as well. When Max was checking me out, I must have given the guys in Madang Air Radio an opportunity for a really good laugh! One of the airstrips a little distance from the river was called Tsumba (TSU), pronounced 'Zumba', and I had landed there with Max. As I had never seen it written, after takeoff I gave my departure call as leaving 'Zombie', which at least gave Max a good belly laugh, if not the guys at Air Radio who took it all in their stride and mercifully didn't ask for a clarification of my departure point. Possibly it was how I was feeling after having been checked out into so many airstrips all in one day!

This airstrip has another memory for me as well. The Ramu River area is a little over 190 kilometres south of the equator, and as a result is always extremely hot (+35 degrees) and usually has a humidity of around 80 percent or higher. Consequently, it is quite normal for everyone to be hot and sweaty. The Tsumba airstrip is some distance from the Ramu River and I was to take a young fellow to another outstation in the Ramu Basin but he was initially being transported by canoe to the nearest point on the river to the airstrip. He must have known I was waiting for him and to his real credit, he had run from the river to the airstrip which had made him even hotter and perspiring more than normal. The net effect this had on me was that after loading him in with the other passengers, I dry-retched before climbing aboard and flying them to their destination. One perk of being the pilot or the front passenger is there is a large air vent in a Cessna 180/185 just forward and above the front seats, so I was able to direct a good stream of fresh air onto my face in times like these! Fortunately for all the passengers there are air vents available for them as well.

In many places in the north coast area, there was a cult called the 'cargo cult'. I think it probably originally stemmed from the fact that the Papuans couldn't understand how the 'white skins' had so many wonderful things that they had never seen or heard of, and believed that we had some secret from the 'gods' that we were withholding from them. So there was an underlying feeling that one day when they had figured out the secret, cargo of all sorts would materialise for them. They also picked up on different things as possibly being the secret. I know that in the Ramu River area, a local Christian had planted a coconut plantation and because he was conscientious and cared for the palms, he had some very good harvests of nuts. 'Ah ha,' some of the cargo cult people said, 'becoming a Christian is the secret to gaining wealth.'

A similar sort of thing happened with a Lutheran missionary in the Lae area who had laboured for years doing Bible translation until it was time to go back to the United States. He had translated the whole of the Scriptures, except, sadly, for one of the minor prophets. 'Ah,' some said, 'the secret must be in that book, and he hasn't translated it for us so we can know it.' I personally believe the devil has blinded those Papuans with this belief system so as to make it harder for them to come to know the truth about Jesus and his salvation for them.

After a relatively short time, probably because of my accumulated flying hours and the mountain flying I had already done, I was being checked into the highlands' airstrips from the Wewak base, which at that time supplied them all with personal and trade store goods. It wasn't too long, though, before one of the other pilot's wives asked Elsie, 'How come your husband is being checked into the highlands, while my husband has been here for about a year already and he isn't being checked in there yet?' I am not sure what diplomatic answer Elsie gave but that was the last we ever heard of it – thankfully!

But my wife wasn't the only one who heard a complaint about me being checked into the highlands. In about November 1967 I remember one missionary at a highland airstrip complaining that my weight was displacing some cargo that he wanted brought in. I also remember Max's response. He said, 'Well, we have one of the highlands pilots going on furlough over Christmas and if Ted doesn't get checked in, you won't have *anything* coming in for a number of months.' When that reality struck home, the complaint ceased and an air of thankfulness prevailed!

The above interchange happened on the Porgera airstrip which was built towards the head of the valley and was developed on a large landslide that was oh-so-gradually moving downhill. This meant that it had a slight wrinkle in it towards the bottom. As it was towards the head of a large valley with the surrounding area sloping up at approximately the same rate, it gave a terrible optical illusion which made it incredibly easy to get too low on late final approach so you had to actually climb up to reach the bottom of the strip. Not a good idea with a normally aspirated engine at 7,000 feet! I overcame this problem by overflying the top of the strip with a bit of clearance and maintained that height all the way around the circuit until turning onto final approach. It gave the visual appearance of being very high but it was a safe way of making sure I didn't get trapped with the above problem.

However, it was obvious one RAAF pilot got caught on a couple of accounts at Porgera, because there was the discarded fuselage of an RAAF Caribou aircraft on the side of the airstrip, which was being used as a 'boi haus' (boy house). Apparently, (as the story goes) the Caribou was bringing a load of fuel into Liagam from Madang. Someone hadn't been doing their map reading too well as they must have just about overflown their destination to get to Porgera. Nor had they done much studying of their landing charts, as the two airstrip runways lay at approximately right angles. All of this must have come to the pilot's consciousness late on final approach, and possibly because of the aforementioned optical allusion, the pilot tried to overshoot – that is, abandon the landing and try and fly away to either make another approach or at least get things sorted out. But sadly, because it was so late in the approach, the Caribou couldn't out climb the terrain and crashed just above the top end of the strip, minus the co-pilot. Realising what was going to happen and because they had a load of fuel on board, the co-pilot ran down the back, opened a side door and took a leap. From what I understand, both pilots survived!

Those guys weren't the only ones to have a bit of excitement on landing at Porgera. The strip surface was made out of consolidated limestone chips, roughly the size of the larger aggregate used to tar-sealed New Zealand roads. While the surface was far from being really rough, there were numerous limestone stones which were loose on the surface. Once, when I had just touched down, and was bringing the control column back to finish the round-out on the sloping airstrip, it just wouldn't travel any further. Not a nice feeling to lose control. I am sure it was a 'God moment' as I realised what must have happened. A loose surface stone had been flicked up by my main wheel, and had jammed in the counter-balance horn of the elevator. How do you overcome that problem? What I tried, worked. I *very* quickly jabbed the control column forward as quickly as I could and back again. That was enough to release the stone, and I again had control. Thank you Lord!

By the time we reached PNG, the first of the turbo-charged 285-horsepower U206s were in operation out of Wewak and as Max was checking me out, he described its initial climb performance as being like that of 'a ruptured duck', and compared with the 300-horsepower normally aspirated (non-turbo) U206, it surely wasn't great at sea level. However, once you got above about 4,000 feet altitude the turbo really came into its own. In reality, it's said that at 5,000 feet a normally aspirated engine of any sort loses approximately 25 percent of its power. If there are no exhaust leaks and all is going well in the turbo department, the TU206s had sea level performance up to 19,000 to 20,000 feet, which was very handy when operating quite normally at 10,000 feet and occasionally above.

There were restrictions as to how long we were allowed to operate without oxygen above the normal pilot ceiling of 10,000 feet. In my day, we were officially allowed to fly at 12,000 feet for a limited period, even though the pilot whom CAA had tested to determine the safe height and time was a lowlands pilot and a smoker! It is interesting how you do adapt to the rarer atmosphere when based in the highlands. Some years later, when we were based at Kawito, there was a pilots' meeting being held at Wewak and I flew to Mendi where Wal and Elizabeth Job were based, and Wal and I continued on to the meeting at Wewak together.

We set off at about 3:00pm and as can frequently happen, the highlands and the central ranges in particular were clouded in with quite high buildups of cloud. However, Wal had the original TU206 (MFH) at Mendi, and we set off. Before long it became pretty obvious that the turbo's performance was going to be really tested, and as there was only one small oxygen bottle on board at the time, I said to Wal, 'You are flying, you have the lot.' Wal said I went to sleep at 18,000 feet on our way up to 22,000 feet, and woke again at about 15,000 feet on the way down once we were in the Sepik Basin. Being curious about the real effects of high-altitude flying, we did a test on the way back home to Mendi, with me as the test subject again! As we climbed up to 10,000 feet, Wal gave me a set of figures to add up and timed me doing it and we then checked the accuracy of the calculations. Then at 12,000 feet he gave me a second (different) lot of figures to do the same. From that rather crude but effective test run, it was very obvious that I was both slower and less accurate the higher we went, which bears out the reason for a restriction on altitude flying without oxygen.

Chapter 13

Operational Flights

Back in 1967, there was always a daily run from Wewak (except Saturday and Sunday) into somewhere in the highlands which meant essentially heading south for an average of about an hour and a quarter. Wewak was a Government administration town on the north coast of PNG serving the whole of the Sepik basin. While not running anything like a 'Regular Public Transport' operation, we did, for the sake of everyone's convenience, work to a regular pattern of working across the sector from east to west, so Liagam was always on a Monday and during the week, we went to Porgera, Guala (Koroba), Kopiago, Tekin, and Telefomin (every fortnight or so) with a few extra stops each day normally thrown in.

Sadly, about five months prior to my starting to fly these routes, John Harveson, a fellow Kiwi pilot had gone missing while operating in the Telefomin area and so it was an area that was treated with the upmost respect. (John or the wreckage has never been found.) Telefomin was a PNG Government administration outpost relatively close to the border with West Irian (now Indonesian Papua) where the Government offices were situated on one side of the airstrip, with the Baptist mission and now MAF on the other. The whole Telefomin basin looked as if it had been a lake or similar at some point, before the area was drained by the forming of the headwaters of the mighty Sepik river, as the earth there was like a fine white silt. As we only went there infrequently, we never really got to experience the full range of weather that could occur in the area during a whole day.

I am sure that the flight programmers at Wewak genuinely thought they were doing us highland pilots a good turn by not sending us there more regularly and only in retrospect have I realised that instead of reducing the stress, it actually increased it, because by going there only once a month (or less) it was like going into the unknown every time we went to Telefomin. We weren't familiar enough with the area to be able to positively identify just where we were in relation to the airstrip by what we saw through even big breaks in the cloud. This meant that when we arrived overhead on top of broken cloud, we had to call up the mission and ask if they could hear the sound of the aircraft, and where it was in relation to the airstrip. Only then could you safely dive down through a decent break and be sure that you were where you wanted to be!

Modern day pilots will naturally be saying, 'What about knowing where you were with a GPS?' Yes, it would have been great if GPS had been invented then, but if it was, it would only have been available to the military. We were in fact quite short on instrumentation, as the ex-wartime instruments being used were so heavy they were considered a weight burden, and so we didn't have any artificial horizon (AH) or a directional gyroscope (DG). But we did have two small wind screen-mounted compasses which didn't always agree. Sometimes they had as much as 15 degrees difference! Obviously, when that happened, it was time to do a new compass swing to correct the error!

As an aside here, later, when we only had one compass but had a DG as well, there were times when the compass was adversely affected by the cargo we were carrying, especially corrugated iron in a C185. I found that the way to overcome the 'iron effect', was to switch on before loading all the electrics you would be using, along with the radio, and turn the aircraft onto the heading for the track you'd be taking to your destination. Switch everything off and load on all the iron and any other cargo, and after starting up to go switch all the electrics on again, note what the compass reading was then and follow that compass heading. However different it may have been from what would be the normal heading, it would take you to your destination without any problem. This system worked equally well if we had to carry any quantity of iron or steel, such as a big steel gearwheel for a sawmill winch.

Because we were not going into Telefomin regularly enough, there was the feeling that we wanted to get the work done, and get out again before the weather closed in towards the afternoon. At times, the Sepik locals' penchant for fire lighting only increased the problem because of the smoke, but that was made even worse when it was mixed with very light rain falling from a high overcast. I experienced this once. In the morning on the way into Telefomin with a health department person and supplies, I experienced the light rain with quite adequate visibility and asked him to be ready to leave at 1:00pm as I figured that I would have completed the tasks the Baptist Mission had for me to do by then. At about 12:00 noon I happened to be back at Telefomin and saw him with the resident mission nurse at the airstrip. I asked them how the visit to the hospital was going (this was the primary focus of his visit). You can imagine my surprise and disappointment when the nurse, who was a keen geologist, said, 'Oh we haven't been there yet, we've been looking at things in the museum,' including, I have no doubt, her rather extensive rock collection!

I was ready to return by 1:00pm, but no government official! At 1:30pm they rolled up and I put him on with some passengers for Myanmin, a mission airstrip in a valley within the Telefomin highlands area which was easy to get to by following the valley systems. We took off from Myanmin and went to the west of Mt Stoll, heading for Wewak. In the meantime, some Sepik locals had been busy lighting fires, and instead of just light rain, there was quite a lot of smoke mixed with it. It appeared initially that the visibility would be better with some altitude, so I climbed up to about 7,000 feet, but it was actually getting worse, so I elected to turn around to head back to Myanmin and then Telefomin as it was simply a case of following valleys to get between the two. However, I made the crucial error of descending more rapidly than I had climbed, which put me into a very different valley to where Myanmin was located!

To his credit, the government guy must have been paying quite a bit of attention to the altimeter as it was he who pointed out to me that I was now below the level of the Myanmin airstrip. We were clearly at the head of a valley running roughly north and south, rather than Myanmin's east and west. So, I said to him, 'Here is where we get down low and follow the river and see where it leads us.' I am ever so grateful that someone within the Australian administration had the idea of painting the place name on the roof of the May River outpost! As soon as I saw that, I knew where I was, although I had never been there before. The trip home at low level thankfully didn't provide any more problems, even though it was still quite smoky.

However, when you have a wife who is in tune with the Holy Spirit, you can't just arrive home at the end of the day as if nothing has happened. After the normal kiss and hug, Elsie asked me, 'What was happening about 2:15pm this afternoon, as I was prompted to pray for you?' There is no way a guy would get away with a shrug and not own up, so I thanked her for her prayers and told her the whole story. It is wonderful to have a wife like that! This wasn't the only time the Holy Spirit prompted her in this way as we will hear later.

Other airstrips apart from Telefomin bring back memories too. At Koroba, before the new government limestone strip was established, the Brethren (CMML) mission had a strip close to their Guala mission station. It was always well kept and was one way because of a hill at the western end and so had a slight downhill slope for takeoff. Sadly, in the northwest season, there was often a gusty tailwind for takeoff. On this occasion, I was flying a C185, which was normal apart from the fact that one wing had a long-range tank, while the other had a short-range tank, which of course meant carrying two dipsticks but also meant that there was less fuel than if both were long-range tanks which was the norm in all the other C185s. A senior Brethren missionary and his family were moving from Guala to either Green River or Wewak and there was a pretty significant tailwind. Looking at the conditions, I would have preferred to do two shuttles to Tari, a DC3 strip about nine minutes away where I could have taken off into wind but the limited fuel state sadly precluded that. I asked for some things to be off-loaded, which was done, but pots and pans etc. don't make much difference weight-wise and while I felt we should have taken more weight off, I was too new and shy to ask for more to come off – or too dumb!

I used a downwind takeoff technique I had learnt from another pilot when doing the venison recovery back in the South Island, which is to fly clean (reducing any drag component) until you've gained flying speed and then pull on takeoff flap while easing back on the control column. As we hurtled down the strip, I knew we weren't going to have a lot of clearance at the end, and after gaining just enough height, found myself steering the aircraft through the lowest wispy tops of the yar trees at the far end. Fellow pilots: You DON'T get any 'ground effect' off the feathery tops of yar trees!

For any non-aviation person reading this, 'ground effect' is like a bubble of air created when any aircraft is close to the ground, because of the high pressure developed under the wing as a result of the wing's form and its aerodynamics. It can, in certain instances, help to keep you airborne when you otherwise wouldn't be!

On the above Guala occasion, when I had gained sufficient height to turn around into the wind and to set heading, my right leg was shaking and bouncing up and down uncontrollably. My mission friend probably noticed this and said, 'That was a great bit of flying, Ted.' I was tempted to say, 'No, it was a lousy bit of captaincy, as I should have requested you to take some real weight off,' but I think I was just so grateful to God that we had all made it off safely that I probably just grunted a response!

I also have a more pleasant memory of the Guala strip and station. Romance happens at times on the mission field, and on this occasion, I was taking a party into Guala to see and be involved in the wedding of two CMML missionary folk. I had taken the groom in a couple of times from his station in the Sepik and this was to be the day. The first surprise came when I was weighing one of the Brethren folk from Wewak and asked where her overnight bag was. She looked at me aghast and said, 'We are coming back this afternoon aren't we?' I said, 'Yes we are aiming to, but one can never tell whether you'll get out of the highlands in the later part of the day,' which is true. The next thing that wasn't scheduled was when we all got to the Guala station, someone came up to me and shoved a camera into my hands and said, 'Can you please take some photos for us?' I just hope my efforts were good enough. For the record, we did get back to Wewak that afternoon without any trouble.

Tekin, a Baptist mission station some distance to the west in the highlands at an elevation of 5,500 feet, is a one-way airstrip with an inconsistent slope. It is also positioned in an elbow of a main valley with a smaller valley feeding into the crook of the elbow which meant that with wind socks at the top and at the bottom of the airstrip, it was not uncommon to have them pointing in opposite directions! Facing the strip on approach, beyond the far end of the airstrip, was a cliff face of limestone about 2,500 feet high. I think that the official circuit direction was right-hand, which meant that all the time flying in that direction, one had to try and see what was happening on the ground past the front of your right-hand passenger! Also, I figured that should you need to give it away (abandon the landing) as you turned onto final approach, it meant the options were quite limited and required steep turns to get out of it either way. So I always did a normal, but quite tight left-hand circuit which gave me the opportunity to feel if there were any downdrafts off the limestone cliff and what sort of disturbance the little valley was likely to promote, as well as being able to easily observe the windsocks all the time.

Yes, the base leg (the last section of the oblong circuit before turning to land) was shorter, but should one have to abort the landing for any reason when turning onto final, it was relatively easy to just fly up the main valley. This gave plenty of space to reconsider things, because when flying the left-hand base, continuing up that main valley was straight ahead. If one was using a right-hand circuit, to abort when about to turn final would mean at least a 90-degree turn to get away from the situation.

In this early period, I remember that one of the Tekin mission wives needed to be medivaced out to Wewak. She was lying down on the hard five-ply floor beside me with the right-hand front seat removed. As it was morning as we climbed out, I noticed that the sun was pouring in onto her closed eyes and causing her distress. Fortunately, I had something which I was able to hold in such a way that I could shade her eyes for the hour or so it took to get to Wewak. She, and her husband seated behind me, were very grateful that I was able to do this.

I later heard of an amusing, but embarrassing situation that occurred in one of the Tekin houses. The men in this area (and to the west of it) wore a belt of fine vines around their waist into which they stuffed tankard leaves to cover their rear end. To be somewhat modest in front, they covered their penis with a dried, upwardly curving gourd (the longer the better!) which was sometimes supported with bark string from their belt. On this occasion, a sincere expatriate helper from New Zealand or Australia was assisting in one of the mission houses. She had longish hair which she kept in place with a hairnet. Somehow, when she was bending over, the local male house help got the end of his gourd caught up in the hairnet. You can imagine the mutual embarrassment as they untangled that situation, and the amusement of any other person seeing their predicament!

One of the mission staff at Tekin had a weather condition named after him by those of my era. As always, the flight programmer would ask for a weather report from a destination like this, which was not only over an hour away, but also just beyond the central ranges, meaning we had no way of knowing what sort of weather we would encounter as we got closer to our destination. One morning, a chap with the surname of van Akker gave the weather report and said it was solid blue. Now some of you may have observed that at times cloud that is raining or about to rain very heavily can look extremely dark blue or even near black. The pilot who was doing the flight that day ran into these latter conditions, and so that sort of weather was dubbed 'van Akker blue' by many of us.

About three minutes by aircraft away from Tekin was the government station and airstrip of Oksapmin which was in an area shaped a bit like a hand basin. You will ask then, 'Why didn't it flood?' – a good question. In the same way a hand basin has a plughole, so did Oksapmin, in the form of a fault in the limestone structure of the basin. My old MAF mini manual has a note: 'Climb out restriction! Severe turbulence can be experienced in the basin, especially in the NW season. SEVERE DOWNDRAFTS!'

Yes, there certainly were severe downdrafts if you were on the wrong side of the basin in the northwest season, and there was also often a quartering tailwind on takeoff which was a further factor to be taken into account. However I found that in the northwest season, it was very useful to purposely drift towards the southern side of the basin and collect the updraft that was there. The lowest point out of the basin was roughly the extended centre line of the airstrip, which was the eastern lip of the basin, but was on the western side of the Strickland Gorge.

In the same way that the limestone structure allowed water to flow out of the Oksapmin Basin, the walls of the Strickland Gorge were also considered to be possibly porous. An Australian university studied the water flow, etc. of the Strickland River at this point and calculated that in normal circumstances it would be economical to build a massive hydro dam there and cable the electric power to Australia – but for one thing. There was no guarantee that the walls of the gorge would actually hold the water for the dam!

I think one of my more memorable solo events in those early days was taking some people into one of the CMML airstrips at Yebil in the West Sepik. The airstrip was a sloping one that often needed to be buzzed (flown low over it) for the sake of chasing a pig or two off it before landing and it also had a rather different approach path. On right-hand base, one needed to head directly for a low cliff face, and then turn right to line up onto the airstrip for landing. I don't know whether the Papuan passenger in the front seat on this occasion had ever flown before or not, but as we headed for the low cliff, she grabbed her towel and completely covered her face so she couldn't see what was going to happen. It was only after we had landed and she heard other people speaking that the towel came off! To be fair, it must have been a terrifying experience for her if she had never flown or landed there before.

A couple of airstrips in the East Sepik had a similar quirk, and these were Yagrumbok and Jambitanget. They both had transverse slopes for a good portion on the airstrip. That is, when landing to the north, the left-hand side of the airstrip was higher than the right-hand side by a significant amount – enough to make it very exciting when landing on them when they were wet. I was never checked out by anyone into Yagrumbok and was programmed to take the resident missionaries back home there from Wewak one afternoon. The wife was more than a little concerned about this, and I remember Max pacifying her with, 'It's okay, I have confidence in Ted, he has had a lot of experience.' Well I'm glad Max had confidence in me, for as fate would have it, there had been rain in the afternoon so the strip was slippery and to keep from sliding off the strip to the right, it was necessary to use the rudder to point the aircraft about 10 to 15 degrees to the left to maintain a straight line. I had an identical experience at Jambitanget one afternoon in similar conditions. All good fun, as long as you had the experience and the nerve to cope!

Chapter 14

New Experiences

The first year at Wewak was naturally one with many new experiences for us as a couple. Elsie was pregnant with Ann, our firstborn, and very sadly for her, she had chronic, sustained morning sickness which wasn't limited to only the morning This was mighty debilitating for her – so much so, that a stainless steel bowl was her constant companion. One day when she had been down town making some purchases, she decided to take a rest before making the quite significant climb back up Wewak Hill on foot to the house we were living in.

But being new to the territory, she sat on a rock fence in the shade of a coconut palm. An old Papua New Guinean man came along and showed great concern with hand movements and much talking, which of course Elsie didn't understand, but then the penny dropped! Sitting under a coconut palm is never a good idea, for should a ripe coconut decide to fall, it can deliver a lot more than just a sore head! I am aware that some people have been killed with a mature, ripe nut dropping on them unexpectedly. While Elsie couldn't communicate her thanks verbally to the old man, she was most grateful to him for his obvious concern and thanked him as best she could.

In those early days, it was fairly common to hear the expression, 'Only in New Guinea.' The following true story may be a good illustration of how this saying came about. On another occasion, Elsie had been into the only store anything like a supermarket in

Wewak, which was owned by Burns Philip. They also owned a shipping line between Australia and PNG and a PNG coastal service. She had gathered her groceries and was at the checkout when two non-mission 'white skin' women walked past. They were wearing very short shorts, with a leg length of about 3 centimetres, if that. They were like a couple of Pied Pipers who had already gathered a troupe of testosterone-filled young bucks walking closely behind them when, mid-checkout, the young chap who was serving Elsie decided that he too would like to see this spectacle. So he left her standing there while he went out the front door and stared at the procession; possibly wishing he was free to join them. It was probably only when there were so many bodies between him and the 'attractions' that he couldn't see them anymore that he came back in and continued to serve Elsie at the checkout! Yes, only in PNG.

One of the regular weekly operations was to fly persons or supplies into Baiyer River for the Baptist Mission and then bring out a load of fresh vegetables. The main airstrip that was used in the Baiyer Valley was Kumbwaretta where the Baptist Mission's hospital was situated, and so it often meant that there were a lot of passenger movements to and from that point to the four other satellite Australian Baptist Missionary Society (ABMS) airstrips in the area. However, most of the vegetables came from one airstrip (Lumusa) just three minutes away (overhead to overhead), so often it was a case of seats in to take passengers to Lumusa and then seats out just five minutes later to take a load of veges packed in wooden crates back to Kumbwaretta. This was done not once, but several times, as there was a quite heavy (110-kilogram) takeoff penalty because of Lumusa's 550-metre length and 4,750-foot altitude.

Elsie and I wanted to get a decent tape recorder (reel-to-reel in those days) and I had arranged to get one from Christian Radio Missionary Fellowship (CRMF) which was at that time situated at the head of the Baiyer Valley at Rugli. It had been transported down to Kumbwaretta for us and I was to pick it up on one of the 'Baptist shuttle' days. The day came on 14 May 1968 and I returned to Wewak, eager to show the top-quality Akai machine to Elsie. However the day was to be even more memorable than that, for when I got back to Wewak, I was told that Elsie had given birth to our firstborn, Ann, and so thoughts of showing off the tape recorder vanished as I made my way out to the Wewak hospital to see Elsie and Ann. What a memorable day it turned out to be!

I was allowed to go in and have a look at Ann, and although a child at that stage isn't supposed to be able to actually focus on anything, I certainly had the feeling that Ann focused her gaze on me for a short period. Mind you, in reality she was about a month old by the time she was born, because the doctor who was attending to Elsie was convinced that her dates were wrong, and so he let nature take its course. He later apologised to Elsie, as it was obvious that Ann was overdue; her skin was 'over cooked' and it peeled a couple of times. But that was soon overcome and we were a happy trio, though I have to admit – and I honour her for this – Elsie was the one who got up at night when it was rarely needed so as to allow me the opportunity to be well rested for the next day's work. Ann was a very placid baby and allowed us to have almost a full night's sleep which was great and we both really appreciated it.

It was during those initial months at Wewak that we came to grips with the north coast PNG trade language, Melanesian Pidgin. This was later to become the most popular trade language over the whole of PNG, though at that time the south coast mainly used 'Police Motu' which, like Pidgin, was a mix of (sometimes very bad) Australian English and either a tribal language or other languages. The north coast was originally a German colony, which changed after the First World War and was the reason there were place names like Marienburg, etc. One of the best places to learn some Pidgin was at church on a Sunday morning, because we could sort of follow a Bible reading as it was being read in Pidgin, while reading it in our English Bible. Of course there was a long way to go, but I found this gave some of the basics to start with. As most of the MAF staff did, we attended the Assemblies of God Church (AOG) each Sunday morning while we were at Wewak.

The afternoon Anglican services which were held a couple of times a month were in English and were taken by Rev Doug McGraw who had been an MAF pilot, although he was flying for another commercial company by the time we were in Wewak. He was a very experienced pilot, having been in the RAF instructing those who flew the dam buster sorties, but he was also an extremely genuine Anglican minister who read the prayers as if it was the very first time, with the accompanying depth of meaning and expression.

The first printing of the whole New Testament (NT) in Pidgin was in 1969 and initially only a few people got one. At that time Scripture Union (SU) was also producing notes to help people understand what the prescribed daily Scripture readings meant. Interestingly, these same notes were being used by the Catholic mission at Wewak to encourage their catechists. Sadly, as soon as the New Testament was printed, the next month the SU notes referred to one of the new books in the NT which hadn't been printed previously, which meant that a high percentage of those using the notes didn't have the appropriate scriptures to read. One of our senior MAF staff requested from the Bible Society the relevant script for just those portions which the SU had used, but sadly the answer was negative. Not willing that all these young readers should be deprived of the opportunity to read the Pidgin Scriptures, Max went to a missionary whom he knew had translated those particular portions, and got his script (it was just fractionally different) and had them printed off to fill the gap. I am pretty sure that the Catholic mission at Wewak printed those Scripture portions for everyone's benefit.

It is interesting to note that the house we were living in on top of Wewak Hill was known in MAF circles at that time as 'the long house' as it was quite large, with toilet facilities at one end, the kitchen at the other, and bedrooms in between, with a verandah down one side. It had been built for MAF in the early days by one of CMML's very early Kiwi missionaries (Christian Missions in Many Lands – Open Brethren). Kay Liddle became one of CMML's senior missionaries and was a staunch supporter of MAF, both on the field and at home in New Zealand when he came back from PNG. He became the chairman of MAF-NZ's council after many years of wonderful missionary service, including being the principal for a period of Christian Leaders Training College (CLTC), an interdenominational Bible College in the Waghi Valley quite close to Mt Hagen.

Fairly early in our time at Wewak, we hosted an evening Bible study in the large lounge that the long house afforded. I can still remember the question asked by a Baptist missionary who was out at Wewak from the highlands. He said, 'What should we expect from a first-generation PNG Christian?' He then went on to give an illustration to explain the reason for his question. He said that a few weeks prior, he had been walking from one place to another and the CLTC student who was accompanying him said, 'There are spirits in that pool.' I don't remember any definitive answer to the question being given, but I know that when another well-respected ex-CLTC PNG pastor was out with a very well-versed missionary he said, 'There are spirits in that tree; I can hear them knocking.' Keith Dennis the missionary didn't comment, but just accepted that Mundalaga knew something he didn't. I have often said, that we 'white skins' are veritable babes in the wood compared to the PNG people with regards to understanding the spirit world.

Back then, if a pilot had an accident which meant the aircraft needed repair, it was deemed appropriate that the pilot be brought into the main base (Wewak) to work on the damaged aircraft until it was flyable again. Top-down communication back then was a bit lacking, to the extent that people in Australia got to know about staff movements in PNG through the Christian newspaper *New Life*, *before* the affected individuals in PNG did! Granted, communications between the two countries was basically by tickertape telegram. This lack of communication was demonstrated to me one day as a minibus-load of people was going to our place for lunch; Elsie was on the roster to take guests that day. Peter said to me, 'I hear my wife and I are coming to stay with you while I am fixing the aircraft.' Vic Ambrose, the Australian MAF secretary, the one who likely had made that decision, was riding with us in the bus at the time, so I responded, 'Oh, is that so? It would have been rather nice if we had been given a heads-up!' Nobody said a word.

However, it is wonderful how God makes the most of these sorts of situations. While we were at Ballarat earlier, this couple had lived next to us and we had become good friends, so it wasn't any great imposition. But more than that, Flo, who was pregnant, said it was wonderful because Peter hadn't up to that point seemed to be at all interested in small children – until they came to stay with us. It thrilled her to see Peter interact with our baby Ann, which brings out the point that God can use unfortunate circumstances to fulfil a need.

As you can imagine, the cargo shed attached to the MAF hangar at Wewak was filled with all sorts of goods to be taken to outstations, including large bags of rice to be sold in the various trade stores. One thing which became very obvious to me quite early on, was the difference between bags of brown rice compared to bags of white rice. The weevils knew where the good tucker was! If the bags had been there for a few days, the bags of brown rice would be covered with weevils, but there was not one weevil on the bags of white rice, even though they were side by side! Somewhat telling, isn't it?

So you can imagine my dismay when one of the commodities we brought into Wewak for the AOG pastor's hens was rice bran from the factory at Maprik which was making brown rice into white rice! I suppose at least the chooks were going to have a healthy diet and the eggs would be of top quality

Talking of diets, one needed to get used to the differences in the way white cultures responded to the tropical norms. As on all MAF bases, the wives provided hospitality for transiting people. On this occasion, it happened to be an American pilot from over the Irian Jaya border, now referred to as West Papua, or Indonesian Papua. He had come for breakfast and Elsie opened a new packet of Weetbix to give him as well as some toast. When the guy put some milk on the Weetbix, a few weevils floated to the top and he pushed it aside. (We would have just skimmed them off and proceeded to eat.) Elsie thought to herself, 'You fussy fellow,' and asked him how long he had been in Irian Jaya, to which he replied, 'Just a few months.' Ah! Elsie thought he hadn't been in the tropics long enough to know weevils and Weetbix often go together! She then gave him an egg on toast and was somewhat nonplussed when she saw him proceed to put jam on his spare piece of toast. She thought that he had just forgotten what stage he was up to in his menu, but no, the jammed toast and egg all went down together. New experiences for us all!

Of course, we also carried passengers in abundance and it was on another flight in from Maprik to Wewak that I had my eyes opened to the strength of the local women. I was about 32 at the time, brought up on a farm and thought of myself as being fairly strong in the arms. I can still remember with utter amazement, what one woman did. I guess she was possibly a little older than me. I unloaded a bilum (native string bag) which I regarded as mighty heavy, from the cargo pack (pod, or Pidgin 'bel') which was attached to the underbelly of the aircraft. Bilums were locally made string bags made from the finely twisted fibrous bark of a tree, capable of carrying almost anything, depending on the size. The normal method for women carrying a bilum was to have the handles of the bag on the forehead while the weight of the whole bag rested on their bent back. As I figured the bilum was so heavy, I asked the woman if I could help her to lift it up so she could carry it. She effectively said, 'No, it's okay,' and with a well-practised twisting swing, she slung it up onto her back and head. I thought 'Wow, how did she do that?' But that was just the start. She then lifted her little toddler up and sat it on her shoulders as well and walked away! Bent forward for sure, which was the typical stance for women carrying anything heavy that way. I would estimate she was carrying at least her own weight on her back, if not more. It was a most enlightening and also rather humbling experience!

In that first year at Wewak, we experienced several earthquakes, as the north coast of PNG is an area very prone to them. In the Readers' Digest World Atlas there is a special map which shows earthquakes as a black dot. The north coast of PNG is like a heavy black line, since there have been so many quakes there. For a period of time, they were so often and regular each fortnight, that the occupants of one mission's two-storeyed house evacuated the top storey and camped in tents on the lawn until the swarm of quakes was over. In the long house, Elsie and I had a bit of a routine as soon as we felt a quake start, especially if it was at night. We'd both jump out of bed, and while Elsie went to the meat-safe cot that Ann was in, I headed to the bedroom door leading onto the verandah to make sure it would open, as the house moved quite a lot and the door could easily jam closed. We would either stand in the doorway or on the verandah as it was too dangerous to go outside in case coconuts fell on us. We had noticed that there were other times when Ann would whimper while lying in the cot and we often wondered why, until we realised that she was probably feeling the very slight tremors that we couldn't feel when walking around.

The meat-safe cot was quite like the meat safes we used before refrigerators became common. In this case, it was like a large oblong box on legs, which meant the bottom of the box was a little lower than waist height to be comfortable when dealing with a baby inside. While the bottom of the cot was solid, the rest of the box was a framework covered with fly/mosquito wire. One side was the fold-down 'door' that gave access into the cot and because the framework wasn't particularly rigid, it would flex with the movements of the quake, so Elsie would have to keep a constant pull on the 'door' so that it released when everything was in line to free it.

To illustrate how much movement there could be during a quake, one night our pillows got wet! Because of the heat, we did not have glass in the windows; just openings covered with flywire for the sake of coolness and to keep mosquitoes out. Outside our bedroom was a water tank near the head of our bed and one night when we were having a reasonable shake the tank sloshed water through the flywire and onto our bed, all of which added to the inconvenience of the earthquake. While we had heard of earthquakes when still at home in New Zealand, we hadn't experienced any of this magnitude!

We heard of one tank that didn't fare so well in Kompiam in the highlands. Instead of a rocking motion like the one that sloshed water onto us, the quake must have produced a more vertical movement. The tank, being made of curved corrugated iron, reduced in height like a concertina with each shock, so it ended up almost half its original height, and likewise half its capacity!

It is possible to see an earthquake or its effects from the air. One afternoon, I was flying back to Wewak into the old Wirui airstrip and saw a wavelike ripple in the tops of the sago palms in the swamp nearby. On landing, I asked if they had had an earthquake in the last few minutes, and the answer was, 'Yes!' So that was a rather interesting observation.

During the regular periods of shakes referred to earlier, we used to move all the aircraft out of the hangar and park them outside as there were things inside the hangar that could damage the aircraft if they fell down or fell over. It was quite common after a decent shake to find the big 45-kilogram gas bottles that we had standing on their ends strewn all over the floor. Our Papuan workers had a different take on the reason for parking the aircraft outside. We heard that they thought the aircraft were outside so that if the earthquakes got too bad, all the MAF staff would take off in them!

After our first year we were due annual holidays. Where would we go? We wanted to see what it was like for missionaries on outstations so that was our focus. The only folk who had indicated that they'd be happy for us to visit were the Apostolic missionaries at Porgera in the highlands. Ian Stephenson and his wife didn't have children, so consequently when we arrived with Ann, there was a lot of interest in this little white 'pikinini' and many of the local ladies wanted to touch her or pinch her. The pinching wasn't being nasty, it was just wanting to confirm that this little white baby was really made of flesh – not like a similar looking doll! There was no cot on the station, so we made a bed/cot for Ann out of a large luggage trunk we had with us, the lid propped open with a piece of wood! It actually worked really well.

Today, Porgera has a very large goldmine roughly in the same area where its mission station was, but in those days (1968) it was very much a bush setting with little to no cash economy to speak of. Some individuals had cash, having been carriers for a government patrol, or some may have found gold in the river at the bottom of the valley. On the second Sunday there, I was invited to speak in church through an interpreter which isn't as easy as it might sound, for you had to remember exactly where you were up to or the next piece of the talk didn't fit in properly. The missionary there had taught tithing (the giving of one tenth of crops or harvest to the

Lord) and while there was a little receptacle for cash, the vast majority of the parishioners brought an offering of what they had, usually 'kaukau' or sweet potato. It grew into a surprisingly large pile.

In talking with Ian afterwards, he said that this offering of their staple food would be given to the Papuan pastors. He pointed out that they only needed ten parishioners to be truly tithing to support a pastor family at the same social level as his congregation. I have often wondered how this would work in our society? For instance, how many parishioners' offerings does it take to keep one of our ministers on the same financial footing as their average congregational member?

Apart from being a pastor to the locals, Ian was a keen photographer who did his own developing in a dark room. Elsie showed an interest in the whole process and one afternoon said that she'd be happy to watch Ian if he was going to be doing some developing. Ian sheepishly said, 'Well I'm sorry, but I am going to the bedroom to get under the blankets to remove a film from my camera.' Elsie delayed her observations!

Many highlanders have a habit of a certain sort of yodelling when anything out of the ordinary is happening, whether it is in fun or fear or war. During the time we were there, a total eclipse of the moon occurred one clear night and while it was quite eerie for us who knew what was going on, it was even more frightening for the locals, most of whom were unaware of it and so the whole valley erupted into a chorus of yodelling.

It is sad that another mission used this event to cement their beliefs into the minds of the local people who attended their services. We heard shortly afterward that this mission which was also operating in the valley but not worshipping on Sunday like the Apostolics, had been telling the people that if it went all dark that night, the locals would know that it was they who were telling them the truth! Sadly, we were also aware that in another area, they used to give a small quantity of rice to those who came to their services, making them literally 'rice Christians'. Worse still, in yet another spot, because there was a local building project going on, they dropped some bags of nails on the airstrip, and not all of them were picked up! They probably hadn't double-bagged them. I wrote to them complaining about this, as it was dangerous for our aircraft which used that airstrip quite regularly.

Chapter 15

Next Stop Mt Hagen

Our first annual holiday over, we moved for a couple of reasons to Mt Hagen (or Kagamuga where the airport was located) where I would become the second pilot. The main reason was so I could become familiar with the highlands area I would be flying into from Wasua on the Fly River in the southern lowlands where we were to be stationed next. The other was to help Wal and Elizabeth Job who were being stretched with the amount of work that was developing from the Mt Hagen base. As it was a transiting point for people from quite a large area, many people stayed overnight in the MAF guest house situated on the compound, but there were no food-making facilities like a motel, so all meals were provided by the MAF family and compensated for by MAF. Up until the time Elsie and I arrived there, Wal and Elizabeth had had only one meal as a family by themselves in three months! They were relieved to have some help.

A second standard MAF house had been built but was not quite finished by the time we arrived. There were instructions to *not* use the toilet as the cement hadn't yet cured. We could use it the next day, but would we just cross our legs and hold on in the meantime? I remember that we ate our first evening meal off the large luggage crate we had brought from New Zealand and which had been used to transport some of our goods up to Mt Hagen. Initially, hot water for washing for both families was obtained by dipping a bucketful out of the cooling water tank of the old Lister diesel engine that drove the generator as there was no town electricity at that time. It naturally had a slight diesel smell to it, though I don't remember it being at all oily. This was then put into a bucket shower – a bucket with a shower rose attached to the bottom. It made for quick showers, as some buckets were only the regular size!

Within a few days of our arrival at Mt Hagen, the aircraft Wal was using (VH-MFH) needed an engine change which had to be done at Wewak. Wal was more than happy for me to stay and help Elsie unpack and set things up, but the field leader said, 'No, Ted has to come out to Wewak and help with the maintenance,' which I did. It was a bit tough having to leave Elsie and wee Ann in a rather unsettled state with only blankets up at the windows as no curtains were yet available. The two wives had to start the Lister engine for the generator to have any power for lights and to keep the big freezer running for outstation goods. While starting it was fairly sure-fire, winding up the big flywheel enough to get it going once the valve lifter was released did take a bit of effort! However, to their credit, both Elizabeth and Elsie survived quite well until we got back a number of days later.

As the new compound was just being established, the fact that Wal and I were a couple of old farmers had its benefits when it came to putting up a security fence. Making a concrete strainer post together is one activity in this process that I remember well; not that anything went wrong, but mixing concrete in a wheelbarrow wasn't unfamiliar to either of us! With our farming backgrounds, we had a lot in common and Wal and Elizabeth were a great couple and easy to get on with. So that I could become familiar with the Southern Highlands, we flew together a lot and that was great too. I vividly remember a couple of flights we did together.

On one, we were heading out into the Jimmi Valley and all of a sudden while in cruise, the turbocharged engine lost a fair amount of power because the manifold pressure had suddenly dropped, giving us roughly 80 percent of the required power. What could it be? We didn't try to continue on, but immediately headed back to the Mt Hagen airfield where the MAF hangar was so we could sort it out. After doing a fairly comprehensive search, we found a tiny speck of carbon was partially blocking a bleed hole in the absolute pressure controller (APC), a vital part of a turbocharged engine. After this incident, a filter was put into the line through which the APC oil flowed.

Wal is one of two people I have got to know well who was an excellent pilot as well as a great engineer. When flying, he was quick in his assessment of a situation and when he was engineering, he was masterfully methodical. You see, ideally, pilots and engineers have slightly different personalities. For a pilot, it is often necessary to make a split-second decision, and carry it through, sometimes with varying results! For an engineer a somewhat slower, more methodical personality is ideal.

The other flight was from Mt Hagen to Vanimo (almost three hours) which is close to the border of West Papua. A plane (not one of MAFs) had gone down and we were making our way to take part in the search and rescue activity. As it was a reasonably long flight with no passengers on board, I took along my travellers' chess kit. It is a small, compact board, and each piece had a peg on the bottom that went into a hole on the board. Wal was flying, but once things were set up, what do you do but bring out the chess kit? He was my sort of chess player too, quick to make a move and very occasionally regretting it afterwards! I must confess that when I played chess at high school, those who could spend five minutes or more working out the next move really did irk me! When we got there, the area we were allotted to search was not where the commercial aircraft had gone down.

Wal did a lot of my general familiarisation into the Southern Highlands area, but a fellow Kiwi, Laurie Darrington, who had been based in Mt Hagen previously, also did some more specific route and strip training. I well remember one afternoon we were due to head southwest from Mt Hagen to take some frozen goods etc. beyond the Ialabu Basin about half an hour away. As I looked in the general direction, all I could see was some very big thunderhead clouds developing. With my relative lack of experience in the area, I would have readily not tried to do the flight. I remember Laurie's words, 'You can't say you can't do it until you have gone and had a look.' You see, Laurie knew something that I didn't at that stage. Yes, there was a line of storm clouds between Mt Ialabu and Mt Wilhelm, but there is a weather weakness right alongside Mt Ialabu which can be exploited. It was like a mini mountain close to the main one and frequently the space between the two was quite clear. Laurie showed me where to go, and once through, there was glorious sunshine on the other side of the line of clouds and the Ialabu Basin was wide open.

Today, MAF's byline is 'Flying for Life', meaning flying for spiritual life by moving what is needed for churches and missions to operate, as well as for human life by transporting people to where they can receive medical treatment. When we went out in 1967, the tagline was 'The servant of missions' because at that time, the vast majority of our work was for the many and various missions we were enabling. Obviously, it was our desire to serve every mission which needed our services. In general, the missions cooperated with each other and agreed on areas in which they would work. However, and very sadly, while I was at Mt Hagen, we terminated our service to one American mission because of an individual and his son who were being a thorn in the flesh to a mission nearby, in that they were not cooperating at all. The reason for their stance was possibly because they had the idea that they were the only ones by God's sovereign grace who had been ordained to spread the gospel in PNG and so wouldn't observe any gentlemen's boundaries!

One trip I did by myself was from Mt Hagen to the Mt Bosavi airstrip (45 minutes away) with an anthropologist. At Wewak, I had flown quite a few anthropologists into the Telefomin area and I hadn't gained a very high regard for them, as it seemed that all they wanted to do was to make use of our mission services, criticise what missions were doing for the people, conduct their research and gain a PhD qualification. I didn't see or hear of anything much they did that actually helped the local people. The chap I had on board to Bosavi seemed to be very similar, in that he was critical of 'how the mission is changing the locals' way of life.' Inwardly I agreed that the mission was changing their way of life but it was definitely for their good and for the better! As I had a whole lot of his supplies on board with him, I said, 'Wow, you are going to have to make quite a few trips to get all this cargo out to the village you are staying at.' His reply was just what I thought it would be. He said, 'Oh I won't be taking it all out to the village; I'll be paying some carriers to take it out there for me,' to which I replied, 'Well you are changing the people's way of life too, by getting them to work for you and by paying them.' He was nowhere near as confident or talkative after that! I just hope he did some thinking.

So much for what was being done during the week, but what about on Sundays? Wal had developed a ministry to workers on the 600-acre tea plantation a short way out of Kagamuga. As my Melanesian Pidgin had developed a little, I helped Wal for a time, and then took over that patch while he developed another area. This was done prior to the regular Baptist morning service each Sunday which we attended and where I also used to preach later, but in English.

Chapter 16

To Wasua on the Fly River

We enjoyed our time at Mt Hagen but it was only a temporary posting for a particular purpose as previously explained. So on 7 December 1968 we moved to Wasua which was going to be our new place of ministry for quite some time. The house was built out of bush materials with flywire instead of windows, but there were also large shutters made from flattened 'pit pit', which is like pampas or toitoi stalks. This was woven into a matting which covered the shutters and could be lowered when a storm or heavy rain was in the offing.

It had a roof made from thatched sago palm leaf which was completely waterproof and silenced the sound of rain falling on it. There were a couple of runs of corrugated iron at one end, the water from which was ushered into a tank which kept us in water. The place had a 'coal range' though it was fired by wood and not coal and it had cracks in the firebox which under certain circumstances belched blue smoke! Elsie used to buy the wood for the stove from young boys who would collect it and bring it to the door. On one occasion, she realised that the little tykes were taking the wood from our own stack at the back of the house and then bringing it around the front to sell it! Elsie only got caught with that scheme once (that she knows of!) It reminds me of an old American Indian proverb: 'You catch me once, that's your fault, but if you catch me twice, that's my fault.'

As was the norm, Elsie had a house girl to help with the added upkeep of the house as it was not so easy to keep clean as one back home and this also freed Elsie to volunteer to help with making up freezer orders etc. for outstations. Having a house girl also helped the local women learn new skills as well as giving them an income. On one occasion, Elsie was in the process of making some bread, when she had to fly to another mission station, so she asked the house help if she could please finish the process. The house girl thought she would make a special sort of bread like she had seen Elsie do. It was just a pity that she had used black pepper instead of cinnamon! However, we still commended her on her initiative. An illustration of how much the local people lived very much from day to day occurred one Monday morning. The house girl asked Elsie if she could go home as she had run out of her staple food item, sago. Elsie asked why she hadn't gone to her village over the weekend to get it. The reply: 'I hadn't run out of it then!'

There were no cupboards to speak of in the kitchen at Wasua, and all the cooking utensils were on shelves with cloth material draped in front of them like curtains. These provided a bit of protection but allowed various vermin to get past them. One night I was in the bedroom when I heard a bloodcurdling scream come from the kitchen. Thinking that Elsie may have burnt herself on the old stove (or had an accident) I ran to see what was the reason for the bellow. On reaching Elsie, I saw by torchlight a large green frog on her neck. I must confess that I think I said something like, 'Crikey, it's only a frog,' to which Elsie responded with something like, 'What would you do if you had a wet, cold, clammy, pulsating thing holding onto your neck?' I have to admit it must have been a nasty surprise in the dark! All the interior walls were made from the same sort of material as the shutters while the exterior was from split limbon palm which gave it a weatherboard look. But it was a house that Elsie made into a home and we enjoyed living there.

Wasua was the PNG headquarters for what was then known as

the Unevangelised Fields Mission (UFM) which has now become part of Pioneers Mission. The Wasua location was chosen in the early days because it was on the banks of the mighty Fly River but, at the same time, was somewhat sheltered from the main flow of the river by a small island some distance from the bank. At that stage, there was still a reasonable flow of water between the bank and the island; sufficient for a boat from Port Moresby to come in with ease with all the supplies needed to keep the mission and its personnel functioning. It was the site of the mission's headquarters as well as their main supply store and distribution centre, workshop and shipyard, all of which contributed to the reason for MAF being based there.

The Wasua airstrip was very adequate when dry, with the A185 having a nil penalty for takeoff or landing. It was a bit like an aircraft carrier though because if you ran off the end one way, you went into the Fly River; at the other end there was, most inconveniently, a large pond that was used for baptisms! Of course this was the main reason for the mission's existence, in that those who were baptised were signifying their faith in Jesus as their Saviour, which meant a radical change in belief and actions.

I remember attending a baptismal service one evening and thinking to myself, 'Don't run off this end.' As misfortune would have it, a little while later while we were still living at Wasua but operating out of Kawito, on a trip from there to Moro at Lake Kutubu (less than 55 minutes), I had one of the many radio failures I had to put up with while still using the old valve radios before they were upgraded to solid-state ones. As I was due to give a position report at seven degrees south when the radio failed, I needed to head back home as quickly as I could, get on the ground and use a ground station to inform Air Radio at Madang or Moresby that I'd had a failure and was safely on the ground. This was necessary as we only had a three-minute grace period after either a regular position report was due or a destination arrival report, before Air Radio would set search and rescue in motion by calling you or asking other aircraft in the area to do so.

It was obviously the southeast season as there was low cloud and persistent light rain falling when I reached Wasua. Now I don't know whether other pilots have this problem, but I have noticed that while I could do a bounce-less landing in the dry, whenever there was rain on the windscreen, I would land high, with the inevitable bounce even though it may have been only 15 to 20 centimetres too high! Cessna's springy legs on their tail draggers were quite unforgiving in these sorts of situations. Yes, you guessed it, this time I bounced, but worse, the airstrip was wet and as I aquaplaned down it with no surface braking at all, I had visions of the baptismal pond at the far end!

I thought to myself, 'Now this is not good,' as it isn't thought very smart theologically to be baptised twice and most certainly not in an aircraft! As the possibilities were growing greater with every 30 metres of airstrip disappearing behind me, I decided to do a ground loop. Yes, I know, the one when I went to pick up the venison wasn't successful, but at least there weren't any rabbit holes here to thwart my best efforts. So I steered the aircraft towards the right-hand side of the strip, booted in full left rudder and put on power, increasing to full power the further around we went, until I was heading in the other direction. Ah, the sweet feeling of success! It was then a case of letting Air Radio know I was safely on the ground. Apart from needing to replace the radio which caused all this drama and inspect the leg attachment box after the heavy landing, I called it a day as the rain just kept falling.

Some readers may wonder why I purposely went right, and then spun around to the left. The reason is that with the engine turning the propeller clockwise (from the pilot's view) the down turning blade produces a greater thrust effect than the upcoming blade, so a turn to the left is enhanced. This is also the reason why this type of tail-wheeled aircraft will swing to the left when the power is applied for takeoff, if compensating rudder isn't applied.

But not all days were like that. At times there was very, very thin fog with the sun shining through it covering the Wasua area. Fortunately, because of the close proximity of the river where it was normally reasonably clear, one could take off, head out over the river to see how thick or thin the fog was and get back down on the airstrip again if necessary. One morning I had to take a number of people over to Balimo where the mission hospital was located, only about nine minutes away. As I couldn't be sure the fog would be similarly thin at Balimo, I decided to go over low-level through the thin and dispersing fog. I can still remember the comment of one of the more senior mission personnel when we arrived safely: 'Now we can scrape the leeches off our feet.' He felt we had flown so low we could have got leeches on our feet, just as if we had been walking on the ground! The time difference though was considerable. To walk between those two points would normally take at least four and a half hours.

Talking of leeches which were quite common in the lowlands, scraping them off was the wrong way to get rid of one if it had attached itself to you. This would mean its jaws were left in you, which invariably caused infection that would fester. Smokers would often touch them with their cigarette butt which very effectively detached them and we found that a drop or two of methylated spirits had the same effect. In fact later, when we used to walk up and down the Kawito airstrip (for a Sunday outing), Elsie would always take the very small bottle of meths which was normally used for lighting the kerosene pressure lantern to deal with any leeches that might attach to us as we walked.

I once saw a leech climbing up the rear edge of the left-hand strut of the aircraft as I was flying. Being of a curious nature, I wondered what speed would be required for it to lose its grip. Like a caterpillar, a leech progresses by holding on with its rear while stretching out to grip with its front; then it brings its rear up to reach where its front is and so progresses with a repetition of this. At normal cruise (120 knots) it got pretty stretched as it switched ends, but it still made progress. It eventually came off at around 135 knots in a shallow dive which was a remarkable achievement, I think!

I guess it happens in every occupation, but one thing that became very obvious to me was the way most individuals, when asked to pass a message on over the two-way radio, would almost invariably give their own interpretation of what you had asked them to say. This didn't always convey the message that was intended. However, I have to honour one lady who would pass on a message verbatim. Sometimes she would say, 'It doesn't make any sense to me, but I guess it does to you,' (the recipient). I knew I could always trust Barbara Wade (later Mrs Talents) to pass on exactly what had been requested. One other mission radio operator must have been told *to always* ask for an aircraft's estimated time of arrival (ETA) before signing off. It used to slightly amuse me that after she had told me the weather at her location was un-flyable with heavy rain, she'd top it off with, 'What is your ETA?'

Of course the programme from Wasua had the normal range and types of work that were being done at this stage for the many missions and the country's development. As previously indicated, much of the work entailed moving the mission supplies that had come in from Port Moresby by boat out to the various mission stations as well as moving people around. Sadly, there were the medical emergency flights as well. One that happened on a Sunday afternoon from Wasua was for a little girl who had been running around under one of the local houses where some fishing lines had been hung, and she had got caught with a fish hook through the eyelid of her right eye. Talk about being brave! When I flew her to the hospital there was no crying, just a rather sad look on her face. We thank God that the hook completely missed her eyeball and she was able to come back home a day or two later when the medics were sure no infection had set in.

When we went to Wasua, we followed the system that had already been in vogue for some time as far as the programming was concerned. This meant that the mission we were serving directed the programme by telling me where to go and what to do. This sounds fair enough when put that way, as they knew what needed to be done. But after we had been there for some time, I was getting somewhat frustrated with the way the mission didn't take into account the weather-related problems this caused. They would have me flying around in the lowlands in the morning and heading into the highlands around midday when the weather was starting to build up and turn nasty. I had asked for a more regular programme but was assured that it just wouldn't work. One night I was so uptight with the tension, I vomited for quite a bit of the night. The next day, we contacted our chief pilot and we were sent on our second annual leave to Samberigi (55 minutes away).

This was my opportunity! While there I figured out a systematic programme catering for those mission stations which needed a weekly or fortnightly call, as well as allowing a period for doing maintenance. When we went back to Wasua, I showed it to the mission and was again told it wouldn't work, to which I replied, 'We will try it for at least a month and see how it goes.' It worked wonderfully and in a rather lovely way, God honoured it too. In the northwest season, there can be very large storm cells dotted around in the lowlands and before long, I noticed that when I was due to fly to the northeast, there was a blocking cell to the northwest and later in the same week, when due to go to the northwest, the blocking cell was in the northeast. I didn't put that down to just being coincidence. I firmly believe that God was in the positioning of those storm cells! And interestingly and significantly, the mission staff away from headquarters relished it also, because they knew up to six months or more in advance (as the system worked on a four-week cycle) what day I was due to be in a certain area and so they planned their meetings, passenger movements, or whatever to coincide with when I was going to be there on schedule. It worked well for me and others, and soon those who said it wouldn't work were happy to use it also. Praise the Lord!

Something that I did note when at Samberigi though, was the way in which pilots not keeping to their forecasted timing or not telling the mission station of a revised time really did seriously inconvenience the mission station's programme. On one occasion, the missionary Don Mosely was due to have a Bible school session in the morning; it was put off until the afternoon because the pilot from Mt Hagen had said he would be arriving about the time the Bible school class would be in session. However, the plane didn't arrive at the time which had been indicated but came in the middle of the afternoon, so once again the Bible school class had to be postponed. Now I know we can say, 'The pilot must have been held up,' and yes that is a real possibility, but that mission had a radio call scheduled every two hours (or if really needed you could break in at any time) to let them know of a revised ETA. This observation was a help to me to see what happens at the other end of our flying ministry, so I resolved to try and keep to time or let folk know when I couldn't.

In fact, it was in both parties' best interest to do so. About 13 years after having been stationed in the area, I needed to fly to Balimo and subsequently heard of this little conversation:

Dr Kath: 'When is the aircraft due?'

Respondent: 'In about a quarter of an hour at 10:55am.'

Dr Kath: 'Who is the pilot, do you know?'

Respondent: 'Ted Crawford.'

Dr Kath: 'Okay, let's get going as Ted will be on time.'

Keeping as close to time as possible not only gave them some certainty, but also meant that I could get a lot more done in a day as I didn't have to wait around until passengers, or whatever, arrived.

Chapter 17

Moving to Kawito

As mentioned, Wasua was on the bank of the Fly River, but sadly the area between the bank and the small island started to silt up, which made it more and more difficult for the coastal boat from Port Moresby to call in there unless it was on full tide. So the process of developing a new inland mission port and MAF base had started before we went to Wasua. The mission, foretelling the day that the boats couldn't call at Wasua, had already established a new depot at Kawito (KWT) some 10 minutes north on the Aramia River. This river was relatively narrow but 27 metres deep, so there was little chance of it silting up. Our predecessors at Wasua, Jim and Ruth Charlesworth, had already moved most of the MAF base necessities such as the refuelling facility over there. The mission had built several houses for those operating the base as well as a new goods distribution centre and a workshop. The house for the MAF family to occupy was the last to be built. The time came when it was forecast that it would be ready sometime in January 1970, the month that Elsie was due to deliver our second child.

Quite naturally, during the month of December, Elsie was in pack-up mode in the Wasua house. I endeavoured to help her and discourage her from overexertion so was not prepared for what happened on 24 December. As so many wonderful and faithful supporters sent the missionaries gifts, parcels, letters, etc. to help them enjoy Christmas when away from home and family, I had a full load of these sorts of things to distribute all around the Papuan lowlands on my 'Father Christmas run' that day.

However, part-way around, I also included moving Barry Waldeck from Debepari, with material to a somewhat remote airstrip. After I had landed at Honinabi, I got a call from Christian Radio Missionary Fellowship (CRMF) which was the coordinating umbrella mission for all the various missions' radio communications, asking if I was on the ground. When I replied in the affirmative, the voice said, 'You have a daughter.' I think my reply was something like, 'Yes I know I have a daughter,' thinking of Ann. The voice came back, 'No, you have a new daughter!' What? That wasn't expected! What do I do now? It would have been nice to head back home at that point but we continued to unload the goods, expecting to continue on with the programme as it stood.

Within minutes there was another call, 'There is a medical emergency at Wasua.' I immediately said, 'Is it Elsie?' thinking of what I had previously heard, but they said, 'No, it is someone else. Can you please come back ASAP and move her.' So I left Barry in the remote location and headed home at maximum cruise power. On arrival at Wasua I found that Elsie, who had recently given birth to Gwen, needed to be moved to the mission hospital at Balimo, along with our neighbour. Two medicals on the same flight – what a fantastic deputation photo! But alas there was so much objection to the idea that no photo was taken. Elsie was to go for a checkup with the Balimo doctor, and the other woman for advice.

The other missionary wife, after diagnosis, was later required to go to Port Moresby. I didn't have the flying hours available to go that far, so had to take her to the provincial headquarters at Daru, expecting a commercial flight to be able to take her through to Port Moresby that afternoon. However, it was the day before Christmas and the commercial pilot's celebrations had already started, so

Lorna had to stay in the Daru hospital that night, cared for by the nuns who served there. She was taken to Port Moresby the next day and had to stay there until her baby was born a good while later.

I later heard this little story about Elsie: Dr Kath and some other helpers had come in the mission Land Rover to the airstrip from the Balimo hospital which was about one kilometre from the airstrip, but alas, when they went to start it to head back to the hospital, the battery was too weak to start the engine. So, it was all hands on deck to push. Elsie got out, expecting to join the pushing team but the doctor, who was already in that position, said, 'No you get into the driver's seat and steer. You've done enough pushing today already!'

For me, after delivering Lorna into the care of the folk at Daru, it was back to Balimo to pick up Elsie and fly home to Wasua and see our new daughter Gwen who was born in our own bedroom. The mission nurse assisting Elsie was an Australian lass who had been a district nurse in Tasmania and had only been in PNG about 10 days. On the station at that time she was caring for many Papuan women who had come to Wasua for the Christmas Convention. Gwen was cradled in a neighbour's new, locally-woven clothes basket, and though six weeks premature, didn't need a special humidity crib as we were in the Papuan lowlands, and every day was at humidity crib temperature and humidity! On reflection, Gwen's early arrival was (selfishly) a real blessing to me personally, as it meant that Elsie didn't have to go out to Wewak three weeks before her due date. If she had needed to do that, I would have been baching for quite a while, though probably some of the other missionaries would have taken pity on me!

You may be wondering why we called both our daughters by short names – Ann and Gwen – with longer second names. It was to some extent a result of my personal experience of being called Edward, and for the sake of going with the flow later becoming known as Ted, as no matter how many times I introduced myself as Edward (for my mum's sake), I was always subsequently called Ted! However, the idea didn't fully work out, as a good friend started to call Ann 'Annabels', and many people thought that Gwen *must* have just been a short form of Gwyneth or Gwendolyn!

Christmas Day saw me loading up again and heading away to complete the run I had to leave half done the day before, for who could leave a guy (Barry) in a remote location away from his family on Christmas Day? Even his own home location of Debepari was fairly remote and in the middle of a vast jungle area. So remote was Debepari that they rarely saw another European, apart from a pilot and the very occasional visit from a government patrol officer. Being aware of this, I used to try and time being there (or other such remote stations) at lunch time so I could afford to take a bit more time and have some fellowship with them as a normal turnaround time of 20 to 25 minutes was far too limited.

Once, after Barry had been to Port Moresby for dental work, he bought a home perm kit for his wife Pam as an act of love, not realising that she couldn't do much with it by herself. To the credit of both of them – her for letting him have a go, and him for actually doing it – they used it together. The next time I called in there, without thinking, I said, 'Wow Pam, your hair is looking great!' I meant it, but it was the sort of compliment I haven't paid to any other person's wife before or since! I think at that moment they both grew a few centimetres taller as it meant so much to them that someone had noticed and commented favourably on their combined result.

Back at Wasua after the Christmas Day run, we all settled down for a week or so before we eventually moved over to the Kawito house, which wasn't fully finished but was in a liveable state and finished within a few weeks.

The Kawito house had a rather unique entrance. It was up on stilts to catch as much breeze as possible, but it was also alongside the Aramia River which had a very large swampy area on its south side. As a result, mosquitoes were in abundance, so much so that the last record catch that I heard of was 13 in one go with just *one hand-slap* on the leg! With so many mossies, the Kawito house had a little landing at the top of the entrance stairs with two doors – one facing the stairs, and the other into the house. The idea of this was to reduce the number of mossies entering the house with you, by acting as a two-stage entrance and a sort of mossie trap.

In 1972 when we had a drought, we needed for a time to use a neighbour's long-drop toilet as there was only just enough condensation trickling into our tank from the roof to supply drinking water for us, even though it had a somewhat smoky taste! A visiting pilot, after having been to the long-drop came back and said, 'There were so many mossies there that they almost lifted me off and carried me away.' After he had sat there for a little while, he reckoned he was due for a blood donor's badge!

The Kawito house had a good-sized pantry, and we needed it, as the boat from Port Moresby came about monthly to six-weekly, and at times skipped a month. Both Elsie and I are really thankful that we were brought up on farms in New Zealand, as it meant we knew how to stock a good pantry, among other handy skills that served us well in many areas in Papua New Guinea.

Another memorable event at Kawito happened one day when Elsie was going down the back steps with some washing to put on the lines strung under the house and she saw a goanna tree lizard (which looks to the uninitiated a bit like a small crocodile). It got itself up on its sturdy legs and moved away from the bottom of the stairs. When I came home after flying, she described it all to me, and to my shame, I poured cold water on her story as to its size because I had never seen such an animal! Perhaps God was teaching me a lesson in humility or something because less than three weeks later, I was at Mapoda and a couple of boys there were parading a goanna that they had just killed on the airstrip. By way of apology to Elsie, I took a photo of them holding its full two-metre or so length so as to say sorry to her for not really believing her story in the first place!

The work done from Kawito was the same as had been done from Wasua and with the new scheduling system working well, there was plenty to do. I moved two out-of-the-ordinary passengers around from there. One was an archbishop (Right Rev Marcus Loan) who was up from Sydney to speak at both the Upper and Lower Fly Asia Pacific Christian Mission conferences. He was a very humble, godly man whose ministry was very much appreciated. The other was a dentist who voluntarily came up to help missionaries as well as locals, and even though at times his ministry was painful, it too was very much appreciated! He had a mobile dentist's chair with him, which I remember was extremely heavy and mighty awkward to get into the C185 due to its large base. It meant taking out both the passenger *and* pilot's seats to get it in, and then replace them afterwards, but his services were really valued by all. Somewhat ironically, his name was Mr Payne!

A few years later, when we were based at Mt Hagen again, Elsie acted as his nurse. He had to extract a PNG chap's tooth but didn't reckon on how well rooted it was and decided it would be the last one he would try to take out.

To give an idea of the time that MAF saved some of the missionaries going to and leaving the Upper Fly Conference, I was taking Rex Nowland from Atkamba to the conference at Pangoa on Lake Murray and he said to me, 'I wonder if you realise the time saving this is for folk like me and my wife?' I really didn't know, so asked him to elaborate. He said that the trip we covered in 25 minutes would have otherwise taken them three days going by other means, with two overnights in the jungle. Little wonder that MAF's work is so deeply appreciated!

While based at Kawito and visiting various mission stations, I sometimes had lunch at Pangoa and other places, which I very much appreciated. On one occasion, folk at Pangoa served me some freshwater prawns, which I liked and enjoyed. Sadly, the prawns didn't like me, and by the time I reached home at Kawito they had caused me to feel quite off. As I was taking people further on to Balimo I had a good old dry-retch before flying them to their destination. I tried prawns again another time, thinking my first experience may have been something to do with that first batch, but sadly, the results were the same, so now, prawns are definitely off the menu for me.

Elsie and Ted in their Queenstown uniforms.

A windy wedding day.

Top: Ted's home until he was 17.
Bottom: Ted with a Cessna 185 – the Queenstown workhorse for remote areas.

A load of deer from above the tree line.

Top: Another aircraft arrives for assembly at Ballarat.
Bottom: Elsie's Ballarat timbrel group outside our barracks accommodation.

Top: Dress code in the highlands, 1969.
Bottom: Missionaries can be romantic too! The wedding of Bruce and Ruth Mulholland of CMML, in Guala.

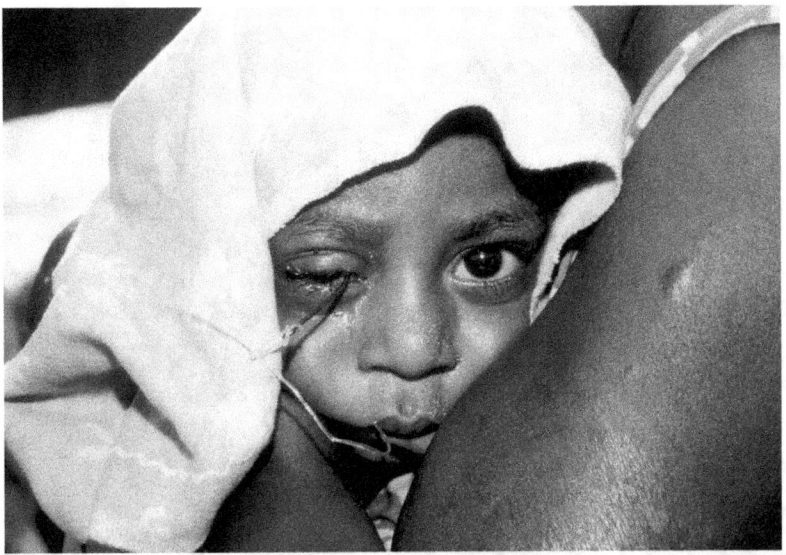

*Top: Medevac of a brave kiddie with a fishhook in her eyelid.
Bottom: Keith Dennis, Tom Hoey and Steve Cochrane,
the first mission staff to enter cannibal territory.*

Top: Tom Hoey and Ted with a group of Biamis.
Bottom: The Biami church after a few short years.

Top: What else will fit in the pod?
Bottom: Moving house mission field style.

Top: A fairly normal load. Where next?
Bottom: CLTC students arriving.

Top: Another group eager to learn.
Bottom: A floatplane on medical patrol from Kapuna Hospital.

Drying those little red chillies!

Top: Elsie buying fruit at Wapenamanda.
Bottom: Elsie's sewing group of nurses.

Top: Ted on the radio 'sched' at the Wewak programme board.
Bottom: Schooling a replacement before Ted leaves Wewak.

*First furlough. Top: With Elsie's dad and mum.
Bottom: Ted with his family.*

Top: Ted in the MAF-NZ office at Ardmore.
Bottom: Some of the Tedz-Cars fleet.

Chapter 18

Our First Furlough and Second Term

In December 1970 it was time for our furlough, as we had been on the field for just over three years. The system was to have a month's holiday and a month's deputation for each year of field service. Elsie and I elected to have some holiday to start with, which gave me time to get a slide presentation together as well as time to get somewhat used to the differences in New Zealand since we had left. Before that, we had time with the New Zealand Council and one of the members who was a businessman asked us how we were doing financially. We replied that we were going fine; in fact, we were saving the child allowance portion of our total allowance for the sake of our girls' higher education. 'Ah,' he said, 'Give three people $5 each and by the end of a week, one will have $10, one will still have the $5 and the other none.' We were and are thankful to God for our financially careful upbringing out in the country where there was no corner store. It was not the first or the last time we heard that others struggled to make ends meet when we were able to save just a little on our MAF allowance.

One of our MAF-NZ council members had a four-metre wooden-framed caravan which he loaned to us, and which became our home away from home for our first deputation period. This started in Queenstown and went to the bottom of the South Island, up the east coast of both Islands as far as Whangārei, and then down the west coast of the North Island as far as Foxton. I can't remember exactly how many meetings we had, but certainly more than 60. Many times, it was a case of have breakfast, move to the next location, set up and have a meeting that night and then on to do the same the next day. For our young daughters (both under the age of three), having the same bed each night gave a real sense of stability, and we made a point whenever possible of having breakfast as a family in the caravan before starting out for the day, even if our hosts offered us to have breakfast with them.

Like many others of the mission's community at that time, we were the recipients of the generosity of a Rootes Group agent (Doug Mawson) based in Dargaville at a time when cars in New Zealand were at a premium. Towing the heavy caravan with a 4-speed gear boxed 1592cc Hillman Super Minx could at times be a bit 'exhilarating'. I remember that on two occasions I had caught up to a cattle truck which was crawling up a steep, windy piece of road, once in the Mangaweka Gorge, and the other on the road around East Cape. Before the new upgrade was done, the road through the gorge was very windy and in places quite steep, with some pretty scary drop-offs on the left-hand side! In both instances, I was in low gear and struggling but was still going faster than the truck in front of me. I knew I wouldn't have the power to do a standing start on the incline (even if the handbrake held the weight of the caravan), so what could I do? Passing wasn't a possibility because of the windy nature of the road, so I resorted to doing what I thought I would never do, and that was slipping the clutch for short periods. By the time we got back up to my family's place at Silverdale towards the end of furlough, we had to replace the clutch. No questions need be asked as to why!

On the trip around the East Cape, we had a meeting at Ruatoria with a rather interesting evening stop. After our evening meal, Elsie decided she wanted to clean her teeth at dusk beside the only tap available. It didn't take her long to realise that the paste she had put on her brush was not toothpaste but hand cream! You may wonder how we got to have meetings in so many out-of-the-way places. It all came down to Ken Nobbs, who was a travelling fabric salesman at that stage. At almost every place he stopped, he seemed to manage to find someone who was willing to be an MAF representative, and so, even though the MAF office secretary was new to her job, she was able to arrange many meetings for us.

In July 1971 we got back to Port Moresby and after the furlough of six months when I had done no flying, I needed to do some circuits to regain currency and to get my 'air legs' back again. As we had requested to return to Kawito, we were soon back into things again there, after flying the Kawito aircraft from Port Moresby which had been dropped off there by the pilot we were taking over from. The folk who had filled in while we were away hadn't fully packed up, owing to parental health circumstances which meant a quick exit, so we had the job of finishing their packing while doing our own unpacking. Back then, every time you went on furlough you were supposed to pack up as if it was going to be the final one, so that if for any reason you couldn't or didn't return, it was simply a case of addressing your containers. As we had already lived in the house, Elsie and I were really surprised at the way Ann (aged three) remembered exactly where so many things had been previously and was able to take small items back to the correct place for us.

While we were at Kawito before going on furlough, I had someone take a photo of me doing routine maintenance on the engine of the aircraft in light rain, with bare feet and wearing a raincoat as there was no hangar to do it in. I know it pulled a few heartstrings (as it was designed to do) even though it was perfectly genuine! Some months after returning, a full hangar with an earth floor was erected. This made maintenance and loading much easier, especially in the southeast season when light drizzly rain was almost the daily norm.

When I say we had plenty to do, it was often a case of working to the maximum permissible flying hours for any given period, which was either 30 hours per week, 100 hours in a month or a total of 900 hours in 12 months. These hours were supposed to include the time taken in flight preparation, loading and unloading, plus the paperwork at the end of the day, which was at times considerable, although we really only included the actual flight hours as there was so much work to do. When working to the maximum hours, it was necessary to keep a daily graph to see how many hours one had available for any particular day, if it had been a very busy period the previous year. As I have said at many a deputation meetings, I couldn't have fulfilled the amount of flying work that I did if it wasn't for the fantastic support Elsie gave me.

This wasn't just in the emotional arena, but also in the very practical way she got loads made up for me while I was away flying. I would tell her where I was going to next, the weight available and any priorities I knew of, and with our wonderful cargo handler Byama, she would make up the load, ready for when I came back. Elsie also taught Byama how to make up loads; so well in fact, that shortly after we left Kawito he was asked to go to our main base at Wewak where, after a short time, he became the head cargo handler. I think this was in no small measure due to the time and effort Elsie had put into training him.

I also taught him how to load the aircraft. Much of it was fairly straightforward and we both learnt some lessons as we went along. The containers that our flour came in (because all missionaries had to make their own bread) were 18-kilogram steel drums which had a press-on lid over the 180-millimetre opening. This normally worked fine, as one had to really work hard to get the lid off, unless you had it on top of a load with the drum facing forward under the restraining net! At about 6,000 feet the pressure inside the drum overcame the tightness of the lid. With the minor explosion that occurs when the lid pops off at that altitude, not only does the lid come off, but a quantity of flour gets expelled at the same time, and if the drum is facing forward, the pilot gets a powder coating! One experience of that was enough, so from then on, the drum was either near the bottom of the load, or lay sideways in the aircraft if it was on top.

While we were both loading the aircraft one morning, I turned around and saw a thin black snake about the diameter of a pencil moving quickly across the dirt floor towards us. I alerted Byama and he was around the front of the aircraft like a shot, vigorously stamping on it. It was a poisonous viper. Snakes were fairly common at Kawito, but they didn't always win! A python thought that one of our neighbour's hens would make a great meal and went through the wire netting around the hen run. However, when it came to back out, the hen it had swallowed made such a lump in its body that it couldn't back out of the hole it had come in through. It was firmly stuck there – to be dispatched later.

It is amazing how quickly a snake can move. One of the first times I realised this was when I was approaching to land at Kawito and a snake about 1.5 metres long crossed the airstrip in front of me while I was on late final. About a quarter of its body was raised up vertically with the head bent forward so that it was approximately parallel with the ground and it was making a remarkable speed. I don't know how a snake propels itself, but from this one's performance, it appears to be extremely efficient.

A bit of a fun story here: Helping in the mission's main supply store at Kawito was an English woman (Pat Christon) who had originally emigrated to New Zealand from the UK. However, before she came 'down under' she did her research, and finding that Australia had snakes, but New Zealand didn't, she opted to go to New Zealand. After being in New Zealand for a while, she became a Christian and was sure she should go the mission field; and yes, she felt that PNG was the place to go – snakes and all! Dear Pat was convinced that God has a real sense of humour. Much later, after she had returned to New Zealand, a colleague who had worked with her visited her in hospital and while the prognosis wasn't good, he said, 'You can never tell with Pat; she's a tough old bird!'

The local people were very afraid of snakes and gave the same treatment – death – to all types whether they were harmless or not. Some snakes were actually helpful, especially in thatched roofed houses where they would stay in the roof thatch and eat any vermin that came to live there. However, on the other side of the coin there were those that one needed to steer well clear of, like the viper, the Papuan black, and the taipan. The latter has a large strike area, and if someone moves within it, the snake will strike whether it is being hassled or not.

The Kawito house we lived in was long and narrow with the living areas grouped at one end and a long passage with bedrooms and office off it. One evening I was still in the office and Elsie was heading for bed a little earlier than me, when I heard a scream coming from our bedroom at the end of the passageway. I immediately went down there to see what had caused Elsie to utter such a bloodcurdling scream, to find her standing on the bed. I said, 'What's the matter?' to which Elsie replied, 'There is a snake in the wardrobe.' Now there are times when a bloke has to appear calm and collected even if he isn't! 'Okay,' says I as I see the problem. I went to the place we always kept a bush knife and spade for such an occasion as this, hoping it would never happen! With Elsie still up on the bed, encouraging me from a safe distance, I managed to flick the snake off the wardrobe's hanger rail and then hold it between the spade and the bush knife as I carried it outside to dispatch it. It may well have been a harmless one, but who knows?

Elsie had another encounter with a snake. It was just before Christmas while we were still at Wasua, where a big group of people had gathered for the Christmas Convention. We were all sitting down on the grass and suddenly, Ray Elvery, who was sitting on Elsie's left, put his hand on her knee and held it extremely tightly – like a horse-bite – so much so that Elsie looked at him, only to see his eyes focused on her feet where minutes before, Ann had been sitting until Elsie had lifted her up onto her other knee. I was sitting on the other side of Elsie, and noticed her looking at her feet, only to see a snake sliding over them! Ray recognised it as a deadly one and of a type not normally seen on the north side of the Fly River. When it had completely cleared Elsie's feet, he immediately stood up, pounded its head with his heel and killed it. Thank you Lord! Perhaps it had been in a canoe that had crossed the river with a load of people for the convention.

An old missionary used to deal with supposed snake bites in a rather novel way, especially if there was no real evidence of the bite. For a bite to be genuine, there should be four puncture holes where the four fangs have entered. Then you know it's the real thing. If someone came to this missionary and there didn't seem to be any evidence of a snake bite, especially if they had been in the water, he would give them an Aspro and sit them against a wall. If they recovered he knew that it may have been a stick or something that had touched them, but if they got worse after about half an hour, he knew that he had to give the anti-venom. He reckoned that he saved a lot of money by using this screening method, as the cost of anti-venom was quite substantial. In the area around Balimo and Kawito, it was well known that Dr Kath Donovan would ask that the culprit snake be caught and brought in with the patient. The reason for this was that a snake-specific anti-venom was infinitely cheaper than a broad-spectrum one.

When we were in the lower Fly River area in the late 1960s and early 1970s there was one geographical area that we initially weren't allowed to fly over because it hadn't yet had sufficient government patrols into it and cannibalism was known to be still practised there. The restriction was of course for our safety, in case we had an engine failure and went down in that area. However after the government patrols had been in there a number of times, three missionaries gained approval and went into the area with the idea of making good contacts and then establishing a mission station there, as it was known to be relatively well-populated.

One of those three (Tom Hoey) was destined to establish a mission station in a location called Mougulu in the heart of the Bedamuni (Biami) language group. Tom and his wife Salome were ex-farmers from the tablelands west of Brisbane and Tom was exceptionally good at picking up new languages. In just six months after arriving in PNG, he was preaching in Police Motu, the trade language of the southern half of PNG at that time. Melanesian Pidgin has since taken over as the trade language of choice for all of PNG. Tom's initial trek made good contacts but failed to find a suitable airstrip site. The possible site they were shown by the locals was unsuitable. As you can imagine, using an interpreter to try and convey the idea of an airstrip to people who have never seen an airstrip or an aircraft on the ground can be a real challenge, especially when the area is covered in jungle.

Before long, Tom and Salome were living on the closest government station at Nomad River and on a subsequent trek into the Biami area found a place that they felt would be suitable for an airstrip. Tom and the locals cut the trees down and I surveyed the area from the air to make sure there weren't any small hills in the approach areas at either end, as there were several not too far away. In fact, a volcanologist said they were mini volcanoes that hadn't grown. Apparently the very large Mt Bosavi nearby (like Mt Egmont/Taranaki for Kiwis) had released the earth's internal pressure by discharging an estimated 104 cubic *kilometres* of material according to a volcanologist. As you can imagine, that amount of material being spewed out needed to settle somewhere and I, with many others, believe that it became the basis of what is now called the Papuan Plateau which stretches from the Coral Sea to the mountain ranges which are the backbone of PNG.

Several reasons seem to confirm this. Firstly it is said that a very early explorer whose charts were accurate everywhere else plotted that he sailed across this area. Then there is the personal experience I had when I was flying after a wet period with another pilot, and I was in the right-hand seat looking at the silver ball of light under the trees (which was the sun shining on water) that lasted for at least half an hour (111 kilometres) as we flew directly north from Kawito. One could very logically ask, 'If there was jungle forest covering the area could that have grown in just a few centuries?' To which I would answer a resounding 'Yes' having seen a tidal mud-bank turn into an island with four to six-metre high trees on it after just 14 years!

Before too long the area for a house was cleared by the Hoeys at Mougulu. Now the spirits with whom the locals were in communication had told them that if they grew coconuts, the ground would open up and swallow the people up, so Tom asked me to get some sprouting coconuts which I airdropped to him and he planted close to the house area. This was a fairly dramatic way of pointing out to the Biami people that the spirits were lying to them. It reminds me of Jesus' words in John 8:44 when speaking of the evil one: '… there is no truth in him. When he lies, he speaks his native language, for he is a liar and the father of lies.'

As Tom was learning the Bedamuni language, he had three constant companions: a notebook, a pencil and a tape recorder. Which of the three he used depended on the situation. On one occasion he was in one of the long houses recording for the sake of furthering his language skills when the locals broke into a spirit trance. The interesting thing about this was the fact that when he played the recording back later, it was recording perfectly before and after the trance session, but the trance period came out as an unintelligible scream. It would seem that the tape recorder wasn't able to record the sound of the language of the spirits. In fact, not making a recording could possibly have been for Tom's ultimate safety. I heard the story of someone on the West Papua side of New Guinea who took a photo of some people. Because of the location there was a long delay in getting the film developed, and by the time the photos came back, one person in the photo had died. This caused quite a stir as the locals accused the photographer of stealing the person's spirit and there was a lot of talking and explaining to do to quieten the situation down.

While the Hoeys were still stationed at Nomad River prior to their house being built amongst the Biamis, some concreting work was being done at the Awaba high school. As there is no sand or gravel anywhere in the lower Papuan plateau where Awaba is situated, I back-loaded sacks of sand and small gravel from the river which Tom had organised for the concreting at Awaba.

Naturally, having a house to live in close to the airstrip site with the planted coconuts was a priority, but all the time that was going on, there was an airstrip to be built and the various arrangements for the equipment for this to happen were being organised. There was a period when the Hoeys were out at Mougulu but the airstrip hadn't yet been built, so they would come back into the Nomad River airstrip to get or send items on the aircraft. I have a vivid memory of Salome running down the track to the end of the Nomad River airstrip. She was obviously wanting to catch the plane and I was waiting there for her. I don't remember the reason, but have an idea that it was to post something to one of their children who was at high school down south in Australia. She was a little puffed, but still the happy, smiling person that Salome always was!

I can't remember whether it was on that same trip or not, but for some reason we had a dearth of eggs for a period in the Western Province and to quote the proverbial, they were as scarce as hen's teeth. I don't know where I had been before getting to Nomad River, but someone had given me half a dozen eggs for us personally and they were in the aircraft pod. Salome saw them and asked if she could have them as she wanted to make a birthday cake for one of her older children who was coming back shortly from schooling in Australia. I chose to say, 'Yeah, fine,' but I spent the next 15 minutes on the way over to my next stop at Debepari wondering how I was going to tell Elsie that I had given away the eggs that had been given to us! This is certainly *not* meant to reflect badly on Salome, but rather to be a reflection of the fantastic working relationship that existed between us, as with many missionaries.

But the Lord was obviously in all this, because when I landed at Debepari, Barry and Pam Waldeck greeted me with: 'I understand that you guys are having an egg shortage. We have hens, so here is a dozen eggs for you!' Wow! One hundred percent increase in 15 minutes; wouldn't a financier love to hear of that sort of interest rate? Not to mention that it gave my faith a real boost, as well as making it very easy to tell the whole story to Elsie when I finally got home!

The items for the development of the airstrip at Mougulu were imported and shipped by road to Tari, a main base in the highlands about 25 minutes from Nomad River and 70 minutes from Kawito. They were a Ferguson 35 tractor and scarifier which were broken down at Tari into components that could fit into a U206 for flying to Nomad River. Special extra wooden floor coverings were made to distribute the concentrated weight of some of the bigger items (such as the engine or the rear axle unit) to comply with Cessna's maximum weight per square foot for the floor. While some individual items were mighty heavy to get into the aircraft, the most awkward that I remember were the tyres off the rear tractor wheels.

They were too big to fit through the Cessna 206's large cargo door, so we had to put cargo straps around them and squash them down into an oval shape so they would fit! A one-metre scoop cut in half was flown into NDR by another aircraft.

We managed to get everything to Nomad River with our fixed-wing aircraft, but that wasn't at the new airstrip site where it was all going to be used. That is where the Summer Institute of Linguistics (SIL) helicopter came in, to shuttle all the components the 15 minutes to the Mougulu airstrip site where it was all reassembled. The scarifier and scoop were welded together again as they had been cut in half to fit in the aircraft. Being ex-farmers, Tom and Salome took turns at the massive task of making an airstrip out of some moderately undulating terrain, which had been de-stumped largely by the locals with Tom helping them. Salome drove all day and Tom drove all night, moving 24,000 cubic metres of soil to make a very worthwhile 655-metre long airstrip with a mere one percent slope to the southeast.

Someone might wonder why it was necessary to call on an SIL helicopter to do this job. Why didn't MAF have a helicopter? It's a fair question. In fact many years later, a helicopter was offered to MAF provided the donor's name was put on it. We didn't take up that offer, even though our sister organisation, MAF-US, operated one over the border in West Papua/Irian Jaya. Why not? There were several reasons and they were mainly operational. Back then, helicopters were slow (particularly the one that had been offered) and while it could lift a reasonable load, it could only be used on special jobs. On top of that, it would have needed specialised engineering as well as special pilots and we really didn't have that sort of expertise or time for the amount of work that would be required to make it a viable operation. So how come MAF-US over the border was able to use one? The answer is the Vietnam War. Proportionally, many more Americans were involved in that war, so there was a pool of expertise (both in engineering and pilots) in America to draw from which MAF Australasia didn't have. We figured that it was much better stewardship of resources to ask SIL to do that sort of work when needed.

However after the Mougulu airstrip was officially opened with much whooping and fanfare as only the PNG locals can do, there was one slight problem. At the south-eastern end of the strip, there was a very large spirit tree which the locals wouldn't let Tom cut down during the initial clearance. It encroached into the approach and departure area at that end and would certainly make things safer in all seasons if it wasn't there. So I hatched a plan with Tom. Any time I was light enough to take off or land safely using that end, I would make it obvious that I was avoiding this tree. After some months of doing this and with the locals now appreciating the things that came and went on the aircraft, as well as Tom and Salome's ministry amongst them, they came to Tom and told him that the tree should come down. Tom didn't need a second invitation; I think the chainsaw was probably going as soon as they finished speaking!

As you can see, the spirits were a very important part of these people's lives, and much was done in fear of them. Another missionary close to Mougulu went out one afternoon with a local couple to their garden. The husband watched while his wife did the hard work of digging and planting. It was the accepted norm that the men felled the trees and cleared the land and the wives cultivated, planted and harvested. The missionary, who was relatively new to the area and its ways, casually remarked on the way home that the man had had a quiet afternoon, to which came the reply, 'No, I was working hard all the time, keeping my wife safe from the spirits.' When you know that the noise of a branch breaking off a tree in the wind can be interpreted as something much more than the simple fact, you realise how much the spirits rule their lives.

When we were at Kawito, we developed a great relationship with Tom and Salome, possibly because we all had farming backgrounds. We were certainly spiritually in tune, and the four of us really appreciated each other. Their children frequently used to overnight with us when they went south to Australia for their high school education and on occasions we would go to Mougulu for a weekend, as we also did to several other mission stations where we were warmly welcomed. The rapid development of the Christian Church in the Biami area was quite dramatic and the Hoeys were forward thinkers in the natural realm as well. A weir for a hydroelectricity system was built, then a medical aid-post and a school and a hospital. An FM radio station was developed with solar panels to back this up; and the list could go on.

After the severe earthquake in 2018, the weir survived, but the adjacent walls of the stream didn't. With repair and the planting of a special grass to help hold the soil together, it is operating again, but with more solar panels added to act as a more substantial backup. The primary school has been named the Tom Hoey Primary School. This shows how much the locals and provincial people appreciate what Tom and Salome have done for them, even though they themselves are somewhat embarrassed by the naming of the school like that. In 2020 a high school was built there, called the Nomad Mougulu High School. One of Tom and Salome's daughters, Sally-Joy Lloyd who is now stationed at Mougulu, is heavily involved in this along with her husband, Ian. Since originally writing this, the high school is now operational, with Ian as the headmaster.

It has been said by an anthropologist that there have been two, if not three different civilisations or cultural waves through PNG. Very evident at Mougulu were the stone mortar and pestle artefacts, indicating that at some time in the past there had been a culture which grew some form of grain – something the current locals know nothing about. Tom also showed us a very lethal-looking weapon made out of stone, not currently made or used by the Biamis. Imagine a *very* course gearwheel with five or six rounded teeth, 130 millimetres or so in diameter and about 50 millimetres thick on the end of a very substantial stick, and you have some idea of it. In close combat, it would inflict much more than a sore head!

As mentioned previously, anthropologists can often give insights into the past which aren't apparent on the surface. However, so do the traditions and stories that are embedded in local folklore, like the one already mentioned about Amanab. Then there is this one from the Orokana Valley, about 130 kilometres away from Mougulu. The local folklore had a story about a great flood that covered the whole earth, and this idea was there before any missionaries arrived! They also had an idea of a massive building, which appeared to be a picture story about a pyramid. How these stories got there no-one knows, unless they came in one of the cultural waves referred to earlier, but at least the flood was a good point of contact to couple with the biblical event.

In many parts of the country, traders have penetrated into remote areas, buying up artefacts for a pittance, which they then take back and sell to museums and the like for a massive profit. Knowing this, and seeing its emergence of it in the Biami area, Tom immediately offered the local people a reasonable price for many bows and arrows etc., and when we used to go there in the 1970s, he had quite an arsenal stowed in the ceiling of their house, ready, I presume, to sell for a fair price to any traders who came buying in the area.

It has been fantastic to hear (in 2023) that Tom and Salome's daughter and her husband as well as a son are now involved in the Biami ministry. When there was the big earthquake in 2018, Sally-Joy was the official United Nations interpreter for those distributing food to the people in that area who had lost so much; as she can speak the Bedamuni language just like a local. For me, it is simply wonderful to hear about the children of missionaries who are going back to consolidate and continue the work their parents have started, or who have gone as missionaries themselves to other countries. I am aware of this happening with at least six families who we used to serve.

Chapter 19

I Thank God for a Praying Wife

I have mentioned previously about how Elsie prayed for me when I was in a sticky situation out of Telefomin. The second time happened one afternoon originating out of Orokana. I had taken a mission education secretary into Orokana so he could assess the school and the teachers etc. there. I had given him a time to be back, which would have easily given us enough time (about an hour) to return back to Awaba where he was living. The elected time came and went, so much so, that I asked the Lord for a sign. Orokana is located in a relatively narrow, longish valley, with a 'break-through' gap at one point on one side, with the river which drains the valley running through it. As the time passed, I said to the Lord, 'If, when I follow the river through the gap, I can see blue above me, I will proceed, but if I can't see any blue, then I will turn around and over-night at Orokana.' One specific error with that prayer was that I didn't specify how low the blue was to be(!) – for when I got through the gap, there was the blue.

As I proceeded, it was obvious that low-level flight on track wasn't going to be possible, as there was a line of build-ups along the Woolley Hills, which are like a low ridge (about 1,200 feet) of limestone extending from Mt Bosavi almost right out to the Gulf of Papua. So the only alternative was to climb and see if there were any breaks between the clouds roughly on track.

The track from Orokana to Awaba was 200 degrees. As we proceeded, the passenger who was late noted that we were actually tracking 150 degrees and asked if this was the way home. I replied, 'It is the only way we are going to get there now and I am trusting there will be a break in the clouds that we can exploit.' Thankfully, after a while there was one, and a heading of about 270 degrees got us to where we wanted to go. Once again, the Holy Spirit had prompted Elsie to pray, and this time she included our eldest daughter Ann who was about three with her as they prayed for me. Was that the time where there was a break? According to a comparison of times, I would say, 'Yes', and it gave us a safe trip home – the needed result!

Another mission station that has a particular spot in my heart was the one established at Mt Bosavi. In our time at Mt Hagen and early Kawito, I had moved people from various points to Bosavi for outreach and ministry, but none were stationed there. However, the time came when Keith and Norma Briggs were to move there to live and minister. The day of the initial move wasn't the most pleasant, as there was a cyclone over northern Australia which was having an effect on the weather and winds on the south side of PNG. Although I tried from both above and below the cloud to get to the Bosavi airstrip, the cloud was just at the level that covered the airstrip, so back home we went. The next day was much better and we made it okay. Because flammables couldn't be carried with passengers, I drained a few litres of fuel out of the aircraft's tanks once we landed so Keith and Norma would have some fuel to run their little power generator with.

It was not long before Norma was teaching some young teens how to read and write, using mini blackboards like slates, with desks made from a section of a tree trunk cut to the right height, and seats from a similar source, only shorter. Keith was into building their house and also putting up a tower with a wind-driven generator to charge batteries. The local Bosavi people were in no way nomadic, in fact, it is said that the majority of them never ventured more than about eight kilometres from where they were born. Like most PNG people, they had a real respect for the spirits and made efforts to keep evil spirits from spoiling their garden, etc. It was rather telling that one of them, after he had come to a saving relationship with Jesus, said to Keith one day, 'Why has it taken you so long to come and tell us about this Good Spirit? We always knew that there was a good spirit, but it was easier for us to relate to the other spirits and besides, we didn't know how to be in touch with the good one.'

The Bosavi airstrip sloped quite definitely towards a gully at the approach end but was relatively flat for about two thirds of its length, but because of the initial slope it had a 3.5 percent slope overall, which meant it was classed as a one-way airstrip. This was fine, except in the northwest season, when the winds could be quite strong and gusty. As the strip was roughly northwest/southeast, it was sometimes safer to land the wrong way before the house and power generating tower were built.

Some time after the Briggs had settled at Bosavi, I was flying from Tari to Kawito (70 minutes), a route which virtually overheads Bosavi, and I had a distinct inner feeling that I should land there and see if everything was alright. Essentially it was, but Norma needed some medical help. She wrote down the details and I took them on to Balimo. One doesn't necessarily want the whole mission to know some personal details by using the mission radio! In the meantime they called Balimo for Dr Kath to come to the airstrip and after reading the symptoms Norma had given, Kath wrote out a prescription on the back of the DC3 captain's flight plan, so that medication could come out on the next scheduled flight from Port Moresby. Talk about all things working together for good for those that love God! If this wasn't an example, I don't know what is!

Apart from helping missionaries establish and maintain mission stations with everything that normally comes to a person's home by car or truck, the work out of Kawito did of course entail some medical emergencies. Normally these would be initiated by a doctor or perhaps an aid post orderly who had been in touch with a doctor for approval. I have to confess that after one particular incident, I made it a rule that the doctor decided whether a case was a medical emergency or not and then I would assess whether the weather was flyable.

It came about one soggy, low cloud and drizzly afternoon in the southeast season that the aid post orderly from Suki called in to Dr Kath Donovan at Balimo Hospital with a case. I also happened to be on the base radio at the same time and from what the orderly said, both Kath and I thought the case could wait until the morning. I think Dr Kath was also assessing the weather as she thought about the patient. When we called up in the morning, we learnt that, sadly, the patient had died in the night. There was also the possibility that the orderly hadn't provided enough information. As their whole culture was so used to death, at times there didn't seem to be the same sense of urgency as we might have felt under the same circumstances. This event was the trigger for me to make it a rule – the medics would tell me whether the case was a medical emergency, and I would determine whether it was possible to safely fly a return trip to the destination or not.

I clearly remember some medical emergencies. One was late on a Saturday afternoon, when a missionary's pregnant wife at Debepari was haemorrhaging. I realised that I would really be pushed for time as it was getting late in the afternoon already so I went immediately, fuelled the plane and put on a trade store load. I then flew to Balimo just seven minutes away to pick up Dr Barb Ellis, then flew directly to Debepari (55 minutes) and dropped the load. On landing at Debepari, I gave a time we needed to get away by so that we could get to Rumginae (30 minutes away) before last light. The norm was to get to your destination considerably before last light unless you declared it a mercy flight with all the associated explanations and paperwork.

After assessment by the doctor, the patient arrived on a blanket as there was no stretcher, five minutes later than I had requested, so it was a quick get in and buckle up or strap down onto the hard plywood floor for the patient, and head off. Fortunately, I had previously done a few trips from Debepari to Rumginae and had done something one of my check pilots, fellow Kiwi Laurie Darrington had advised me to do. He said, 'Ted, when the weather is good, get down low-level and see what the terrain looks like so that you know what it's like if you ever need to fly low-level because of weather.' I had done this and had noted that away in the distance (actually over the border in West Papua) there was a little sugar loaf hill and if I headed directly for that, it would take me right over Rumginae. On the evening in question, I took off and turned in the general direction of Rumginae and there in stark relief in the golden glow of the setting sun was the sugar loaf. Thank you Lord for a fine night! We managed to get to Rumginae a couple of minutes before last light and the patient's husband, who was already there for meetings, was visibly relieved because his wife was now in safe medical care. A few months later a healthy baby boy was born who now lives in Western Australia. Again, thank you Lord!

However, not all medicals are accomplished like that. Late-ish one afternoon, I was heading back home to Kawito from Rumginae and the Pangoa mission on Lake Murray called up asking for a patient to be taken from there to Balimo. As it was only a small diversion, I said I could do it. However, when I arrived over Pangoa, I saw that it had recently rained, and worse, there was a very strong wind blowing at right angles across the strip. I think the folk were somewhat surprised and dismayed to hear me tell them that I considered it was too unsafe to land in those conditions and I went away without picking up the patient. While every MAF pilot always desires to help, they have to work according to the prevailing conditions and on this occasion it was necessary to say, 'Sorry, I can't do it.' These are the times when the prayers of faithful partners at home for a pilot's wisdom in assessing the situation are most necessary!

Many years later when Elsie and I were in the MAF-NZ home office, we had a person contact us who was studying to become a doctor and was enquiring about flying training with the idea of becoming a real flying doctor. I immediately saw a problem, and while normally we tried to encourage folk to learn to fly at the Flight Training Centre, I strongly discouraged it this time. Think about it for a moment. The concept of being a flying doctor sounds great at first but, in reality, at some stage the person is going to have to make an almost impossible decision. A doctor with a patient on board strikes bad weather on route; which is going to be the stronger emotion – saving the patient the doctor knows they can help, or being the pilot, knowing the weather is deteriorating in front of them, and they really should turn back? Or take the situation where the flying doctor is answering an emergency call, and again the weather is bad and getting worse, does the pilot in them say 'Sorry,' and turn back, or does the doctor in them try and push on? I pointed out these sorts of scenarios to the person and they never communicated again. I hope they saw the reasoning, but I don't know if they did, or whether they went and learnt somewhere else, though to date I haven't heard of that sort of person actually operating in any mission.

Before I relate the next most memorable medical emergency flight, I need to explain a couple of terms. Firstly, 'fingers of cloud'. Since PNG is close to the equator, it is in the path of the inter-tropical front which sits between the two trade winds (northwest and southeast) that prevail in that region. The front follows the sun, moving from north to south and back again. Or should I say more correctly, it follows where the sun is overhead as the effect of the movement is actually the earth tilting on its vertical axis. In any case, on the south coast of PNG, it produces two very distinct, but different weather patterns. The front can be kilometres, or even country wide, or it can be quite narrow at times. I have flown under the front in quite heavy rain, leaving a southeast tail wind on one side and coming out the other side into a northwest headwind on a trip from Kawito to Rumginae.

The northwest season is regarded in the Papua lowlands region, south of the main highlands area, as being the dry season, even though the rainfall is within only 12 centimetres per year, compared to the wet southeast season. This is because in the northwest season, it is usually fine, sunny and hot in the morning with storms developing during the day. The sun licks up the moisture between the thunderstorm cells which often merge together in the late afternoon. The ground underfoot appears to be drier than in the southeast season when it is constantly being kept wet with drizzle and light rain coming out of low to medium height cloud, with the occasional heavier shower.

In these conditions, in either season, once the low cloud starts to lift, there will frequently be small fingers of cloud rising up out of the jungle in vertical columns and meeting up with the low cloud ceiling above. It is still quite flyable, depending on how long it has been since the heavier rain fell that caused it.

The other item to explain is what I mean by the bomb scow. This was a small flat-bottomed barge with (I think) a single-cylinder diesel engine as it had a very distinct 'pop, pop, pop' sound when travelling. Originally it was used in WW2 for carrying either bombs or depth charges out to Catalina flying boats where they were attached to the bomb racks under the wings. The local mission had acquired one after the war and it was used for transporting personnel and some cargo travelling between Awaba, Kawito, Balimo and occasionally Mapoda, all on the Aramia River. While the scow always got there, it certainly wasn't a speedy mode of transport, especially going upstream and it was quite open as there was no actual cabin, though there was a covering over the top of it.

Two things were happening on the day of this memorable medical emergency. Apart from the medical, the Minister of Education and some education officials were coming out from Port Moresby to the Awaba high school for a special function. I hadn't been booked to provide any transport for them so when the medical came in, I set off for the Nomad River airstrip. The medical was for an Seventh Day Adventist pastor who had his arm mauled by a crocodile. Apparently the chap had caught and tied up the crocodile the day before but when he went to claim his prize the next morning, the croc had managed to loosen its ties during the night enough to get the pastor's arm. The Nomad River aid post orderly had done his best to stem the flow of blood and patch up the arm but it needed more work done on it by a doctor, hence the medical emergency.

The weather was one of those days when there had been heavy rain in the night and there was a mass of fingers of cloud rising up out of the jungle. As I had previously flown a search and rescue flight on almost the identical route when a commercial twin-engine aircraft had gone missing, I elected to head west of track. By doing this, I knew I would strike the Strickland River downstream from a very useful landmark, a red clay bank (very distinctive then, but later covered with vegetation), from which one could head roughly east-northeast to Nomad River or west-southwest to Debepari.

All went well with the flight until I was called up and told that the commercial aircraft bringing the government officials from Port Moresby had landed at Kawito as the pilot had (very wisely) thought it was unsafe to land at Awaba, so would I take the party to Awaba when I got back? Knowing just how slippery Awaba was when wet, and with drizzle still falling, I responded that no, it would be too unsafe for me to land there as well, so please ask them to travel upstream to Awaba on the bomb scow, which had a top covering but open sides.

Getting to the Strickland River, I flew up it at very low level without having to worry about any fingers of cloud as they only rose up out of the jungle. From the distinctive red clay bank I turned and got to Nomad River without any trouble. The pastor was quite mobile and was able to sit up on the return journey to the hospital at Balimo following much the same route.

On arriving back at Kawito, you can imagine my surprise and dismay when I saw the government party waiting for me. Apparently the mission representative had told them, 'Don't worry, Ted will get you there.' This was even though the Port Moresby pilot had taken his plane (a Britain Norman Islander) and done an empty dummy run landing at Awaba which confirmed his original thought that it was far too slippery to land there safely with a load of passengers, as it was only 518 metres long. In one sense I didn't blame them not wanting to spend two hours or so travelling up the river on the bomb scow, but again I said, 'Sorry, but I'm not going to risk everything with a landing there.' This is the constant tension MAF pilots have. They want to serve and do what the mission wants, but have to assess a number of things, and at times it is very hard not to be affected by the pressure that is put on them. Sometimes one has to say a polite, but very definite 'No.'

It was now lunchtime so what were we to do with about nine people? Elsie asked the other mission wife on the station if she could take some, and she took two. It was just as well Elsie had a well-stocked pantry, as all the rest of them piled into our lounge room and Elsie and the mission rep and I hastily prepared some tuna and rice for them. To their credit, they saw the problem and didn't hold anything against me for refusing to make the flight and in fact the Minister of Education wrote a very nicely worded letter to Elsie thanking her for stepping up and providing such a good meal at short notice.

The above incident was, from memory, only the third time that I couldn't – or didn't – fulfil a task I was asked to do. I have to confess there was one time I refused to do something for the mission, even though I was asked to do it. I had flown Grahame a single, young Australian missionary chap several times from Suki, where there was a European family, to Arufe (25 minutes) and got to know him reasonably well. These trips were for just a few days; he was encouraging the local pastors and gaining further insights into the culture and the language. While he was willing to go and live amongst the people for a short time, I assessed him as being a rather shy person, although this was shown later not to be wholly correct!

One morning on the radio 'sched' (which we pronounced as 'sked' – short for 'schedule'), the mission asked me to transport him from Suki to Kiunga. With no mission station at that time at Kiunga, which was a government station, I asked them where he was going to live. They replied that he would be living with the mission's Papuan pastor family there. I said that no way would I take him to a 'Siberia' situation like that, which naturally didn't meet with cheers of approval (although a couple of missionaries later did say privately to me, 'Good on you'). I came up with the compromise of taking him to the Rumginae mission station and hospital which was about three hours away along a passable, though poor road from Kiunga. I think when they saw I meant what I said, they agreed.

Unknown to me, Grahame was delighted with the outcome, as he had bright eyes for one of the nurses at Rumginae Hospital! Eventually, they got married, and at the time of writing (2023) are still happily married and living back in Australia, but still servicing the Arufe people with visits, encouragements and translated

Scriptures. So, what about this incident and the final outcome? Coincidence? Good luck on Grahame's part, or God's will? I prefer to think that in making this decision, I was just a small cog in God's great purpose. I have to honour the mission involved though; they can't have mentioned it to the MAF leadership, as I was never asked for a 'Please explain'. Like a number of missionaries' children of that era who were brought up on the field, their daughter has served Jesus in Peru for 10 years, and like her parents, continues to support the work there after returning to Australia.

When I sent the above to Grahame for his approval, he came back to me with this portion of his life's story from his perspective. It can be found in Chapter 20 of his book *Fighting to Live: A story of Spiritual Warfare In Papua New Guinea* and I insert here excerpts from that chapter with his permission:

> No good thing will God withhold from those whose walk is blameless. These words from Psalm 84 gripped me. I had been praying for a partner, because the loneliness was almost unbearable and this seemed to be a promise of what God was planning. I opened the latest mission magazine and noticed that a new missionary was coming to work in PNG: a nurse named Elizabeth Abbott. I wondered if there was any connection between her and the verse in the Psalm I had just read.
>
> Shortly after this, I was moved to work at the mission's supply base at Kawito. I was shocked by this move, because God was blessing the translation checking, the youth ministry at Suki and the literacy work at Arufe. ... As I motored along, a small voice said, 'It is not the mission that is moving you, but I, the Almighty God am taking you out to meet Elizabeth Abbott and you will return together to continue the ministry in both Suki and Arufe.'

... Two days later as I flew out of Suki for Kawito my tears flowed freely. It was hard leaving the people I had come to love, but in my inner being, I knew God had a purpose. ... On November 27th Elizabeth arrived at Kawito on her way to the hospital at Rumginae. ... We met and the next morning I went to see her off and teach her the greetings of the Aekyom people of Rumginae. ... Things looked promising so I prayed about the next step: 'God, you have introduced me to Elizabeth, but how am I going to overcome the 300 km distance between us?'

A couple of weeks later, the mission director told me I was to move to Kiunga to maintain the missionary supply line. I couldn't believe my ears; Elizabeth was only 25 km away from Kiunga. When the director told Ted Crawford ... that I was to move to Kiunga, he responded, 'That is very isolated, it is like moving him from Moscow to Siberia. ... I suggest that he be sent to Rumginae to manage Kiunga from there.'

It is not normal for the pilot to contradict the director over personnel movements. But the director realised that Ted was more aware of the situation than he was, so my destination was changed to Rumginae. I was unaware of this discussion so Ted came to me, and said, 'I had better tell you of what I have just done. The director wanted you to go to Kiunga, but I refused to do it. I said I'd move you to Rumginae. Is that okay?'

'Is that okay??' I looked at Ted, being very surprised at how fast God was working things out according to his perfect will. 'Ted, you don't know what you have just done, but one day I will tell you.'

Grahame and Elizabeth were married on 14 March 1973. It reminds me of Romans 8:28. God has his ways of working!

About the search and rescue mission for the missing commercial plane referred to in the story of the Nomad River pastor above: I was assigned the job of tracking 18 kilometres west of the track that the plane would have taken from Balimo to Nomad River. It subsequently came out that the pilot had only recently obtained his instrument rating which could have been a temptation for him to fly in cloud or heavy rain that wouldn't have been possible for a visual pilot like myself. When I was abreast of the highest of the mini volcanoes referred to earlier which I knew to be on track, I called the Civil Aviation Authority Search and Rescue (SAR) via Air Radio and suggested that I have a look at that volcanic hill which at the time was basically in the clear. The answer came back, 'No, just continue on with your assignment.'

Over the next few days, a number of us were engaged in flying around in very much less than normal visual conditions trying to find the missing aircraft. After about four days (as I remember it) it was found on top of the knob that I wanted to have a look at on that first clear afternoon! You would have thought the SAR coordinator could have taken a local guy's idea as being worth following through on, but apparently not. It caused much added expense with many extra hours flying, as well as exposing the searchers to flying in worse than marginal conditions in an attempt to find the missing aircraft. In fact I found an area that from a normal height looked flat, only to discover that there was a big depression in the treetops there! This probably gives you an idea of how close to the treetops we were flying because of the weather which, when looking for a missing aircraft doesn't give a particularly wide range of vision!

Medical evacuations were generally pretty random, but one area seemed to specialise in broken arms and legs and when you know how they came about, you will understand why. The coconut milk in a green coconut is normally quite like fizzy drink and is most refreshing, but apparently if you open a green nut up a little early and let water in, that fizzy turns into a real top-shelf sort of drink. It would seem that the Suki area men liked the top-shelf drink, and would climb a coconut palm and open a nut up and leave it for some time, then after a period, climb up again and taste their brew. Sadly, for some of them, the delights of their enterprise would suddenly and abruptly cease as they lost their grip on the tree and fell to the ground, breaking one or more limbs. It was happening so frequently that the missionary felt it was unfair for the Government (with Australian aid funds) to be constantly paying for the medical flights for such endeavours, and so imposed a fee to get the plane to come and pick them up. However this only slowed things down for a little while, so great was their desire for their home brew.

When we were based in the Western Province at Kawito, leprosy was still moderately common in PNG. At Mapoda (downstream from Kawito and Balimo) there was a leprosarium and at times I was asked to fly a patient in there. We naturally robed them up so that they wouldn't infect anything and then disinfected the seats, etc. after carrying such a patient. If a patient had a leprous ulcer, one needed to open up the air vent and try and keep one's nose in the stream of fresh air, such was the distinctive and overwhelming smell. Because of a significant drop-off of leprosy, the hospital was later converted into a Bible school, but sadly (as of 2023) leprosy has apparently once again become a significant disease in PNG.

After a while it became apparent to both mission hospitals in the western province (Balimo and Rumginae) that there was resistance from the locals about going to hospital; that is, until it was found out they were saying in effect, 'Don't go to hospital because you die there.' This was, of course, a significant problem for a culture where, like many others, dying in your home place had so much meaning. The main reason this thinking came about was the fact that the local people would try all their own remedies and potions before going to an aid post which would soon see that treatment was beyond them and send patients to hospital. In other words, the hospitals were receiving patients so late that a cure for whatever was wrong with them was doubtful or impossible and so the patient died.

So with that happening, how did the hospitals counter it? They overcame this problem by sending the patient back to their home place when they realised there was a slim chance of full recovery. As time went on and the locals gained more confidence in the missionary hospital's cures, they started to come earlier to the aid posts and hospitals which gave the hospitals a better chance of curing them.

Another positive aspect of the work done out of Kawito and many other bases was taking student families to Christian Leaders Training College (CLTC) in the PNG highlands. It was wonderful that quite a number were going for training and, initially, I could get two families in on a C185 flight as their luggage was so minimal. Much later, it was only possible to take one family at a time as their essentials had increased so much! However, even that amount was truly minimal compared to what a European would have taken. It was on one such flight that I found the answer to what I thought was going to be a really serious problem. All of a sudden the aircraft started to 'hunt', that is, the engine seemed to be surging for no apparent reason, even though all the power settings were correct and the instruments showed no problems. My first thought was I might have a propeller problem as it seemed to be surging, but the revs were stable. Then out of the corner of my eye as I was checking the instruments I saw what it was. The young mum in the seat behind me was bouncing her little child on her knee (as you do) and that was causing the terrible effect we were experiencing.

CLTC depended on MAF to bring their students from all over PNG, and we had a wonderful rapport with them. It was obviously not known to one mission coordinator in a South Island east coast town when we were on our first furlough though. He apologised profusely for a double-up with ourselves of MAF and Garth and Ruth Morgan of CLTC scheduled on the same night at the same venue. We both assured him that it wasn't a problem as we worked well with each other anyway. My slide presentation showing MAF taking CLTC students to the facility, and Garth's presentation showing an MAF aircraft bringing others to CLTC would have demonstrated to him how much we did work together, and hopefully put him at ease.

Knowing a physical area fairly well can sometimes be helpful to others. One Saturday afternoon, I saw the oil company helicopter (there was now a camp on the other side of the airstrip doing seismic surveys) coming in at a speed that I had never seen before. I thought there must be something wrong and he needed some help, so I went down from our house to meet him. In fact it wasn't him that needed help, but a private pilot (not MAF) up from Australia who had got lost when travelling from Port Moresby around the coast of the Gulf of Papua to Daru – the customs exit point for light aircraft out of PNG to Australia. The helicopter pilot asked me to get on my aircraft radio and communicate with Air Radio in Port Moresby who were coordinating the problem because the aircraft was running low on fuel, as he had been reckoning on refuelling at Daru.

Air Radio told me two facts – the route he had been taking, and the fact that he was over a few iron-roofed buildings. I immediately figured what the problem was, because it was in the southeast season with relatively low cloud with drizzle and reduced, though adequate visibility for flying.

What had happened was that he had been following the coastline so closely that he had flown up the side of the wide estuary at the mouth of the Bamu River without realising it, until it narrowed into a river. I asked the pilot if there was a point downstream from the iron-roofed buildings he was over where it appears as if another river had broken through into the one he was over? The answer came back, 'Yes', and so I told Air Radio that he was over the Bamu River mission and the closest point for him to get down would be Balimo. The helicopter quickly took off to escort him there.

It was rather nice to learn later that the Civil Aviation Authority had written to Max Meyers my chief pilot thanking him for this. 'Your guy at Kawito somehow managed to identify where a lost plane was and so averted what could have been a tragedy.' It was equally nice that Max immediately passed that message on to me.

In fact, what had happened with the two rivers (Bamu and Aramia) was that they had been quite close to a natural breakthrough when the local people dug a trench between them for the sake of easily moving their canoes across the narrow neck of land and after that, the water flow did the rest. It was when flying over the Bamu River once, upstream from the mission, that I saw a bore in action. It appears to be like a wave, sometimes of quite significant proportions and speed moving up the river, and is caused by an incoming tide flowing into an ever-narrowing estuary and then up the river. This can happen on any river that has a wide mouth which gradually narrows. I am aware that one of the UFM mission boat captains, when heading upriver on an incoming tide, would shelter in the lee of an island and then move out onto the bore wave, as it travelled much faster than the boat could have under its own power.

It was good that from time to time council members from both Australia and New Zealand came up to PNG and had a little look at the reality of life there. The padded centre seat of the Cessna 185 had been replaced with what we called a sling seat which comprised a low crossbar between the two rear door posts below knee height and another bar about shoulder height a little way further back. Between these two bars was a piece of heavy material which formed a reasonably comfortable sling seat. At times when the amount of luggage was too much to go into the pod (the cargo pack under the aircraft), you could slide a suitcase or similar under the sling seat, meaning the centre passengers were effectively sitting on their suitcases which admittedly was much harder and less comfortable than the sling seat.

On one occasion a very sincere Australian MAF council member was up and overnighted with us on his way to Mt Hagen. Elsie told him of the trouble I had been having with my old valve radios failing, having been away because of this problem 14 nights in one month. This was in the days before solid-state radios were readily available. Once I had two radios in the pod going for repair and the operational one gave out on me on the way there! To get the repairs done, we took our radios to Christian Radio Missionary Fellowship (CRMF) at Rugli near Mt Hagen. One time, my field leader said I should head home as soon as I had one serviceable radio in the aircraft. I politely told him I wasn't moving from Hagen until I had two serviceable radios, one in the aircraft and a spare. The aforementioned councillor remarked to Elsie, 'Ted will be having more than radio problems if this situation doesn't change soon,' meaning Elsie would soon be getting tired of it all. To her credit, I don't ever remember her ever complaining about it, except feeling really sorry for me with all the radio trouble I was having.

When I took this council member up to Mt Hagen (80 minutes) I slipped his case under the centre seat as we flew to what was then called a 'pilots' meeting' which in fact incorporated all operational staff including the much-needed and respected engineers. At the meeting, this chap complained about sitting on his suitcase, to which I replied, 'You ask any missionary which they would prefer – sit on their suitcase on the flight and have the suitcase with them when they arrive, or leave it behind? I know what their answer would be 100 percent of the time!' All the others pilots agreed with me. The poor guy made no progress with his complaint, but got a dose of what real mission life was like.

I think the later solid-state radios were better sealed than the old valve type that we were using in the late 1960s and they needed to be! One morning as I taxied out, I had just finished giving my taxiing call and a puff of blue smoke came out of the front of the radio and it went dead. I was able to go back and cancel my taxi call with Air Radio with the base radio and then investigate the problem. It was easy enough to find. A small cockroach had been wandering across the circuit board and had stumbled across a couple of high voltage points with the result that it was instantly turned into a piece of carbon. Fortunately I had observed what the professionals did in such circumstances and I drilled a hole to eliminate the piece of carbon and hey presto! – the radio worked again, so I was able to proceed with a 'holier' radio than before.

An explanation here for those not familiar with pilot radio procedures: For the sake of search and rescue, when you are away from a controlled airfield (i.e. one without an air traffic control tower), the pilot calls the relevant air traffic Air Radio station that covers the area you are in, with a taxi call alerting them that you are about to make a takeoff. When airborne, you give a departure call with an estimated time to your destination, or a reporting time if more than 30 minutes away. When you arrive at your destination, you give an arrival call and can ask Air Radio to cancel their SAR (Search and Rescue) watch for you. Or you can nominate to report on the ground to cancel the SAR watch. In PNG in my time, the grace time was three minutes before Air Radio would start calling to see if you were okay or had a revised ETA. Air Radio's initial SAR was often just getting another aircraft in the area to call you on a different frequency to alert you that you were past your SAR watch time.

On another occasion when a high profile Air Pacific Christian

Mission (APCM) councillor was up to the PNG field, he was booked to go with me from Balimo to Samberigi and then Samberigi to Port Moresby a couple of days later to catch a flight south which he said he *had* to catch because of meetings in Melbourne he *had* to attend. This conversation took place on the airstrip at Balimo, with a DC3 waiting to load to go to Port Moresby. The weather at the time was very poor and so I said to him, 'If you *have* to get to Port Moresby in that timeframe, please get on this DC3 flight right now, as I can't guarantee to get you to Port Moresby in your timeframe because of the seasonal weather conditions.' I don't think he liked it too much, but he did get on the DC3 as he could see I meant what I said, and the weather was backing me up with drizzle out of low cloud! A typical southeast season day.

It is interesting to hear how a person is affected by the realities of things once they visit the field. Another APCM council member I had moved around a few places said to me as we stood together on the Rumginae airstrip, 'You know, down south we are terribly arrogant, trying to dictate what the folk on the field can and cannot do.' The background to this was that there had been a time in the recent past when the council in Melbourne would determine some very minor things, such as the maximum size of a hen run because of the amount of wire netting needed, and hence the cost!

I have no doubt this was because just before this time (around 1969), they had a centralised payment system where everything that happened on the field was paid for by the home council, including individuals' allowances from the donations they received. Once the mission took up the concept of personal support where individual missionaries raised their own prayer and financial support, things became much freer. This particular councillor was the accountant for a big, well-known firm, but I think he went back a changed man from what he had observed during his field visit.

Once, when a person with a little baby was up from south for a field wedding, the Port Moresby pilot was out at Wasua to take the little family back to Port Moresby (three hours flying). As things were being packed away, the pilot Eddie asked the young mum if she wanted her bag in the cabin, to which she replied, 'Oh if I need it, I'll get it.' Eddie patiently reminded her that she wasn't in a car and that it wasn't possible to get the bag from the pod (the cargo pack attached to the belly of the plane) while in flight! So she stowed it by her feet. I must confess here that I am so glad that we had a couple of small children in the early years of my flying in PNG. It helped me understand how many necessities there are when travelling with small children; otherwise I am sure I wouldn't really have understood the need to take so much aboard.

Not many places had a system such as at Kawito, where the aircraft fuel was decanted into an underground tank from which it was pumped mechanically into the aircraft. All outstation depots had drums of fuel which we tried our very best to get people to leave on their sides. If left standing up, even though they were double-sealed with rubber seals, when they heated up (especially in the tropical sun) a certain amount of fuel vapour escaped past the seals. Then when they cooled down or if it rained, some water from on top was sucked in past the seals which could cause serious problems if the water got into the aircraft fuel system. However, it was good old Eddie who, with much hype and encouragement, managed to get some local boys on an outstation to pump with a hand pump so fast that the small venting hole in the pump wasn't sufficient to fill the vacuum which was fast being created inside the drum. The result? An almighty pop, and the round drum became a triangular one around its middle.

We were fortunate to be able to get fresh vegetables once a week from Wapenamanda (75 minutes away) in the highlands. The Wapenamanda aircraft would normally make the trip, and then I'd distribute the veges according to how they had been ordered. There was only one problem with the system – if we ordered, say, 5 kilograms of potatoes, and they didn't have them, they would fill the total order with cabbages, of which they seemed to have an endless supply! Elsie tried her best to camouflage the cabbages by serving them in many different ways with recipes from her mum and sisters but sadly I developed a real aversion to that vegetable, which still persists today.

The fact that a pilot, after having been in one area for some time, is able to operate safely there when others don't want to, was demonstrated to Elsie on one of these vege runs. The Wapenamanda pilot had brought the vegetables down from the highlands a little later in the day than normal, and when he set out to return, he wasn't happy with the weather he saw ahead of him and so wisely turned back. He was complaining about this to Elsie and comparing it with the fact that I was still flying. In fact, I was operating in a quite different area, so localised at times is the weather; a factor Elsie reminded him of. He eventually took off for his home when the weather changed and arrived home safely later that afternoon.

In 1972 there was a very severe drought in PNG, something which I later observed seemed to occur roughly every seven to ten years. With the drought in full swing, everything dried out and all the locals seemed to have a fixation on burning anything that was burnable! It got so bad that after a while, I refused to carry any matches out to the trade stores, which was a futile attempt to give the message that they should stop burning everything in sight. The first burn would take all the undergrowth and singe the higher material and the second burn would burn the singed and dried stuff and singe the tops and the last burn was the tops of trees. Eventually this happened to all trees so that in time they were burning their staple food tree, the sago palms.

The smoke from all this burning became so thick that one time when lining up to land at Balimo, I couldn't see the far end of the strip (1,300 metres). Another time, coming home from the west on top of the worst of it, I didn't see the ground through it until I had descended to 1,500 feet. On another occasion when flying from Pangoa to Kiunga I thought it was getting a bit too thick, so I timed how long it took me to get to a tall tree up ahead. I figured that 15 seconds wasn't enough, so turned around and went back to Pangoa. On another afternoon, when flying from Kawito to Pangoa (45 minutes), a commercial pilot must have spotted me on his left before I saw him, with the result that the first I saw of him, he was zoom climbing from about the same elevation as I was flying as we approached the same circuit area.

As the houses we were living in only had tank supply for all water, it became quite critical as the drought progressed. Water for washing could still be fetched from the Aramia River which was close by, but drinking water was more difficult. Interestingly, there was sufficient condensation off the roof each night to keep our tank at a certain level all through the drought. It tasted a bit smoky even after a good boil, but when it was either that or river water there wasn't any real choice.

As I flew from Balimo to Kawito one Saturday (six minutes), I noticed that there was a fire front in the dry kunai grass (which is a bit taller and coarser than paspalum) moving towards Kawito. This was before the oil company was based on the other side of the airstrip. I told the villagers on the far side of the airstrip that they really needed to cut a firebreak in the long grass to stop the fire's advance. They did do something, but it was far too narrow, so on the Sunday afternoon we heard a roar like a train and then what sounded like explosions. It was the bamboo by the river burning. The airtight sections of the bamboo exploded and sent sparks everywhere. This was getting far too close to all the buildings and to the 40 or so drums of aviation fuel lying on their sides on the near side of the fairly bare grassed airstrip. We went and helped with fighting the fire front and as it was close to the mission's afternoon two-way radio sched time, Elsie asked the mission for prayer that the fire wouldn't cross the airstrip to where the fuel, distribution centre, workshop and houses were. When she came back from the sched, Elsie brought some orange drink to quench the thirst of those of us beating out the oncoming flames with wet sacks. One dear old Papuan lady took a sip and I guess because she hadn't tasted it before, spat it out – and had to remain thirsty.

Up until this time, the strong breeze had been from the south-east. It devoured an unused hut with a sago palm thatched roof in the most spectacular fire I have ever seen! The bright red flames from the dry thatch went up about 15 metres and were topped with jet black smoke, just like a large pile of burning tyres. After a short while, the wind changed from southeast to due south and the fire went down the right-hand side of the airstrip away from the fuel and the buildings. Does God answer prayer? For sure he does!

Sometimes, I believe God answers others' prayers for us when we don't even know we need them. I had a situation which I think exemplified this. In the early times at Wasua and Kawito I had to go to Mt Hagen for the aircraft's 33-hourly maintenance and inspection (which was later extended to 50 hours) and to Wewak for the 100-hourly. In this instance at Wewak the spark plugs and oil filter were changed by a reasonably experienced Papuan worker while I inspected and worked on the airframe. As is always the case after any engine maintenance, I had done a complete run up with the cowls (the covers around the engine) off and had inspected the engine for any oil leaks, etc. before cowling up again to fly home. On the Saturday morning, I set off for home at Kawito which took me, via Tari, right across the Central Highlands area of PNG, a trip of about 2.5 hours. All had gone well, and I was glad to get back home to Elsie and the girls.

On Monday morning, I was scheduled to do a 50-minute trip

up to Lake Kutubu with goods which Biyama (our cargo handler) and I had just been loaded into the aircraft. The helicopter pilot from the oil company camp came across the airstrip and asked me to take him over to the commercial flight at Balimo because his helicopter battery had suddenly failed (as lithium batteries are inclined to do) which meant he couldn't fly himself there.

I was loaded and all set to go and while I was contemplating the answer, the scripture came to me: 'Do unto others as you would have them do unto you.' Okay God, I get the message, so I unloaded again to take him the six minutes to Balimo. As it was time for the mission radio sched, I told the folk at Kutubu I wouldn't be coming at the expected time because I was taking the heli pilot to Balimo. When Balimo heard this, they asked me to track via the Aramia River on the way, as the bomb scow was overdue.

All went well and I caught up with the bomb scow in the Balimo lagoon not far from its destination, so was glad to be able to report that all was well there. After the heli pilot got out, I went around to the starboard side of the plane ready to put a new helicopter battery into the place where his seat had been. And then I noticed it! All down the right-hand side of the pod (cargo pack) there was oil – lots of it! So I went back to the port side again and looked at the oil dipstick. It only showed four US quarts, when we normally ran our aircraft on 11 US quarts. This meant of course that in the space of eight minutes, I had lost overboard more than half of my oil. It was subsequently found that the oil filter had been torqued (tightened) up to the same feet per pounds as the spark plugs, which was over-tight, and somehow the seal had popped thus allowing the oil to escape. But I had flown home for 2.5 hours on the Saturday without any problem. What was going on? Possibly the cooling off and reheating again had something to do with this, though no-one has yet come up with a logical answer that satisfies me.

What would have happened if the prayers of faithful supporters for all MAF pilots' safety – and our own that morning – hadn't been offered and I hadn't responded to the Holy Spirit's prompting from Scripture? The undoubted result is that the engine would have seized in about 20 minutes or so, which, if I was still heading to the Lake Kutubu airstrip (50 minutes) would have meant I would be over tall, thick jungle with no place to land. So thank you Lord for the faithful prayers of supporters and your undertaking in this situation! As this happened shortly after we had returned after our first furlough, I took it as a definite confirmation that we were doing God's will and that he was looking after us.

I have mentioned 'goods' several times and that is because, apart from the frequent passenger movements, the normal cargo was made up of mission freezer bags, mail and general supplies for the mission station and trade stores. In fact, if you think of anything that is transported to your home by any means, these same things reach many mission stations by light aircraft. The cargo at times included live creatures like young heifers, pigs, goats and fowl of various sorts, all tied and trussed up for safety. This 'live cargo' was usually for the sake of starting a new breeding program. Also, cassowaries into the highlands seemed to be the order of the day at one time. They were used for bride prices there.

As mentioned, the main supply base had moved to Kawito and had been taken over by the mission's trading subsidiary Papuan Supply and Welfare (Pasuwe) Ltd. To run it, they had brought someone up from Australia to be based in Port Moresby, who initially had no idea how to supply remote mission outstations. For instance, as a family of two adults and two small children we bought our toilet rolls in cartons of six dozen, as one could never tell whether the boat from Port Moresby was going to come on time, or miss a month! Though it didn't happen to us, we heard of one family getting just six rolls with a note: 'What is the matter with you folk out there, have you got diarrhoea or something? Use some apple paper if you run out!' Now there were two problems with that suggestion; we couldn't get apples where we were living, and if we did get any (although they were prohibitively expensive), they were cradled in paper mache like present day egg cartons. Not a very ideal substitute for toilet paper!

The mission decided after a short while that this new manager needed to get out onto a mission station and face the realities of those he was serving. As I was to fly him to a place that wasn't too remote to start with, he overnighted with us. When it got close to bedtime, Elsie asked him whether he would like a cup of tea, coffee or Milo. He said, 'Did you ask if I'd like Milo? That's for invalids and pregnant women!' Elsie, who was getting a tad tired of his patronising, woman's-man attitude, replied rather uncharacteristically, 'Now which of those are you? I'll make you a coffee.' Fortunately for all concerned, after about two weeks spent on a couple of more remote mission stations, he got the message!

Apart from MAF being there, the Air Pacific Christian Mission (now Pioneers) had their general supplies store with a well-equipped workshop and a large freezer room attached. In the workshop was a Lister single-cylinder diesel engine which supplied power to the houses, the store and of course the very large home-made freezer which was big enough to store the freezer supplies for the whole mission for several weeks. Because it had been constructed on the field, it had a number of external pipes, some of which would frost up when the freezer was running.

At Kawito, as she had done at Wasua, Elsie often helped to make up the freezer orders for outstation families. On this occasion, she was helping another mission wife with this task, and the other wife had her young son with her. He saw one of the frosted-up pipes and decided to give it a lick. Yes, you may have guessed it, his tongue got stuck on the pipe. Both the women were amazed at how long a kid's tongue can be when he tried to back off! They had to pour water on the point of contact to release his tongue. Now you have every right not to believe this, but blow me, if he didn't try and give the pipe a second lick, with exactly the same result! I think that even his mum was a little annoyed at what he had done.

As you can imagine, keeping the diesel engine going was very important, especially when a ship had just been in and the freezer was full. One Sunday afternoon we were somehow alerted to the fact that the old Lister engine had died, but worse, the engineer wasn't on the station at the time. Now, just after our family back in New Zealand had bought our 1953 Fordson Major petrol tractor for the farm, Ford brought out a diesel model, and as part of the promotion they had meetings where they showed how you can actually dunk a burning match into diesel. The match goes out just as if it was dunked in water. Diesel needs to be vaporised for it to burn, and they had an injector tester there to show the effect of this.

At Kawito, we all knew that if the old engine didn't get going again, we could lose hundreds, if not thousands of dollars' worth of meat, etc. in the freezer. Equipped with this scant and very elementary knowledge from about 20 years earlier, I took the injector out and cleaned it, found the tester and adjusted the injector to what I thought looked to be about right, and put it back into the engine. Praise the Lord, it came back to life again, saving all the freezer products, as well as giving us all power that night!

The supplies came by smaller coastal boats from Port Moresby roughly every month to six weeks and there was normally a lot to be unloaded at Kawito because it was the mission's main supply base. With only a few families living there, a number of women would canoe down from Aketa Village upstream to help transfer the goods from the bank into the wharf shed. They were fantastic workers. At the end of the day they would get into their skinny little canoe and paddle upstream back to their village. And when I say 'skinny' I really mean it! Whether it was because it was a women's canoe or not, I don't know, but the one in question was so narrow that the women didn't have space to put their feet together on the bottom. It was clearly made for the paddler/s to be standing up all the way.

Once, I happened to be down at the wharf area after a boat had come in and saw about four women take off in one of these canoes which was so small you couldn't possibly sit down in it. There looked to be about a hand's breadth of freeboard on the side of the canoe. And then it happened – the Steamships' coastal boat took off upstream to unload at Awaba. I thought to myself, 'Now this is going to be interesting. How is that skinny little canoe going to stay afloat when the bow wave of the larger boat catches up with them?' I need not have worried, because I was about to see what I think was one of the most skilful exhibitions of group coordination I have ever seen. As the bow wave started to affect the canoe, all the women did exactly the same strokes, first a couple on this side, then one on the other side in absolute unison and the canoe just rocked a bit and then settled down again. I can still visualise this truly amazing sight of the skill and coordination of those women!

Not everyone had the same skill. One afternoon, a senior teacher from Awaba High School needed to come down to Kawito to make a connecting flight to Port Moresby for a meeting. He asked his class who would like to take him down the river by canoe. Several hands went up and he chose some, not realising that a high proportion of them were highlanders who weren't familiar with canoeing. There was an unwritten law amongst lowlanders that if you lost your balance, you would jump overboard and so not upset the rest of the canoe. Sadly, the highlanders either didn't know that rule, or were unwilling to abide by it, and so we felt very sorry for the Australian teacher when he arrived, not only wet through but with water draining out of his briefcase! I guess he would choose a little more carefully after that experience.

In fact, those guys had a good reason not to jump out of the canoe – crocodiles! Yes, there were crocs in the Aramia River, and several were killed by locals who spent many nights hunting them for their skins with powerful torches and a gun. However, there were still enough around to be a disincentive to swim in the river, unless there was a group of people making a lot of noise with much splashing around. The most dangerous time for people to go to the edge of the river was in the evening, especially if the water was glassy and looked dark. In those conditions the croc is the master of the situation, as it can see the person/s plainly, but you can't see them! A person should never, ever go alone, unless it is absolutely necessary in such conditions.

One croc did get caught, killed, dragged up onto the wharf landing road and left there. Sadly, the children of one mission family (not MAF) thought it was a plaything and sat on its back. They wouldn't have survived if it had just been basking there in the sun like crocs are so apt to do!

Some areas had croc farms. One was at Daru, the provincial headquarters, and when I was there once, I saw a 5.6-metre-long 'big fella' that almost filled its enclosure. I also went past another enclosure where there were numerous small crocs, which I would estimate were about 0.5 metres long. As I went past, something must have spooked them and I was absolutely staggered at the speed with which they moved and disappeared. It was, in fact, somewhat frightening!

I have two more croc stories, both of which are true. One involves a government project croc farm at Pangoa on Lake Murray, which is on the western boundary of PNG. When those who were erecting the fences for the proposed farm asked the locals if the fences were high enough, the locals said, 'No, in a really big wet, the water comes up much higher than that.' Probably thinking that they were building to the higher mark, the fences were erected. Old

Keith Dennis, the resident Kiwi missionary on the other side of the lake said that if they had looked carefully, they could have seen much higher marks on the surrounding trees, but obviously they weren't bushmen like he was. A couple of seasons later, there was a really big wet. The water went higher than the fences and many of the young crocs swam out to freedom!

The next story involves an Australian man who was married to a Kiwi. They were moving out to Suki mission station up the Suki River which is a subsidiary of the mighty Fly River where crocs abound. For whatever reason, they hadn't made it to their destination by nightfall, so they camped on the bank of the Suki River. The story goes that during the night, the wife woke up, claiming there was a noise outside their small tent and her husband passed it off, asking her to go back to sleep. Whether she did or not, I don't know, but in the morning, there were the unmistakable tracks of a crocodile which went right around the tent! Obviously, she had heard something!

While we were at Kawito we were really looking forward to a visit from one of Elsie's sisters, Shirley and her family who were serving with the Salvation Army in India. Another sister who had been to London as a Salvation Army representative had already visited, but Elsie hadn't seen Shirley in 10 years, and I had never met that family, so you can imagine how much we were looking forward to them visiting us. They told us not to go out to Port Moresby as they wanted to see us on location. One afternoon, just four days before their planned arrival, I was on the ground at an outstation and got a message from our headquarters in Mt Hagen that the family wouldn't be coming as planned, because Shirley had 'gone to be with Jesus'. I waited until we'd had dinner and the girls were in bed before I broke the devastating news to Elsie.

What a sad time this was as we had all been so looking forward to their arrival. However, for a while before this, Elsie had a feeling that for some unknown reason they weren't going to be able to make it. We hadn't had any communication from her husband Dave until some weeks later, when a bunch of aerogrammes came all together. Dave had faithfully written updates on the situation, but as happened often, they had been delayed in the mail. Shirley had needed an operation to remove a cancerous growth, which was successful, although the whole tumour could not be removed the first time. A few days later, her wound burst, making further surgery necessary. Shirley was too weak to survive.

Shirley had spoken with Dave about her death, feeling it would be a catalyst for something worthwhile spiritually, and so it came about. Her death meant that several local Indian folk came into a saving relationship with Jesus, for which, I have no doubt, she praised the Lord while she was with Him. The Indian folk showed how much they had appreciated Shirley and her ministry amongst them by naming a newly-built Salvation Army hall the 'Shirley Millar Memorial Hall' in her memory. Also, back in New Zealand, more than one person felt the call of God to overseas missionary service because of Shirley's death.

On the day the Port Moresby aircraft was due to bring the Millar family to Kawito, Laurie Darrington, a fellow Kiwi who was based at the capital's airfield, brought flowers he'd been given earlier to Elsie and greeted her with: 'Elsie, I'm so very sorry that I haven't got your sister and family on board today,' and gave her a great big hug. This genuine empathy from Laurie meant so much to Elsie.

A very high proportion of the passengers we flew were fellow missionaries, some with particular skills, like language translation, etc. APCM had a couple who had specialist skills in breaking down a language and creating an alphabet for it. They were based at Lake Kutubu but made themselves available to any area that needed help with a new translation project. I only remember taking them to one area in the Western Province, but I am aware that they did visit several places, including across the border into West Papua. Taken all in all, our time at Kawito serving the various missions and church was most enjoyable and they certainly made us feel as if we were part of their mission family.

One example of this was that we used to go to various mission stations for weekends for a break. I have mentioned going to Mougulu and being so encouraged with the growth of the church there from nothing in quite a short time, but we also went to Pangoa to stay with fellow Kiwis, although they were much older than us. While sitting in a cane chair and talking with Keith Dennis there one evening, with a thunderstorm nearby, I noticed sweat dripping off my elbows because it was so hot and humid. We went once to Tari for an annual break too, where the mission had its hostel for primary-aged children so they could go to school as well. I also remember spending a most enjoyable Christmas one year at Debepari with Barry and Pam Waldeck whom I had got to know quite well as a result of my lunchtime visits. It was also at Debepari that I first saw a pit saw working and felt so sorry for the guy in the pit with all the sawdust raining down on him! So while there was a lot of work done out of Kawito, there were times of enjoyment and relaxation as well.

Chapter 20

To Wapenamanda

In January 1973 after our second 18 months at Kawito we were asked to move to Wapenamanda (WDA) in the highlands to serve the Missouri Synod Lutherans. This worked out well for us as a family as Ann, in the later period at Kawito, had been doing 'school of the air' with the base radio, which was a great help with starting her schooling. This was done using high frequency radio with the teacher based at Rugli (not too far from Mt Hagen) where the Christian Radio Missionary Fellowship (CRMF) was then based. Later CRMF moved to Goroka and then after a time became a part of MAF as MAF Technologies. At Wapenamanda, Ann was able to go each day to a boarding school up the valley at Amapyak that was built primarily for outstation mission children; that is, until some road improvements caused a slip to come down, fully blocking the road.

Flying over this in the course of my work, it was easy to see the reason for the slip occurring. There was a curve in the road that was being modified and to do this, a new sloping cutting into a rather high bank was made on one side. All good, apart from the fact that the new cutting also cut across an old and well-worn path (that reminded me of a sheep track) which, when it rained, acted as a trench to catch and divert all the water from the higher ground above onto one point in the new cutting. The newly cut soil could only take so much of this and once it became saturated, it slumped down onto the road.

As the school was a boarding school, Ann and the others from 'down valley' who were blocked by the slip stayed at the school on weekdays for some time until the problem was fixed. It was the parents' task on Monday to take those from 'down valley' to one side of the slip, piggyback their child across the slip to people who came down from 'up valley' to take them to school. The reverse happened each Friday afternoon. When piggybacking Ann through the slush, I was so grateful that she wasn't too big and heavy!

For some reason, Elsie had promised Ann that we would get her a tin of talcum powder while she was boarding at the school. Sometimes, in a place like PNG, it is one thing to say you are going to do it, and a very different thing to be able to carry it out. Waso (the Lutheran mission's trading store) didn't have anything, so it became my job to see if any of the outstation trade stores had some. I tried quite a few mission stores before finding one that had a tin, much to the rejoicing of all!

During this time, work was being done to clear the slip material, but sadly the grader broke through the old road surface and it became quite a bog. Once it was deemed to be okay to traverse this patch, Elsie took some children up to school in MAF's faithful old VW Kombi. However there was very heavy rain before her return trip and on the way back and even the Kombi couldn't make it up the slight slope. No problem! A whole bunch of willing local workers who had been sheltering under a tree started to push the van, but it started to slip sideways towards a drop-off at the side. Elsie managed to get them to stop before it was too late. But again, no problem! The grader driver was called upon to pull her to safety. But oh, what a scary sight it was for Elsie to see this massive grader belting towards her in reverse and only just stopping a couple of metres in front of the van! A tow rope was produced, but it was rather short and because of this and the different levels of the hitch points, when the grader took off with a hiss and a roar, the front of the van was lifted clean off the ground. It left Elsie helplessly sitting there not being able to steer and totally at the mercy of the grader driver. She was ever so glad to get home that day – and I shared in her gladness when I later heard the tale!

The Wapenamanda Valley was the main base area where the Missouri Synod Lutherans had many of their facilities. We imagined it was like a little bit of America dropped into the valley. There was their hospital complex at Mumbisanda, their high school complex across the river at Pausa, their commercial business and supply centre (Waso) at Wapenamanda, their boarding school for the missionaries' outstation children at Amapyak, another compound at Yaibos and a Bible school at Birip. The only missions operating in this valley were the Lutherans and the Roman Catholics. By PNG standards, the Valley was not massive, being only about 19 kilometres long and 1.6 kilometres wide, but it was very densely populated with about 17,000 people (from memory).

The hospital was very well-equipped, with a few doctors, including one Australian, a radiologist with a laboratory, and a dentist, so we were very well catered for medically. One of the things that Elsie did while we were stationed there was to teach some of the Papuan nurses some sewing skills. This may sound quite easy, but many of the things she taught were entirely new to them, like rocking their feet to power a treadle sewing machine. Sounds simple, but have you ever tried it? I have, and at first I wasn't very successful either. Another skill was learning how to use a pair of scissors. Time and patience were of the essence but they soon got it.

When you consider that in 1973 these people had only had European contact for a little over 25 years and the men were still carrying stone axes in their string belts, you might get the picture of just how far they had come in working with European tools etc. in that limited time. I have often said that the PNG people, given the same opportunities to learn and experience things that we have had, could easily equal or perhaps even excel us. Having said that, though, they would leave us for dead when it came to knowing their way around in the bush!

Between where we lived at Wapenamanda and Pausa where the high school was situated, there was a deep ravine with the medium-sized River Lai at the bottom, which was frequently in flood because of the heavy rainfall that was almost constant in the area. The bridge across this river was a Bailey bridge with some planks on it, which rattled alarmingly as you crossed over it. I had been across there once before the afternoon that Elsie and I were to go to Pausa for the first time and so I suggested to Elsie it would be good if she drove the MAF Kombi across while I was with her, figuring that once she had done it once, she would probably cope with doing it again.

Why the caution? Well, apart from the rather unnerving rattle of the bridge, once you got to the Pausa side, there was a sharp turn on a steep gradient. A little further on up the side of the ravine, there was another very sharp hairpin bend to the right with a metal quarry on the *inside* of the hairpin, making for a drop-off cliff on that side. But that was not all! Just after you got around the hairpin, if you looked in the rear vision mirror, there appeared to be a great void behind you, as you were climbing up the side of the valley. To add to the drama, about 50 metres after rounding the hairpin, the road went over a big slippery 'greasy back' rock, with *no* gravel on it for your tyres to grip on! Elsie said later that if she hadn't been at the wheel that first time, she doubted she would have ever been game to do it by herself later. To her *very* great credit, she not only made that trip once, but many times as she went over to Pausa to help with a preschool group there each week.

As a result of this, Elsie built up a great relationship with the other Lutheran staff and we were invited over there reasonably early in our experience there to a 'bung' (collective/shared) meal. As is often done, they politely invited us as visitors to eat first. There was a slight problem with this, as we were confronted with peas encased in green jelly and shredded carrots in orange jelly. The problem to newbies like us was – is it a vegetable dish or a modified dessert? We decided because of the visible veges, it was probably the former.

Wapenamanda itself was at an elevation of 5,800 feet and with its 1,540-metre tar-sealed runway was the headquarters of the Lutheran mission's commercial arm Waso, where they had established a supply centre the equivalent of a large warehouse. There was also a motor garage and a distribution centre for the many vegetables they had encouraged the locals to grow. During our time there, this was producing enough vegetables to warrant a DC3 coming in once a week and taking a load out to Madang, the coastal town.

The woman who was overseeing the vegetable project noticed that some of the vegetables were going missing after they had been paid for, because those working at Waso had no time for their own gardens. She knew about a cultural custom and used it to the firm's advantage. In that culture, if a woman of child-bearing age (and thus menstruating) was to step over any edible item, no male would eat it, so she made a point for a time of striding about over all the laid-out vegetables. The stealing stopped immediately!

Mavis probably knew this custom because the Lutheran mission had a Brethren anthropologist working with them who had found out a number of things which the average mission person wouldn't know. He had also learnt that a local's garden area was the equivalent to our bedroom, in that a man and his wife would go there to enjoy some intimacy. In this area there were men's houses and separate women's houses; in other places a group would all live together, so having places for intimacy away from the living area made perfect sense! Of course we white skin dummies could have easily and unknowingly just gone to 'have a look' at the garden areas, not knowing their particular cultural significance.

After hearing the many things this chap had found out about the culture of the people and how best to approach them, it completely changed my mind about anthropologists in relation to mission. In fact, I now believe that, ideally, if there are to be expatriate personnel involved, a Christian anthropologist should be the first person to enter a new area or language group, to find out so many things that the average Westerner just doesn't know.

As I mentioned earlier, the Papua New Guineans had come a long way in a short time in getting to grips with our Western culture. They had adapted quickly to things like driving on roads. Mind you, they had no concept of 'enough is enough', especially when it came to the number of people who could be carried on a passenger motor vehicle. The most popular one used in our time was a Toyota Stout which was a small ute (about half a tonne). It had a short wheel base, with the tray weight mid-ships over the rear axle, often making the vehicle dangerously light to steer. One person saw one so heavily loaded with people that the steering only engaged when the front wheels happened to hit the ground! It is little wonder that a few of these left the road.

The story about the Yaibos mission station where we frequently went to church was rather intriguing. When the mission moved into the Wapenamanda Valley, they sought permission from the local clans as to where they could purchase land and build their various complexes. The negotiations for the Yaibos area went extremely smoothly with all the local clans agreeing to the land purchase and building there. It was not until after they had put up a number of buildings and a fight between the same local clans broke out that the mission found out they had bought a traditional fight ground which had been, in effect, no man's land as far as the locals were concerned! There were stories about stray arrows piercing the woven 'pit pit' (pampas) walls during the heat of the battle!

Tribal fighting and the ancient payback system was (and still is) a real problem as the Papuans had long memories. Many lives were lost and village houses burnt down just because someone had, in many cases accidently, injured or killed someone from another tribe or clan. One morning, a well-educated Papuan 'didyman' (agricultural advisor) came and asked me to get him and his family out of the valley immediately. I asked why the urgency and he said that a fellow Papuan had been involved in an accident on the road from Mt Hagen the night before with a local who had been injured, and as he was the only Papuan in the valley, his and his family's lives were in danger. It didn't matter that he had no connection with the Papuan involved in the accident, except that he came from the same part of the country. I naturally took them to Mt Hagen before the rest of the day's work so he could get a commercial flight back to Port Moresby and to his home area.

In my opinion, this concept of payback was to hamper the effectiveness of the PNG police after independence, because why put yourself and your clan at risk by arresting and laying a charge against someone from another clan when there was always the strong possibility of them getting even? This sort of thing naturally didn't affect the Australian police when they were there, and so law and order were kept to a much higher and safer level.

As with all MAF bases then operating in PNG, apart from medical emergencies, work for the mission and church was the top priority as well as moving their personnel from place to place. The next priority was the transporting of goods for the mission and trade stores as well as back-loading product the local people had grown or gathered that could be sold nearer 'civilisation'. For example, Maramuni was an airstrip on the northern side of the central ranges where the Lutheran mission had established a station. They had encouraged the local people to grow chillies – the really hot little red ones. When carrying them in the aircraft, different pilots had very different reactions to them. For some, the sneezing and runny nose started as soon as the pilot got into the aircraft, because of the fine irritating dust that came off the bags of chillies. For me, when they were in the aircraft was no problem, but as soon as I got out into the fresh air at the destination the sneezing and running nose started in earnest and lasted almost uncontrollably for about 10 minutes. We normally flew the chillies over the central ranges to Wabag (18 minutes) where they were taken by road to their sales point.

Once, I took a couple of these little chillies home to Elsie and she put them in a stew. There didn't seem to be any noticeable results, so she took one and bit it. Wow, did it bite back! It was so hot she knew never ever to do that again, although I am aware of one Kiwi SIL member who loves to eat them! Another, much more pleasant sort of back-load was taking tree orchid flowers from Paiela out to the road head at Liagam (15 minutes) for an export market. While I don't know if it ever was an MAF load, it was interesting to see the vast areas of white pyrethrum flowers in the general area of Wabag and Liagam. These flowers are dried and powdered for use in insect sprays, etc.

Each base/programme had its own peculiarities. Wapenamanda's was that it had one airstrip which was like the flat deck of an old-style aircraft carrier (not like the modern ones with a curved-up ramp on the takeoff end). This Paiela airstrip called for a pilot with some expertise and experience. It was reasonably short (487 metres at 6,150 feet elevation), so no help there. The Turbo 206 had a 230 kilogram landing penalty but even with that, it still allowed us to service a family there, moving stuff from the neighbouring Porgera airstrip just seven minutes away. Interestingly, because the terrain between these two airstrips was effectively a mountain ridge, it was cheaper for the Government to hire us to fly a patrol from Porgera to Paiela, than to hire a bunch of local carriers. It was a two-day trek for them, which meant hiring extra carriers for the food they needed on the trip, so the accumulated cost made flying the patrol cheaper. The Paiela strip had a drop-off at each end, but when taking off to the north, once clear of the airstrip, there was about 3,000 feet of airspace directly underneath you, which meant one could dive a little to pick up extra airspeed.

As in most areas in PNG, even people from neighbouring valleys were frequently classed as enemies. In some cases, they spoke the same language but over time they had developed slightly different dialects. I heard of one Porgera chap who had been a very respected and effective fight leader who used to terrorise the Paiela Valley people with frequent raids. After the Apostolic mission in Porgera had presented the gospel of Jesus to him and he accepted Jesus as his Saviour, the first thing he did (which could have been very dangerous!) was to go to the people of the Paiela Valley, ask their forgiveness for his previous actions, and tell them about his faith in Jesus. Such is the power of the Christian gospel being worked out in conversion.

Interestingly, even though there was enmity between different highland tribes, they had a system worked out that allowed designated and defined people to go to another tribe and negotiate with them for young women to move across clans/tribes so that there was not too much inbreeding. Sadly, a system like this hadn't been in place in one area of the North Fly and some of their people had deformities and birth defects.

Different areas used different objects as currency. Some used shells, some salt, but in the Wap area it was pigs and shells. Every so often they would have a pig exchange or 'tae', where pigs were used to pay back previous loans with the equivalent of massively exorbitant interest! Borrowed pigs from relatives and friends were used by a young man as a bride price for a wife whose value was based on how hard she could work in the garden or carry a load. As he accumulated his own pigs, he would pay off his loan at a tae to those from whom he had originally borrowed the bride price. The more pigs an individual owned, the wealthier they were deemed to be. Back in 1973, I know that a breeding sow was valued at 200 kina, when a kina was worth about NZD$1.50, as it was being strongly supported by Australia. In that culture, the number of wives a chap had also gave him status, and on the side of the road you would see stakes driven into the ground showing how many wives that particular land owner had which designated his wealth.

When we knew that we were going to go to serve the Lutherans, I studied a few things I knew they believed. One of the main differences was how they treated the sacrament of Christian Communion (the Eucharist). Being a first-step breakaway from the Roman Catholic Church, they had only slightly modified the belief regarding the elements. Catholics believe that *all* the consecrated bread and wine actually becomes the body and blood of the Lord Jesus during the time of the Communion service. The Lutherans have modified this to believe that only that which is consumed becomes the literal body and blood of Christ. Having come from a background where the elements are symbolic, neither Elsie nor I were happy with those beliefs, so we didn't partake in their Communion celebration.

We attended their services (the alternative at that time was the Roman Catholics), as well as their local Bible studies, especially with some a little further up the valley. That Bible study group was classed as being almost charismatic because we sang *Scripture in Song* choruses which were popular in New Zealand at that time. However, one of these people so wanted to identify with us that she didn't take Communion one Sunday. The next Sunday she missed for a health reason and by the third Sunday she was feeling the spiritual lack of not having taken Communion. We assured her that while we appreciated her wanting to stand with us, we asked her not to do this again just for our sake.

While I don't think it is the Lutherans' official stance, I personally felt that these folks had in some way exchanged the taking of Communion with an understanding of the Holy Spirit being with us and Christ's presence being in us because of that. This was illustrated in a way at one Bible study when we got onto the topic of God's guidance. The leader said that you could only know God's guidance in retrospect by seeing how everything had worked out. I believe this can most assuredly be the case in many instances. However, I questioned that concept and said I wouldn't have been serving them there if I hadn't known God's guidance *before* things happened. It was either at that time or another time that one of the leaders asked us, 'Actually, what breed (denomination) are you?' I'm not sure that stating we were members (at that time) of the Salvation Army fully satisfied him or his question! Despite all of these differences (including a chain-smoking Bible study leader) we had good fellowship with a number of these folk and are still in touch with a couple 50 years later.

I hasten to add here, that recently (2023) we have been receiving emails about the Lutheran pioneers who were there before we were, and their stories indicate they had very much the same concept of guidance as our understanding of it, which is quite different to what we encountered with some.

In June 1974 the PNG programme was short of aircraft, probably because one was south for an engine change and/or major overhaul. To cover this shortage, MAF-AIR Ballarat loaned VH-BVY to the programme, a tad reluctantly as I understand it. I think this was because they had taken this ex-PNG field aircraft and had done it up very nicely with extra instrumentation, and it was effectively 'their baby'. Why it was given to me in the Wapenamanda programme I'll never know, but for the best part of the month of June, it became 'my baby'. It was a good old aircraft and performed well, apart from one thing that was a bit annoying and quite embarrassing!

The emergency location transmitter (ELT) had an extremely super-sensitive setting on its G-switch, so that it would switch on the ELT with the slightest bump. Quite understandably, any pilots reading this will think it was because I was making poor landings. Wrong! I even had it go off when I was taking off on a slightly rough strip. This meant that I had to have one of the two VHF radios permanently tuned to the emergency frequency so I knew when it had activated. When that happened, I had to call Air Radio and tell them that I was okay even though the ELT indicated that I wasn't. The setting may have been alright for a tarmac runway, but it was hopeless for many mission airstrips!

Perhaps I do have an inkling as to why it was given to me on a single pilot programme. Aircraft on such programmes were generally better looked after than on a multi-pilot base, because any particular aircraft is no-one's 'baby' there. Perhaps this next incident will help to explain this. At Kawito, the base aircraft was P2-BVJ and one naturally got to know the various positions for the engine controls for differing circumstances. On this occasion we had been to Wewak as a family and were taking P2-MFB, one of Wewak's multi-pilot based aircraft, back to Kawito, because BVJ needed an engine change. This episode occurred at Tari in the Southern Highlands at an altitude of 5,250 feet. As we came in to land, I felt the position of the mixture control and deemed it to be okay as it was in a similar position to what BVJ's would have been, but on touching down, the fuel mixture proved to be too rich for the altitude and the engine started to die as a result.

When I tried to re-start the engine while still rolling towards the parking bay, the over-rich mixture caught fire and so when we stopped in the parking bay, I told Elsie who had eight-month-old Ann in her arms to get out. She swung her legs out to be greeted by the heat of the flames, but kept going. I had got out my side of the cabin, grabbed the fire extinguisher, opened the oil-flap door and directed the extinguisher into the heart of the fire, which fortunately died quite quickly. After it was out, I had to take the cowls off and check that the fire hadn't burnt anything of consequence.

So what were the contributing factors to this happening? Firstly, the mixture control was adjusted very differently to 'my' aircraft, which was something I hadn't recognised, and this caused the over-rich mixture on landing. But also, when the cowls were off, I saw that as it was a multi-pilot aircraft and so no-one's baby, there was surface oil everywhere, which had caught alight. After a very good inspection and a call to the engineers to get a clearance to proceed, we headed home with some good lessons learnt on the way.

Initially within PNG, the only MAF waterborne aircraft was a Cessna C180 full floatplane which could only land and be anchored on the water at Wewak. It was a bit of a drama doing maintenance work on it, as it was staggeringly easy to drop a spanner, not onto a hangar floor from which it could easily be picked up, but into the briny with the associated wet arms and legs to retrieve it! This aircraft functioned well for the work in the Sepik Basin, where it was relatively easy to refuel and maintain. It was used to visit people at remote lakes and rivers around 30 to 45 minutes away from Wewak. However, the folk at Kapuna Hospital in the Gulf of Papua heard of MAF's waterborne aircraft and asked MAF to go there to help with their clinic patrols which normally took about three weeks by outboard canoe. This was when a lot of Australian aid was pouring into PNG, so the Government was giving Kapuna Hospital an allowance for the fuel used to do these patrols with motorised canoes.

Max Meyers (our chief pilot at the time) set off from the north side of PNG in the floatplane, reckoning on landing on Lake Kutubu just south of the highland ranges to refuel, but – oh dear – when he got to Kutubu, it was completely clouded in and his only choice was to continue on towards Kapuna on top of the low cloud, trusting that his fuel would last until he got there! It would have been a most unpleasant feeling, and I guess he had the fuel 'leaned out' as much as he dared for the rest of the trip. He carried on over the top (30 to 35 minutes) and as frequently happens in the Gulf, the cloud started to break up about the coastline and he managed – just – to get there before he ran out of fuel. Thank you, Lord Jesus!

After that experience by our chief pilot, it wasn't long before a set of amphibious floats were bought and fitted onto a C185, which meant that many landing areas then became possible refuelling points. Whether by design or accident I don't know, but they were a set of Edo amphibious floats which were superb in rivers and lakes where the water doesn't get too roughed up more than about 50 to 100 centimetres. And so it was that while we were stationed at Wapenamanda I was asked to start flying the floatplane. This was quite reasonable and possible, as I already had previous experience in Queenstown before going to the field, and besides, the Hagen pilots who didn't have float experience could cover the work that I would normally be doing out of Wapenamanda.

And so on 17 April 1974 David Grace (the chief pilot since Max Meyers had moved to the Melbourne head office) took me down into the Gulf of Papua to check me out on the many water landing areas in the appropriately designated C185, P2-WET. We spent six days there, doing checks into the many places Kapuna Hospital went to on their medical patrols. Kapuna Hospital was established by two Kiwi doctors married to each other – the late Peter Calvert and his wife Lynn, who at 97 was still there, having received a Queen's award but retired from the medical side of things. They were pioneers in every sense of the word and when necessary, did things differently. (As I re-read and revised this in August 2023, I heard that Lynn has just passed into the presence of her Lord after 64 years of faithful service to the people of the Papuan Gulf area.)

I will always remember the day I met Peter for the first time.

He greeted us with his mouth open on one side and told us the reason was because he had lost a cap off a tooth, so he had glued it back on with Araldite – and was trying not to put pressure on it until it set. And this was in the days before the five-minute Araldite glue came into existence! But the Calverts' hospitality was superb and once one got to know a few things about the place, one recognised what a massive impact they'd had on people's health and faith in the Gulf region.

You are possibly wondering how they were able to have an aircraft moving the nurses from place to place instead of using an outboard canoe which one would expect to be so much cheaper. As mentioned, the hospital was given a fuel allowance for their canoe patrols, so how could the expenses of an aircraft be paid for? It came out of the canoe fuel fund! The reason was that since it is a delta area with many rivers running into the Gulf of Papua and so many of the places visited were on different rivers, what could take a day by canoe getting from one river to the next (via the open sea) could be done in three minutes by an aircraft crossing over the narrow strip of land between the two rivers. Using the floatplane to do the job meant saving a massive amount of time, reducing a three-week village patrol to 10 days, because there were so many short hops between many rivers.

Something that took a little getting used to initially was just how slippery the tidal mud on the banks of the rivers could be. Unlike my experience in the New Zealand fiord, it was quite safe to back the floatplane into the bank and leave it there as the tide went out. When you came back, there was the aircraft facing the water which could be about four metres away. It was simply a case of starting the engine and putting on a bit of power and the floats would slide down through the slippery mud into the water similar a skier on snow.

There were a few things to get used to when staying at Kapuna.

Having an outside long-drop toilet wasn't too strange, but having a hen come and sit on the end of your bed in the morning was a bit different! This was possible because all the window shutters were always open to try and keep the house cool, except when they were shut in a storm to keep the rain out. However, there were also the young roosters which, with their immature voices, would start the day a lot earlier than was necessary and while their roost was in a tree at the other end of the house, I never ever appreciated their raucous wakeup call!

Like all the bush mission stations in that period, power was provided in the evenings and for the hospital in times of emergency by a faithful old single-cylinder Lister diesel engine which would 'pop, pop, pop' away with its regular mechanical rhythm when running. Cooking was done on a coal range, fired by wood as at Wasua, and bread was made regularly. Toast was often made by cutting slices off a newly-made loaf and then laying them on the top of the stove. Sadly, if the bread was a bit too new (or even a tad soggy), the resulting toast was a test as to how good your teeth and jaw muscles were. Perhaps this had been Peter's tooth cap problem? I don't remember that it was ever revealed under what circumstances his cap gave way.

As many of you probably know, pawpaw (sometimes called papaya) has a laxative effect. When we were at Wewak, we often used to get them from what we regarded as the 'Garden of Eden' altitude of 2,500 feet. The pawpaws which came from one Baptist mission station at that altitude were really sought after. When pilots went into Telefomin (75 minutes) they would often purchase them at Myanmin and bring them back, much to the delight of the folk at Wewak. Because they weren't overly plentiful, one's constitution could cope okay with the relatively small amounts eaten, with minimal laxative effect. However, not having a plentiful supply of pawpaw wasn't the case at Kapuna. There was an endless supply and while the locals had gotten used them as part of their regular diet, that was not the case for 'imports' to the locality like a pilot from the highlands where we didn't get them very often at all. One had to monitor the intake of the said pawpaw if you didn't want to do a number of quick midnight sorties to the long-drop out the back!

A rather interesting fact about bringing the pawpaws down from altitude was that they had to be punctured with a stick or ball point pen so as to equalise the air pressure inside the pawpaw with the greater external pressure as the descent progressed. If this wasn't done, the inside of the pawpaw turned to mush because of the increased outside air pressure. How that worked, I don't know, but that is what happened.

When flying the Kapuna nurses on their health patrols, lunch was always supplied, even if, as happened on one occasion, it was a packet of cracker biscuits and a tin of bully beef. On another occasion, I must have missed picking up my lunch and I resorted to trying to swallow some locally prepared sago. Now when we white skins think of sago, I guess we invariably think of the miniature balls that become clear when cooked, which are absolutely delicious. However, while sago was a staple diet for many on the south coast of PNG, they didn't prepare it like that at all. After the women have processed it from the pith in the trunk of the sago palm, raw sago is very much like wet flour in consistency and is very heavy. A 'log' of sago about 45 centimetres long and around 20 centimetres in diameter weighed about 18 to 20 kilograms, from memory. We often used to carry these sago 'logs' to hospitals for relatives or friends who were there. Sometimes it was packed in what had been 20-kilogram rice bags, but the sago was about three times that weight.

Where Kapuna was located on the south coast, the normal method of preparing sago would be to roll an amount of raw sago 'powder' in some banana leaves and cook it over an open fire. It would come out from this process very much like a long stick, which was quite hard on the outside but soft and could be gooey in the middle. If that wasn't the norm, it was what the stick was like that was offered to me. I have to confess that to my palate it was tasteless and pretty hard to get down without a lot of liquid to drink. Interestingly, sticks of sago were an important part of a marriage ceremony on the south coast, at least in the Wasua area. The bride would cook a stick of sago and give it to the groom who would break it in half and give half back to his bride (the equivalent of us exchanging wedding rings), and so the marriage was sealed.

This is not to say that the raw sago couldn't be made into something very delicious! When at Kawito, Elsie often used it as a substitute for toast, by mixing sago with some grated coconut and a little salt and frying it in a pan like a pancake. It was delicious, to the extent that we missed it and had withdrawal symptoms regarding it when we came back to New Zealand!

Those on the north side of the main divide prepared sago quite differently, by mixing water with the wet flour sago and cooking it in a pot until it had become opaque and glutinous, similar in appearance to the little sago balls that we are used to. I don't know how they ate it once it got to that state.

I think that most pilots flying out of Kapuna used to try and help the nurses from the hospital when out on the medical patrols. What we could do medically was quite limited, but it didn't take much instruction to paint an area with gentian violet. Many times these patrols were to solitary villages up little rivers where there didn't appear to be much distance between the wingtips and the trees on the banks, but one soon got used to that. Also it was surprising how soon one gained the confidence to 'walk the plank' as it were, on a single, wet, slippery, floating log which was the means of getting from terra firma out to the floatplane, sometimes carrying a suitcase of medical supplies. It is also amazing the negative affect that a wire strung quite high above a river between the banks had. (I imagine it was a type of flying fox to send goods from one side of the river to the other, but I'm not really sure. It certainly wasn't a power line or a telephone line.) I can still remember once having to take off in this situation. I needn't have concerned myself as the aircraft was hardly on the step by the time I got underneath the wire, but I still felt quite uneasy and was glad to get airborne well beyond it.

It was a tad nerve-racking when David Grace was checking me into one place on the lower reaches of the Erave River when it was in flood. Landing was no problem as there was plenty of length to land in the clear, but to take off in a clear departure area, one had to taxi upstream from the village into a narrower portion of the river and turn around to take off heading downstream. Now, when the river wasn't in flood, this might have been a fairly simple task, but when in flood, the swiftness of the river came into play. The floats have small rudders at the rear which are quite efficient when at slow speeds, but not sufficiently effective when turning across the strong flow of the river. I remember hugging as close as possible to the right-hand side, and initiating the turn with full left rudder and a burst of power to try and maximise the turn effect. We did eventually get turned around, but because the river was flowing so fast, we were carried downstream for 60 to 90 metres or more before the turn was completed. I was glad when we were airborne again!

Another time I felt uneasy was when I was operating out of Kapuna by myself and was asked to go to a particular Island on the coast, called Goaribari Island. Some years previously, when taking a new missionary from Port Moresby around the coast to Awaba (three hours), I apparently gave him a lot of concern as we passed over this island. Having (at that time) recently come off the tourist work in Queenstown where we were encouraged to point out places of interest, I said to him, 'See that Island down there? That is where a young Scot and botanist explorer, Rev James Chalmers of the London Missionary Society, was murdered with his party in 1901.' From my perspective, I was passing on a bit of history and never realised that, sadly, those comments stayed with the poor chap for many years. Well, now it became my turn! I was asked to go to this island to deliver some medical supplies and I can distinctly remember thinking to myself, 'I hope those guys have changed their minds about white foreigners!' Thankfully, I needn't have worried.

Some time later, there was an opportunity for MAF to open up a ministry in the then British Solomon Islands. This was first investigated with a twin-engine Piper land plane, but it became obvious that a floatplane would be much more useful and viable, so the C185 on the Edo amphibious floats was deployed there. In PNG, MAF then bought a U206 on a set of PK-made amphibious floats. I don't know why the brands were switched, but I have a suspicion that the comparative prices may have come into it. We really hadn't realised, because we had had no comparison, just how much better the Edos were for the work we were doing in PNG. The Edo floats had two curved 'gull wing' surfaces between the central keel and the chine (the bottom outside edge) which effectively acted as a two planing step levels. This made getting up on the step and taking off much easier than with the PKs. The PKs were essentially just a straight 'V' from keel to chine and by comparison on relatively smooth water it was like trying to fly off the surface of thick grease. In an attempt to improve the performance, on 9 September 1977 we tried altering the set-up angle between the aircraft's horizontal line and the floats, but that didn't make any real difference. In fact the more we diverged from the original angle, the worse it got, so we went back to the original set-up and stuck with that for several years.

We didn't know of a way to improve the takeoff until much later when I saw in the PNG *Post Courier* which, by our standards, was not much more than a 'local rag', an article about a new design of a boat in the UK, which they were able to water-ski behind when it was only powered by a 35-horsepower outboard motor. The idea was simple and vaguely similar to the Edos. The boat, instead of being the traditional shape, was slab-sided vertically. Between the central keel and the outside edge of the boat on each side was a gently curved convex surface and the bow was designed to create spray or foam. The foam was caught under the two convex surfaces and so when the boat was moving fast, it was essentially floating on a cushion of air bubbles.

One thing that the PK floats could do very effectively was create a lot of spay. I mentally saw a connection and when flying that plane next, I took note of the place where the spray went out past the chine. I then asked the engineers if they would please put keepers on the chines from a little before that point rearwards, which they agreed to do. Sadly for me, I never got to fly the floats with that modification because I had to come back to New Zealand to have a gallbladder operation in 1979. However another pilot who did, estimated that it reduced the takeoff distance by about a third, which was a very significant amount. By the time I got back to PNG from my op, that pilot had left for furlough, and the aircraft, which by then had been put back onto wheels, had had an accident and the floatplane as such was no more.

Having mildly condemned the PKs I will say this in their favour – they had a much wider and flatter upper surface which was easier to walk around on and so one felt more secure when walking on them. This was fairly significant for someone like me who couldn't swim! It was a relief to get back onto them the only time I remember slipping off them. But the major difference I found was once when I had to take off in open water which was really choppy with 45 cm deep waves. There they excelled and handled that sort of water very much better than the Edos would have. So I guess the lesson here is 'horses for courses' or in other words, buy floats according to the type of water you are going to be mainly flying off.

At times I had to anchor in a main stream and let the local villagers come with their canoes and get the nurses or supplies off of the aircraft. We had a couple of very differently designed anchors which we used. One was very like the shape of a miniature double-sided plough, which was good for the soft mud that was on the bottom of most of the rivers. The other was similar to four large fishhooks welded together and made from 9- to 12-millimetre round steel. On one occasion, just after I had welded up one of the latter, I needed to anchor in a big tidal stream close to its mouth while delivering supplies to a village up a shallow tributary on one side. All went well until I went to lift the anchor! By this time, the tide was running in up the main stream and there was also a strong wind behind it, so the floatplane was facing towards the coast. Try as I would, I couldn't lift the anchor against these forces which were working against me. Whether the spike anchor had got stuck on a submerged log or similar, I don't know, but one thing I did know was that I wasn't going to spend the night there, as it was late in the afternoon already. I didn't have a knife to cut the rope, so there was only one thing for it – start the engine and put on sufficient power to snap the rope! It worked, after the front of the floats buried and then popped out again.

Several years later when I was chief pilot, a Civil Aviation inspector came to check me out on the U206 amphibious floatplane, but he didn't have a floatplane rating himself, so I had to check him out first and give him a rating on it so he could then check me out! The aircraft was at that time positioned at Mt Hagen and there was reason to move it to Wewak (75 minutes), so we loaded a refrigerator into it (which was a full load for it in the highlands with two pilots) and set off. The U206 on PK floats had a rather different takeoff to any other land aircraft, in that just after lifting the front wheels off in the rotation, it would quite suddenly pitch up quite badly, and one needed to reverse the control column very quickly to maintain a smooth take off. I rather unscientifically put it down to the extra surface of the underside of the floats being exposed to the oncoming air, and the extra lift created by the floats' upper surfaces. I had briefed the inspector about this, and he had coped with the takeoff very well. Just after we were airborne, he said to me, 'The takeoff is rather exhilarating, isn't it?'

But the best was yet to be! Just after we had got through the Yuat Gap, I decided that it would be good for him to know about the alternate fuel system which all MAF aircraft were equipped with at that time. It was a means of providing fuel to the engine rather crudely (but effectively), should anything happen to the normal fuel system. As we were at about full throttle height (you have to open the throttle more as you gain altitude), I started the demonstration by leaning off the normal system and opening up the alternate system, only to find that it hadn't been adjusted correctly and, with a splutter, the engine started to die. Some very quick readjustment got it running smoothly again but when we got on the ground at Wewak, this was rectified smartly.

This was one problem with having the main engineering base at Mt Hagen. It was at 5,350 feet, so you couldn't adjust anything accurately to sea level full power. When based at Kawito (with chief engineer maintenance approval), I had to do a number of readjustments on new engines to get optimum sea level performance, e.g. adjusting the engine/propellers constant speed unit to get the correct revs at sea level full power.

But back to the check-out with the CAA chap. After the readjustment, we did some landings and takeoffs on various rivers and lakes in the lower Sepik region quite successfully. On one, he did a very low-level right-hand turn after takeoff. Not knowing whether he was testing me at this point, I said, 'You know you shouldn't be turning so low and should be turning to your left, don't you?' (Under normal circumstances, you shouldn't make a turn until you reach 500 feet and it is normal to turn left.) His reply? That lake wasn't an authorised landing area, so those rules don't apply! Okay, I hadn't realised that. He then proceeded to tell me he had been flying RAAF Caribous in Vietnam, where they frequently needed to take off and turn *below and within* the arc of artillery covering fire! And he thought the takeoff at Hagen was exhilarating?!

Prior to 1973, the MAF conferences had been held biennially at the main base at Wewak where folk were billeted with other families. Because they were only held every second year, it was quite possible for a staff member to miss one because of furlough which meant that some didn't get to meet their peers for four years or so. But the organisation was growing, and the main base had been moved up to Mt Hagen in the highlands. Where to hold a conference now? I can't remember whether it was offered or what, but it was decided that we would make use of the Lutheran boarding school at Amapyak, just up the valley from where we were based at Wapenamanda, so Elsie and I had the privilege of getting all the arrangements sorted out. One of the items we needed were some cots, if they were available, from the Lutheran mission folk, so I put up a notice on the public notice board at the Waso entrance. To add a bit of humour, I put in brackets underneath the request: 'We're quite a prolific lot', underneath which someone else with an equal sense of humour wrote, 'Suggest night flying!' We got enough cots and the whole conference went off really well.

Once, while based at Wapenamanda, I ended up at Kandep (7,200 feet elevation) because of poor weather, only to find a couple of Civil Aviation Authority inspectors there also, who were flying a much faster aircraft than I was. The Kiwi missionary there very hospitably took us all back to the mission house for afternoon tea which was appreciated by everyone. However, I think in an attempt to glorify the MAF pilots, he started to tell stories, which were somewhat exaggerated, like a fisherman's tall tales. All the time, I was endeavouring to catch his eye and mouth 'No' because of the CAA guys!

As almost always happens with the weather in PNG, the big, high afternoon clouds almost completely rained out, leaving the surrounding mountains in the clear, so later in the afternoon I took off to head home to Wapenamanda which was only about 12 minutes away. The CAA chaps asked me to send back a weather report as they were heading for Madang on the northeast coast which was in the same general direction. Up to a certain point it was quite clear and fortunately for me, I was able to pick up certain landmarks through cloud breaks when over the top of the Wap Valley and I returned home without any drama. Knowing these chaps were instrument rated and flying an instrument-capable aircraft, I reported that the weather was initially clear with quite a lot of cloud in the Wap Valley, but it looked as if they could get out to Madang on top of any cloud without any problem. I found out when I met them again later, that they didn't pursue the idea of proceeding and acknowledged the fact that: 'You guys get to know your pea patch in such a way that it is safe for you, but not for others.' Phew, thank you Lord that they took that attitude!

It was during the time we were based at Wap that my dear Mum died back in New Zealand. While today, PNG has one of the most up-to-date telephone systems in the world, back then it was virtually non-existent. So Mum had died and was buried by the time I got to know of it, as the message had passed through a number of hands before I got it. I was told about it while I was at the cargo shed so I walked back down to the house to tell Elsie. It was alongside a large clump of bamboo that I felt a new revelation come to me, though I don't know whether it is theologically sound or not! I felt that my mother was now a sister in Christ rather than a mother. To me, it didn't depreciate one little bit all Mum had done for me, but rather I felt it gave us a new, mature, spiritual relationship through our mutual Saviour Jesus Christ.

It was also while we were at Wapenamanda that the Mt Hagen programme was plagued for a period with someone tampering with our aircraft until such time as we had an accident that damaged an aircraft.

I will recount the events as I am aware of them, and you make up your mind whether you think there could be any sinister connotation. There was a commercial aircraft operator on Mt Hagen airfield that I'll call 'XX' which treated us as opposition, even though we were primarily serving a totally different clientele. Yes, there were times when we picked up commercial customers, as we were licensed and allowed to do, but we adhered strictly to the licence requirement that we only did so one hour *after* the other operator's scheduled departure time for any particular location. Their antagonism may have arisen because they were so often so far behind their schedule that we had legally picked up a passenger.

Sadly for all, that other operator had a series of accidents. I can't be sure but as I remember it, they were at a time of year when there was a change of weather pattern because of the inter-tropical front moving over the country, as it does twice a year when the sun is overhead. Civil aviation naturally came to visit them to see what the problem was. After some discussion, the inspector came up to our hangar and in effect asked, 'How come XX operator is having accidents, but you guys aren't?' One of our senior pilots offered the suggestion that MAF did a thorough check-out of all our pilots. Whether the CAA Inspector was undiplomatic enough to go back to XX and say this or not, we obviously don't know, but the deadly messing with our aircraft started after that time.

As far as the lack of adequate check-outs by XX was concerned,

I personally know of a couple of glaring examples which confirm this. Once, a new pilot was rubbished by a senior pilot at Mt Hagen for not 'getting through' to a destination in poor weather when that senior base pilot did it a little later. The other was when a pilot from a lowland base was so poorly checked that he had a medical condition every morning he was scheduled to do a run into the highlands from the lowlands, because he wasn't confident of where he was going in the destination area.

While it was only in retrospect that we dropped to the idea, the first unusual thing that occurred was an engine fire, caused because of a leaking fuel line. We naturally thought that an engineer hadn't tightened a junction nut sufficiently. However, God overruled, and the pilot was able to put the aircraft down successfully on an airstrip which was roughly on track for the route he was taking. The next event was after a flight from Mt Hagen to Telefomin (90 minutes). When the pilot turned the ignition off, instead of the propeller rotating one or two times as the engine wound down which is normal, it came to a sudden stop. The pilot wisely took a note of this and called for an engineer to investigate, who, when he pulled the dipstick out, found it smelt strongly of battery acid, which it was later confirmed to have been contaminated with. The next problem was when this same pilot (though he wasn't actually rostered to do that flight, the GM was) was flying from Mt Hagen to the Western Province (85 minutes) and the engine started to vibrate violently. Then the propeller came off and flew into the bushes just as he was successfully doing a forced landing on a sandbar in the Kikori River. The nuts holding the propeller on had been loosened, not with a socket or ring spanner but with an open-ended spanner, as was evidenced by the marks on a stray nut that had miraculously become lodged within the cowls.

The final event was when a mate of mine took off with a passenger from Mt Hagen heading for Wewak (75 minutes). He hadn't gone very far when the motor seized completely, so he turned around and tried to glide back to the airport. Sadly, he couldn't stretch the glide far enough and came down in some tall grass on soft ground a bit short of the runway. The aircraft flipped onto its back and he and the passenger walked away, though the undoing of the seat belts with double shoulder harness wasn't easy when they were hanging upside down! In this instance, some hard plastic had been pushed down the oil-filler tube which had melted when the engine got hot and so completely sealed off the oil pump filter, starving the engine of lubrication. With all the forced landings, not one person was injured. Thank you, Lord! After this accident, things got back to normal. You can draw your own conclusions.

However, it was great to hear a compliment from the pilot of a heavier commercial aircraft that was in the Mt Hagen area at the time, listening to my mate's mayday call. He said, 'I have never heard anyone so calm and in control when facing such a dire situation.' That, I feel, was not only a compliment to my mate, but also a witness to those who heard it of Christ's presence with him in the circumstance. Other operators were aware that all of us MAF-ers were Christians. Yet another operator's pilot was doing work for an oil exploration company and asked the missionary at Mt Bosavi if he would send him a weather report. The missionary said, 'Yeah, no problem, I can tell you what I'd tell the MAF chaps.' The commercial pilot said, 'Oh, you'll have to do a bit better than that, as they have someone special flying with them.' We acknowledge that the Holy Spirit of Christ was, and is with us and we are very thankful for it!

Looking at my logbook, the first week of December 1973 was quite busy in the A185 MFX, probably moving teachers back home to their village or families on holidays, as each day included moving from the highlands back down into the Western Province and back. In the space of just four days, I clocked up 23.10 hours flying, combined with 74 landings and takeoffs. Thank the Lord for the stamina to do this, for if you consider the extra 25 minutes for each landing (at the least), it comes to a good number of hours spent on the job that week.

Some Papuans become very close and protective of you when you are on a single pilot base. At Wapenamanda we took on a young chap, Yalis, as a combined cargo handler and house boy ('haus boi' in Melanesian Pidgin) from those who had been there before us. He was a good chap and became quite protective of 'the missus bilong mi' – Elsie. This was demonstrated to us in a couple of incidents. Firstly, when I was away flying the floatplane, he used to come over each night before he went to bed and walk around our place to make sure all was in order. In the second instance, he heard there was a 'long-long' man hanging around, so he slept in the outside laundry that night to make sure Elsie and the girls were kept safe. The term 'long-long' described a person who was mentally unstable for whatever reason. I personally think that in some cases they were in that condition because of being possessed by an evil spirit, and the average local was very much in fear of them because some of them seemed to gain extra strength when in that condition. To us, this incident showed the depth of commitment of Yalis, who took the name of Kati when he became a Christian. I have no doubt at all that other people could tell similar stories about their house help of whatever gender.

As we were to go on our second furlough at the end of June 1974, I had the pleasure of checking out my replacement pilot into the area. It all went very well for both of us. The only incident that I very clearly remember was one in which he didn't really feature too much. We had been to Kopiago and had been asked to take a pig (all trussed up) with us to our next stop at Liagam (about 30 minutes). We were assured that there would be someone there to take possession of it. All went well until I made the terrible mistake of opening the pod door *before* asking where the person was who was going to take possession of the pig. Out came the pig, which had managed to un-truss itself on the 30-minute flight.

I grabbed the thin plaited rope that was attached to one of the pig's legs, while the new pilot jumped onto the aircraft's wheel to get well clear of the drama. So, there I was like a ringmaster asking the gathered crowd whose pig it was, while the pig ran from one extension of the rope to the other. With nothing but a stony silence from the crowd, what were we to do? The pig made up my mind for me, as just before I let it go, it jumped up and slid its open mouth down my bare lower arm. Thankfully, it didn't break any skin anywhere, but that was enough as far as I was concerned. The last we saw of the pig, it was headed north across the airstrip into the Central Ranges with the rope still attached.

Chapter 21

Our Second Furlough

We left Wapenamanda at the end of June 1974 to head home for our second furlough, which was again six months long. Once again, a caravan was our 'home' for the most of the time, but this time it was a reasonably modern two-axled one with a bit more space for us all. We were most grateful to one of Elsie's sisters and her husband for allowing us to park it near their back door so we could use all their facilities. The one time I did tow it to another location – to Elsie's sister's place out in the country – I was surprised at how much heavier and harder it was to tow than a single-axled van. Of course, once again, the towing vehicle was a Hillman Super Minx! We had a break and then took a good number of meetings. On our first furlough, we had the distinct impression that many people had put us on a pedestal purely because we had gone to PNG. In my preaching, I endeavoured to correct that idea by using Romans 12:2 to point out that it all depends on what God has called any individual to do. The thing is, have people sought to know God's will for them, or are they just doing what they like doing?

Now that Ann and Gwen were of school age, they attended the local Foxton primary school. While this was a positive experience for the most part, sadly one of them was once called a 'rudey' by the Kiwi kids when asked what the children in PNG wore. They answered, 'Sometimes nothing,' which of course was true, but unbelievable for the Kiwi kids to imagine, hence the name-calling. Thankfully, one of the teachers was wise enough to realise that what our girls had said was true, and they needed to be backed up in order to clear the air. The teacher asked me to go to the school and show the class some photos which showed the PNG culture and the lack of dress worn by many PNG children. This was enlightening for the school class and there were no more rude remarks afterwards that I am aware of.

Once again, this furlough included a good deal of deputation work, but often just one of us would be involved so the other could keep company with the girls as they were still quite young. It didn't involve towing a caravan everywhere as we had parked up at Nancy's place, but we still got to move around a fair bit. Once again, we benefited from Doug Mawson of Dargaville's sale of a car to MAF for us to use. He always bought it back so it didn't cost MAF much, if anything, as long as there were no mechanical repairs.

As we were based at Foxton, we did quite a lot of our deputation in the lower North Island. MAF had an extremely keen representative at Havelock North who would get us into school assemblies, old people's homes and many churches – all over a long weekend for us. I remember making up a crude screen for one of the rest homes where there were no facilities, so I could project the slides from the rear.

One thing quickly stood out from our visits to churches of many different denominations – some churches were vague about who their missionaries were and where they were stationed. They often said, 'Yes, we have a missionary up there in PNG somewhere, but I'm not sure just where they are.' The one startling exception was the Open Brethren (now often called a Community Church), who would ask, 'How is so and so who is stationed at XX doing?' Their financial generosity to MAF was equally different. From our experience, the mission fields of the world would be much poorer, both in personnel and financially if it weren't for the Open Brethren folk.

While this next incident could be taken as critical of at least one

Open Brethren assembly, it is certainly not meant to be, as I am just stating some facts. Elsie and I were in the Hawkes Bay. I had just had a cold and we had already had about 12 speaking engagements by the time we got to this particular Open Brethren assembly on a Saturday evening. We were staying with the local MAF representative who could hear that my voice was failing to the point where I couldn't do much more than whisper. This isn't much good when addressing a large group of people, so we decided Elsie would show the slides which had a tape-recorded commentary with them. However, this meant she would also have to answer any questions.

The rep said we'd better check this out, as that particular assembly was very traditional and might not want a woman speaking to them. So he rang an elder he knew who said, 'Well, okay, it isn't as though she will be teaching us is it?' Hurdle one jumped through! But Elsie didn't have a hat, which would have been a problem at this place, so the rep's wife dug around for a couple of old hats that looked respectable, one for Elsie and one for herself to wear as she was also coming to the meeting. Hurdle two satisfied! The meeting went quite well, with the rep doing a bit of an introduction about MAF and then the slide show.

Then came the tricky bit – the questions! There were two young fellows, both in aviation, who got a bit technical with their questions and Elsie was ever so glad that she had absorbed some of the 'pilot speak' that always occurred when she was hosting another pilot for a meal. There were times she looked quizzically at me to make sure what she had said was correct, but rarely did I need to squeak out a correction in reply. And then the breakthrough came! An elder said, 'How about telling us about yourself and what you do?' Wow, what a wonderful relief for Elsie; she was now accepted and felt much freer for it. Taken all in all, it was a great experience for us both, and I was so proud of Elsie that she was able to answer so many awkward flying and engineering questions the way she did.

This was yet another example of what I have said so many times at deputation meetings: 'I couldn't have done half of the amount of work in PNG that I was able to do, if it wasn't for the fact that Elsie stood alongside me and helped me in so many different ways.'

A couple of other memorable things happened on this furlough. As already mentioned, my mother had died while we were based at Wapenamanda and the estate was able to pay out my portion of her will. We had been busy with deputation and keeping an eye on the local newspaper for any reasonably-priced house in Palmerston North. We settled on that city because Elsie's folk had already lost a daughter on missionary service with the Salvation Army in India, and I felt that we should settle within a reasonable distance from their home in Foxton. Palmerston North was the closest city where I thought I could probably get employment when we finally came home to stay, and there was the talk then that a new, large engineering industry was going to establish there, although it never did.

When I think about it now, I can't believe how naive I was to think that we could look for a house, buy it, and successfully rent it out in less than three weeks! But God was most definitely with us. One Saturday night on the last weekend of our deputation period, I saw a house advertised in Palmerston North and I said to Elsie, 'Either there is something wrong with this place, or it is a relative snip.' First thing on Monday morning we were at the agents, looked at it, paid the deposit and it was all go from then on. Sadly, the house was for sale because of a marriage breakup but it was a godsend for us. I can't remember whether it was in answer to an advert for accommodation or by word of mouth, but within days we had a young American couple who were doing research at Massey University signed up to rent the house. They were prepared to pay more if we provided a refrigerator and a freezer, so we bought one of each. When the wife, who was the daughter of a United States Air Force person who had been continually shifting, heard our story and that we were shortly going to be leaving for PNG, she couldn't imagine us departing without at least having a meal there, so she graciously invited Elsie and me for an evening meal. They stayed there for at least three years, maybe more, and really cared for it. Mind you, we were extremely grateful to one of Elsie's high school friends and her husband for looking after the place on our behalf, treating it as a ministry to do so. They worshipped with the Open Brethren chapel in Palmerston North, where the place became known as 'the mission house'. It was empty for only about a week over the seven years they were looking after it for us. Thank you Blanche and Ray!

Each furlough we always asked God to reconfirm our calling about going back to PNG with MAF to continue to work there. God is so good, and Elsie is so wise. As Elsie was aware that we were reckoning on buying a house on this furlough, she had confirmation from God quite early on that we should return to PNG. She put it down to the fact that it gave her a real peace about leaving our newly purchased home instead of settling down into it. In her wisdom, she never told me about her feelings until I too had received the confirmation I needed from God. At various times it was from Scripture, or it was something said in a sermon or message, or a daily reading; yet another time, it was the words of a song, but in each instance it would come with an undeniable clarity. The key to it was, of course, that we had asked God for confirmation, expected it, and were really listening for it with a willingness to do whatever God wanted us to do.

After buying the house in Palmerston North, we were to go to my parents' place just north of Auckland but on the way through, we called in at MAF's medical advisor in Manurewa because Ann had sadly picked up a very bad cough due to the much colder New Zealand weather. He immediately prescribed Bactrim which, even though it was after hours, I was able to get from our chemist friend

Nev Bradley at Whangaparāoa. The transformation was staggering! Praise the Lord! Within two days we could tell things were coming right, but would she be okay to fly out of New Zealand in less than a week? We committed it to God and in faith booked all of us out on the appointed day. By then she was so much better that we had no qualms about taking her on the international flights.

Chapter 22

Our Third Term at Mt Hagen

And so it was that on 17 January 1975 we arrived back in PNG but this time to Mt Hagen in the highlands, only about 13 minutes flying from Wapenamanda where we had been before furlough. The flying work out of Mt Hagen was the same as other bases we had worked on, with a couple of differences for me. I was to be the base manager, which at that time involved caring for and maintaining all the houses and making sure that everything was running smoothly. I didn't have to do the physical and practical work myself, but had a European with a team of Papuans who could do that. I was also a line pilot with check and training responsibilities and at times filled in doing the flight programming.

I am well aware that one change I made as base manager didn't get a tick of approval from everyone. To understand my reasoning for the change, you have to know that for a good percentage of the year, the Mt Hagen airfield was often clear very early in the morning and then came under low cloud at about 8:30am to 8:45am. This meant that if pilots didn't get away before the low cloud came down further, they had to wait around for the sun to burn it off enough for the control tower to open the airfield again, which could be about 9:00am to 9:30am.

It had been the practice for everyone to have morning devotions when we all arrived at about 8:00am. These often lasted until 8:40am, which meant that by the time the aircraft were loaded after that, the airfield was often under a blanket of low cloud and the pilots couldn't get going. However, if the pilots and cargo handlers got going at 8.00am, we could generally get started with our flying programme before the airfield closed, as the control tower was most helpful in letting us out to head for the Baiyer Gap where we could see the sun was shining in the Baiyer Valley beyond. Yes, it did mean that there was a disruption for all the ground staff, engineers, office workers and cargo handlers who then stopped at 9.00am to have devotions, but they didn't have to battle with the ugly highlands weather like we pilots did in the afternoon because of having a late start to the day.

This system worked well until a poorly checked-out pilot (belonging to the previously mentioned 'XX' firm) who certainly didn't know the lie of the land around the Mt. Hagen airfield came in from Wewak one typical morning. To the south of the field, there is a 600-acre tea plantation which was at times reasonably clear as it is towards the head of a valley, and could well be affected by katabatic winds. (Katabatic breezes happen when colder, heavy air sinks and flows down a valley.) The tower told the pilot to approach from there, but instead he must have seen a break over the town, and let down there, scaring himself silly as a result. The trouble with this was that the town is several metres higher than the airfield, and so he found himself in the low-cloud band. As a result, he 225'd the tower. (A CAA 225 report is one that reports a dangerous situation to the Civil Aviation Authorities.) As a result, the tower was told to work to the regulations, and it meant that our early starts were curtailed for quite a period until the chaps in the tower gradually eased back again to the more reasonable and sensible way of operating.

I wrote to CAA about this situation, pointing out that the Lae instrument chart allowed for a visual approach from a much lower cloud base than what the tower had been using. They came back to me with what I considered was an absolutely daft reason for their limitations. They said that because the Mt Hagen airfield was above

5,000 feet elevation, it was subject to the same cloud clearances as any aircraft flying above 5,000 feet in clear air! This, in my opinion, was the sort of response you'd get from someone who wasn't prepared to think a situation through.

We had been allocated house number three on 'holy row' near the Mt Hagen airport at Kagamuga – not the official name for the little stub road, but as the four houses on one side were all occupied by Christians, it got that title locally. There were three MAF houses and the one at the end was occupied by the airfield Mobil agent who at that time was also a Christian. The other side of the road wasn't so 'holy' though, as it was the local tavern from which emanated much noise most of the time we were awake, and sometimes when we were supposed to be asleep! For security's sake, we had high netting fences with barbed and razor wire along the top, so the wives who were at home with small children during the day while husbands were away flying or engineering had some sense of safety.

We were now right next door to the house we had occupied at Kagamuga when we were at Mt Hagen the first time. However, between houses two and three, someone had at sometime earlier planted a row of eucalyptus trees. We hadn't done it, and in fact I don't remember them there when we were based there previously. With the wonderful growing conditions in PNG, all of them had grown quite tall, so much so, that they had got to the stage when they really needed to be cut down, and as I was base manager, it was my job to organise getting it done! But they were *between* two houses, which I would estimate from memory were only about 15m apart, so how could it be done? At that time, there was an old Aussie bushman working in the APCM sawmill at either Tari or Dauli High School in the Tari Valley. I approached him to see if he would do the job. He came out to the base and, one breezeless morning, dropped all of the trees. I was away flying but when I came home, there they were, all lying down without a scratch on anything! In fact there was a very small shrub (about a metre high) in the middle of the front lawn of house number 2 and the trees were lying either side of it like a bunch of pickup sticks. I should have taken a photo of it, because it was one of the prettiest sights one could see and was a real tribute to this old bushman's undoubted skill!

Of course today, one could text to communicate between the houses but back then the phone system that they have now was not up and running, so good communication between all those houses wasn't possible apart from the intercom system I put in, which gave all the wives an added sense of security. The phone system they have now, with repeater towers on the many high mountains, is wonderful. PNG was one of the earliest countries to embrace the new microwave telephone technology and, when it was installed, one of the most up-to-date telegraph systems of any country, certainly in the Pacific region.

On this compound, which had the three MAF houses on it, there was also what had been a guest house – an oblong building with a bedroom at each end and facilities in between. The late Gloria Penberthy, personal assistant to the field leader, came up to Mt Hagen from Wewak when the headquarters were transferred there and after some modifications, took up residence. She had previously worked amongst Aboriginals in western and central Australia before joining MAF. It can be really tough on single people and especially women in situations like this and we felt really privileged to have a good relationship with her, as did many others. Gloria was extremely capable but at times, quite naturally, got a bit frustrated at the way some things went, or didn't go! So who could she talk to, to release that frustration? Thankfully, she felt she could do it at least with us and one evening she came to our place and aired some things outside our house that had been causing her some angst. Elsie asked her to stay for tea, and Gloria replied,

'Thanks, but no thanks, I just wanted to get some stuff off my chest, and I've done that, so thanks for listening!'

Gloria was quite keen on her garden and often on a Sunday afternoon could be seen out tending to the plants she was establishing. She had a practical flair to her gardening too, in that outside her bedroom windows she planted little 'crown of thorns' bushes in case anyone wanted to have a peep! That plant has wicked hard spikes about 25 to 30 millimetres long, which thankfully I haven't had the misfortune of encountering! Sadly, Gloria died of a brain tumour well before what one would have thought was her time, back in her parents' town of Sydney.

On 16 September 1975 Papua New Guinea gained independence, or autonomous rule. I have to say that the Australian administration was generally doing an excellent job of schooling the Papua New Guineans towards independence, but they were aiming for about 1985, rather than 1975. The reason for it coming before the aimed-for date was because the UN, stirred on by Russia, was demanding it earlier, and Australia either succumbed or was instructed to give up their administration of the country.

This was a real pity, as the Aussies were doing a good job in trying to develop individuals in particular areas, but hadn't really explained enough at that time what independence meant. We heard that some Air Niugini airline cargo staff in Port Moresby thought that once PNG gained independence, they would instantly become pilots! Also, because of the lack of time, people were being thrust into positions that they hadn't received instruction for or had a background in. A short time (nine months?) after Independence Day it was promulgated that the whole education system would be nationalised, i.e. expatriate teachers teaching in mission-funded and operated schools could no longer teach there. This was far too soon, as it didn't give the Australian administration time to help get up to speed those who would be taking on extra responsibility and it meant that some were asked to do something they had never done before.

I was personally involved in helping one man at the Lake Kutubu school who was apparently a very good teacher, but suddenly became the school headmaster without much idea as to what that entailed. It was mentally disturbing him to the degree that the education secretary for the region asked MAF to go and rescue him from the situation. He was to be flown out to Mendi (15 minutes) where he was helped medically and psychologically. Not knowing how he would react to being asked to leave Kutubu, I was very glad that the CEO of MAF Australia, Jim Charlesworth – a former field pilot and a strapping big chap – was available to come with me and sit alongside the teacher. We were so relieved that he presented no problem and was a willing passenger.

Another area in which nationalisation was a struggle was with the PNG police force. As mentioned earlier in the example of the Papuan wanting to exit the Wapenamanda Valley in a hurry, the old tribal concept of payback was, and still is, alive and well. Payback applied even to policemen. So sadly, from the time of independence onwards, after the Australian police force went back to Australia, law and order in PNG deteriorated significantly. However, there were things that you had to laugh at and if you didn't, you just wouldn't last the distance. I remember one of our MAF wives was berated by a national policeman for parking on a pedestrian crossing in Mt Hagen town. She said, 'But there are no markings on the road to indicate that this is a pedestrian crossing or I wouldn't have parked here.' The reply? 'I know, but there was a pedestrian crossing here before they put the last lot of tar-seal over it!'

Much later in our time after the next furlough, we were located in the Mt Hagen township on another compound in an ex-Dept of Civil Aviation house which was up on stilts. It had a laundry under it which was broken into one night and some clothing was stolen, including one of Elsie's blouses. A few days later, she saw it being worn by a local man at the market, so she went to the police station to report it. The policemen said, 'Well, did you catch him?' I think Elsie said to herself, if not under her breath, 'I thought that was your job!' Ah well, things like this did happen in PNG!

In Mt Hagen there were a few churches that catered for the expatriate population. We settled on going to the morning service at the Baptist church where English-speaking Papuans and expats worshipped together. In the evenings we went to the Wesleyan service. It was a privilege to be able on occasions to expound God's word to those who gathered together at these churches for fellowship. I well remember taking a Christmas morning service at the Wesleyans' one year and a definite prerequisite before going to church was for the girls to open at least one present each. You simply couldn't deny them that privilege!

While we were at Mt Hagen, I was again flying the amphibious floatplane as the need arose. One such time was after a long period of rain when MAF was asked to lift some artefacts out of Munduku. This was a Swiss mission station, close to the lower reaches of the Karawari River about 45 minutes from Mt Hagen. The airstrip was close to the river, with the mission buildings between the airstrip and the river. A trader had been further up the river purchasing artefacts and, to be fair to him, he had arranged for a larger commercial aircraft (a Talair Twin Otter) to come in and pick up the artefacts, but with the amount of rain that there had been, the airstrip was too wet and soft for that aircraft, or even one of ours to use. The obvious solution was to use the floatplane in the river alongside.

The pickup needed to be done 'right now' because the Papuan Christians at Munduku had come to the Swiss missionaries and told them that they wanted the artefacts gone. Of course the local people had a much better idea of the evil spiritual consequences of them staying there than the white skin missionaries had, and they didn't want them on the mission station where they were kept in a storeroom.

I went to do the job of taking these artefacts out by using the amphibious floatplane to take off from the river and land at Kompiam airstrip (25 minutes) where the larger aircraft could come and pick them up. All okay, but the amount of rain that had fallen in the area meant the Karawari River was in flood, moving very swiftly, and worse, bringing debris down. This wasn't nice, as a very useful timber called kwila was of such a specific density that it floated just beneath the surface of the water and could cause a lot of damage to the floats if they were hit at speed. This wasn't too much of a problem when landing, because if you looked down, you could see something that could cause a problem, but while taking off, it was another matter entirely. It was more helpful if trees coming down the river had branches sticking up in the air, as it was so easy then to see them and avoid them.

After landing and securing the aircraft, I went with the missionary to the aforesaid storeroom. I realised then why the locals wanted the artefacts gone. I guess we've all heard of the saying: 'Your hair standing up on the back of your neck.' Well, that was exactly how it felt for me; the evil coming out from that room could indeed be 'felt'. And I had to put that stuff in the plane and fly it out. I thank God that the Holy Spirit is much stronger than any of the spirits associated with those artefacts and the whole operation was done without any incidents, but for a number of reasons, I was doubly careful that day. Praise the Lord!

Some readers may question some of what I have just written – understandably. Sadly, missionaries often buy artefacts without realising that many are an intrinsic part of the Indigenous people's spirit rituals and worship. A senior missionary friend of ours had done this, and taken artefacts back to his home country and stored them in the attic of his house. The next time he went home on furlough, the family seemed to be continually plagued with ill-health. Then he thought, 'I wonder if those artefacts have anything to do with it?' He took them down and disposed of them and the family's health quickly improved and they remained in good health for the rest of their furlough. He didn't feel it was any coincidence.

Soon after we arrived in PNG, Elsie and I had fallen into this new missionary trap and bought a carved crocodile amongst other things and when home, had given them to my brother to store at the farm. However, when we heard about the above from a person whom we knew well and respected, we wrote home and asked my brother to dispose of what we had left with him. We later found out that the crocodile was the god of the Sepik River people from whom we had bought the carved one. Something that makes some of these artefacts even more evil is the fact that many have either been included in the spirit worship of the people, or they have been dedicated to the spirits prior to sale.

I heard of another incident along a similar theme when I was in Greenlane Hospital having my gallbladder removed in 1979. A Christian visitor to the man in the next bed told of how she had taken possession of a house at Papamoa Beach that had a lot of South African artefacts left in it. She removed them and burnt them, and she said that when they were burning, she could hear screams coming from the fire. I know that seems incredible and out of this world but having 'felt' the evil at Munduku I didn't have a problem in believing her story; I trust you can believe it too.

Because the local people had such a good understanding of the evil spirits' powers, when they became Christians, they expected the Holy Spirit to do things that we so-called enlightened people perhaps wouldn't think of. This was because the missions had quite correctly told them that the Holy Spirit was more powerful in every way than the evil spirits they were used to. The thing that impressed me about the way Christian locals approached a problem, was they *always* based their request for a miracle on a miracle that is recorded in Scripture. Now, stand by for a few 'believe it or not' stories!

If you have a convention running at night and it goes a lot longer than expected and the kerosene storm lanterns which are your only means of lighting start to go out, what do you do? One group prayed saying, 'Lord you turned water into wine, and we don't have any more kerosene here, but we need the light for the rest of this convention. Please turn this water into kerosene so our lamps can keep burning.' They put water into their kerosene lamps and they kept burning! Now, I wouldn't expect too many of my readers would have done that. I must confess, I wouldn't even have thought of the idea, or had the faith to do it. Perhaps this is an indictment on me for my lack of faith.

A very similar thing happened to some people who were going on an evangelistic outreach up a feeder river of a large highland lake when their outboard motor ran out of petrol. Using the same concept of water into wine, they prayed; this time it was water into petrol and the outboard motor kept going. That is *practical faith* in operation!

Just a little way downstream from Erave (which is in the foothills of the highlands at 3,400 feet elevation) on the Erave River there was the small native village called Waitari. (Interestingly, in a couple of areas in PNG 'wai' means water, as it does in Māori.) When I was being checked out into this area of the river, I noticed that while the people had small canoes, they hadn't developed a paddle like the lowlanders had, and were simply using lengths of large-diameter bamboo as their paddles. Surprisingly, they could make reasonable progress with them, even when going upstream.

The Wesleyan mission took up the challenge of ministering Christ's love to these people and placed a pastor by the name of Yaweja amongst them. He was a dynamic man of faith and had been to Mt Hagen to get an aid post orderly (male nurse) to take back to Waitari to help with the newly-formed health clinic there. However, he struck a problem, for when they came to a river they had to cross to get to Waitari, it was in flood and the bridge made from vines was under water.

So what did Yaweja do? He prayed to the Lord, 'Lord, you can see the problem we have. This fellow will turn back if we can't get across this river. In the same way as you helped the Israelites cross the Red Sea, please help us get across this river.' Within minutes, the water had lowered enough for them to see the vine bridge again and go across on it. As soon as all the party was across, a log came down the river with a branch sticking up which caught the vines supporting the bridge and demolished it. This effectively meant no going back for the orderly. This is another example of asking for supernatural help based on a Scripture miracle.

Waitari and Yaweja have another couple of miracles in store for us. The first relates to the building of the church out of native materials which were free and readily available. The roof was going to be thatched painstakingly with sago palm leaf. When the building was ready to put the roof on, Yaweja had everyone go out and gather as much sago palm leaf as they could. I don't know whether the village thatcher was part of that group or not, but he was recognised as someone who could estimate by eye how much leaf was needed to thatch any given roof. He adamantly said that they didn't have enough, even though they had scoured far and wide to find what they had. Again he said, 'Not enough,' but in faith they started and the 'not enough' became 'sufficient', reminiscent of the widow's jars of oil in 2 Kings 4:1-7. I don't know if Yaweja had prayed for a miracle, but knowing him as I did, I think he would have.

Running parallel with the Erave River, just upstream but on the other side from Waitari village was a flat area suitable for an airstrip. It was determined that an airstrip could be built there, but those building it were going to be using some small mechanical equipment which needed fuel, so once again yours truly was to take the fuel in using the amphibious floatplane. Because of weight restrictions, the floatplane could only take half a drum of petrol at a time off Ialabu which is at about 6,000 feet elevation. Loading a 200-litre drum into a land-based Cessna 206 was relatively easy, but it was a whole different story loading it into the amphibious floatplane which is so much higher off the ground. The fuel was brought to me on the back of a small truck which was carefully backed up towards the aircraft and loaded into the aircraft off the truck.

The Erave River at Waitari is adequately wide and has two fairly straight stretches joined by an S-bend. At about the middle of the lower bend there is a rock big enough to cause a lot of damage to a float, but with normal river flow it is exposed so it can easily be seen. The fuel was to be unloaded at a point upstream at the top of the upper straight stretch.

Because of the rock in the S-bend which was to be avoided, I decided to land in the upper straight stretch. There was plenty of room once one slid down between the treetops, with the occasional wing lift to avoid a branch on the way down. It was good fun and quite stimulating. The fuel unloaded, it was time to take off again for another load, but while I could land on the top stretch, it wasn't long enough or clear enough to take off from, so it was a case of heading down and around the 'S' bend with the rock in the middle and taking off on the lower stretch. While both the floats had small rudders on their rear, they were not very effective in a strong current, so I decided to get up on the step (30 to 45 knots) on the upper stretch and use the much more effective aircraft air rudder at that speed to negotiate the bends. Passing the rock at that speed with only about three metres of wing-tip clearance on the port (left) side from a rock face and about the same distance from the right-hand float, was once again a somewhat stimulating experience!

Some may think that navigating around a rock at speed in a floatplane was a miracle, and I don't in any way depreciate it, but rather thank the Lord that it was able to be done safely.

Yaweja wanted to reach out to some villagers downstream past the S-bend and recruited some of his highland friends to take part. The Wesleyan mission at Fugwa to which he belonged was based at 5,720 feet in the highlands, whereas the village to be visited was a little lower than Erave at around 3,000 feet. These friends, not being used to canoeing like lowlanders, set off even though the river was in flood just enough to cover the rock. Yes, you guessed it! The canoe came around the first bend and as they were passing through the second bend, it hit the rock, flipped over and everything in it was tossed out. Then a series of miracles took place. Highlanders are not strong swimmers, yet all of them got to the bank, as did a borrowed steel-headed axe, and at least one Bible. The Bible is possibly understandable, as it was in a plastic bag to keep it dry and there may have had enough air trapped in it to keep it afloat, but a steel headed axe? It reminds me of what is related in 2 Kings 6:5-6. Yes, miracles still happen today, but they aren't spoken about so much in our society for fear (I think) that others just won't believe the person telling about them! (I trust that you will believe me!)

As has already been indicated, women were treated pretty much as a commodity (to our Christian-influenced cultural way of thinking) and at times they were the victims of absolute cruelty. I remember one case I had to bring in to the Mt Hagen hospital; a woman had been slashed on her arm by a machete. I don't know the reason in that case, but other instances seem to have been quite petty, or something that could have been talked through.

However, at least in some highland areas, women had a means of getting back at a husband who was being unreasonable. In most highland areas men covered their rear private parts with broad, coloured Tankard leaves stuck in their belts which were made from small vines. They always had a patch of these tankard plants growing in their garden, so they could easily renew their 'pants'. At times, an irate wife would get back at her husband by pulling up all his leaf plants, leaving him without any new trousers! In a culture that hadn't had time to absorb much – if anything – of our Christian standards, the arm incident could well have been punishment for creating a 'no pants' situation.

In the Bosavi area, the fine vines used for belts also functioned like a box of matches, as a couple of pieces could be broken off and rubbed together vigorously to start a fire, provided the other material was dry. The women in this area wore bulky string skirts, presumably made like many other things from the woven fibres of tree bark. These skirts were metres long and the women wound them around themselves many times to make the skirt. Much further west in the highlands, the women's skirts covered them well in the front and were longer at the back, so when they were bending over or walking up a steep incline, they were still well-covered, even though there was no covering on the sides of their thighs.

In another highland area (Porgera and Paiela Valleys) there was a tree that grew big bunches of nuts, which the locals really loved. There were two problems. The outer shell of the Caracas nut was so hard that a European would take to the nut with a hammer to break the shell. Of course the locals didn't have a hammer, so they used their teeth like a vice and would try and crack the shell that way. Those times that it didn't work too well meant that a person had to be brought into a hospital to get their tooth fixed up or removed. There was another problem too in that the trees were tribally owned by the people of that particular valley or clan. And woe betide someone from another tribe or valley found stealing the nuts off 'our' tree. They really took a dim view of that, and it could easily start a tribal fight if the offender was killed.

Medical emergencies were one of the many tasks carried out by

MAF aircraft, and I have already touched on a couple of instances when we were based in Kawito, but here are a few that I remember from our time in Mt Hagen. Sadly, quite a large proportion of our medical emergencies were women with birthing problems, mostly breech births. It was great being able to help in this way and get them to hospital care, but on a few occasions that didn't happen. Those putting the women on the aircraft would always steadfastly assure the pilot that there was no way she would give birth in flight. Really? Thankfully, I never had a birth on board, but the last I heard, Jim Charlesworth had the highest tally with three children being born as he took 'impossible' birthing problems to a helping facility. The closest I got to anything like this was when I brought a poor woman in from Lapalama to Mt Hagen (25 minutes) with the baby stuck halfway out which must have been shockingly painful as well as awfully embarrassing for her; but there wasn't a whisper of complaint.

At times, though, medical staff can unwittingly put a lot of pressure on a pilot with regards to a woman with a birthing problem. Much later, when I was chief pilot, I remember when a pilot based at Anguganak was informed by the nursing staff very late in the evening that they had a woman with a breech birth that really should get out to Wewak Hospital for the attention she needed. The pilot initially made the correct call by not going, as it was getting dark. There was no doctor there at the time, but the nurses kept giving him hourly updates on how things were getting worse, so the pilot eventually succumbed and attempted to take off in the dark without adequate runway lighting. Fortunately for all, he ran off to the side of the airstrip into some tall kunai grass, which meant he couldn't continue. The woman gave birth naturally a little later that night and all went well for her and the baby.

I guess we have all heard that if a person on a boat is inclined to be seasick, the answer is to give them the tiller. It can work similarly in an aircraft, but sadly there is a bit more to flying a plane than just steering a yacht! I think I can honestly say that there have only been two times that I have felt squeamish in an aircraft. The first time was the rocking of the DC3 on the ground at Whenuapai. The second time was when Warwick Walesby and I had to go to Kudjip to pick up a young girl about eight years old.

I had check and training approval and Warwick hadn't yet been checked into the Kudjip airstrip, so he did the flying. We picked up the mother and the little girl who had fallen from a second-storey balcony and landed on her head, which meant she was bleeding from her nose and ears. Although Kudjip had a good Nazarene hospital, for some reason she needed to get to Mt Hagen. Once again, Warwick was flying for the return to Mt Hagen, but the seating arrangement meant I had to sit in the back seat. I was very glad I managed to hold it all together for the trip of about 12 minutes, although it seemed to be much longer than that! It wasn't Warwick's flying that caused the feeling; I am sure seeing the poor little girl and feeling so helpless had a lot to do with it. She later came right and returned home by road.

Doing check and training could be quite interesting. MAF was brilliant in this regard and made sure that a new pilot was comfortable with a route or airstrip before they were sent out on their own. A couple of times a little extra encouragement was needed, but generally the new pilot picked up what was required reasonably quickly. This often depended on their past flying experience, which determined how quickly they did so. One thing I found most interesting was that as the checker, I could tell the person they were doing well, but for some reason they seemed unsure that I really meant it. However if Elsie related how well the husband was doing to the new pilot's wife, it then seemed to be a lot more valid! Perhaps they thought I was just saying it to boost their morale? I don't know.

Doing checking into tricky places is always an assessment of your own skills and ability. Even though you have a set of controls in front of you, if you want to see whether the pilot being checked has really grasped the situation completely, you have to let them proceed until you feel that the circumstances could be beyond your own skills and ability to rectify. Sometimes this is not an easy task! I well remember telling one pilot as I was checking him into Tekin one windy day, 'You know, I reckon that if we had a lot of smoke in this valley to observe what the wind currents are doing, we wouldn't even try to land here.' And I believe that assessment was true, as at times on approaching to land at Tekin, it was a serious case of full power (because you were sinking), then you'd be caught in an updraft and have to cut power back and so on, much of the way down your final approach to land.

This of course was not quite as easy when we got the turbocharged 206s, because the turbo needed time to spool up after being at low revs for any length of time, so when we did get on the ground, we would leave them to idle for about three minutes for the sake of the bearing between the exhaust side of the turbo and the fresh air side. This single centre bearing between the hot (exhaust) and cold (fresh air) sides was oiled by pressure and had a novel way of not leaking oil at either end. The shaft had a spiral groove which captured the oil from escaping and brought it back to the centre drain. So why the rundown at idle once on the ground? As you can imagine, the whole unit got very, very hot, with the exhaust driving the turbo as well as the fact that the turbo was spinning at very high speeds for quite a time even as it spooled down. If you shut the engine down too quickly after landing, the heat in the unit and shaft would bake the oil in the spiral grooves, which in time meant that the whole oiling system ceased to function properly and the bearing would give out. I don't think MAF ever had any bearings give out on us, but another operator (who didn't spool down regularly) certainly did.

Essentially, our MAF work in the 1960s and 70s centred on five things:

- Moving missionaries and pastors, or those training to become pastors like those to/from Christian Leaders Training College at Banz (Giramben was their own airstrip later)
- Transporting everything missionaries needed, both personally and for the development of their work, including livestock and building materials
- Being involved in medical patrols and evacuations
- Supplying mission run trade stores
- Doing all sorts of government work, including search and rescue.

Back when various missions were establishing their mission stations, a fair proportion of our work was supporting them in that. As a mission station was being set up, trade stores were also started, which had a dual effect. As the work in the area grew, medical aid post orderlies and teachers came to the area from other places and these people didn't have a plot of land of their own to grow their food, as they were essentially 'foreigners', even though they were still in their own country! Having a trade store on site helped these folk with food supplies even though it was very different from what they would normally have in their home area. While the missions didn't make the sort of profits that stores in the main centres made, it was enough to support further developments. To help, MAF flew these goods at a reduced rate compared to a commercial rate.

When we first went to PNG in 1967, each mission had enough goods, passengers, personal effects and trade stores to charter the whole aircraft on the outward journey. It seemed a logical and a reasonable idea to pick up anyone else from another mission on the way back – for free. In many of the MAF outstation bases, we were working virtually entirely for the same mission anyway, so this really didn't matter. However, as time went on, it became apparent (out of Mt Hagen at least), that often one mission was providing the loading for the aircraft out, while another mission was hopping on the back-load for free quite frequently. When this became obvious, I suggested that the cost of the weight of the whole flight, instead of just the forward loading, be split up proportionately according to the weight of the total loading (outgoing plus homecoming), which was fairer and made more sense. Thankfully, that concept was adopted.

Later, as passengers started to become the dominant 'cargo', we charged what was reckoned as a proportion of a normal load per person. As we were not operating a regular public transport service, officially we couldn't charge a fare as such, but it effectively became something like that using the proportionate system. To aid us in this, we were blessed with an electrical engineer (Terry Burn) who was a real wiz in his field, in that he had built his own computer before computers became generally available.

Not only that, he was also well schooled in trigonometry and from the coordinates of any two airstrips was able to calculate the magnetic track and distance between them, and later the proportionate charge for a passenger. All of this went into our mini manual for easy reference when out and about. I have no doubt this is now carried on a mobile phone or tablet.

As you can imagine, all this information in our mini manual decreased the pilot's workload enormously, as there was no Google Earth and GPS back then! It became mighty useful when you were away from base, when for some good reason the programme changed – and change it often did! It was normally because of a need which was not known to the programmer or pilot when putting in their original flight plan. At one stage, when we were based at Mt Hagen, there was a civil aviation flight planning and briefing facility at the airport where we would submit our flight plan. The chaps there would then send our planned route and elapsed times to the relevant Air Radio facility (normally Madang Air Radio) which would monitor our flight for search and rescue purposes. They would write all those details on paper strips which they had in front of them for each leg of our plan, so that they could monitor us for the sake of our safety. I well remember the day when I went to Tari and was then asked on the spot to go to Benaria (15 minutes) and bring a person in need of medical assistance back out to Tari. When I called Madang with a change of plan they came back with, 'Okay, we think that from now on, it will be best for you guys just to put in a plan to your first destination as your plans seem to change so frequently!' The changes, of course meant that all the writing up the Air Radio chaps had done on their paper strips to follow us was of no use, so I quite understood their frustration!

Over the years, the aircraft types changed, while remaining relatively similar. Before our time in PNG, they were using a model of Piper aircraft that was the big brother to the sort on which I had done all my initial training. They were built with a small tubular frame with a fabric covering. Then came the first all-metal aircraft for MAF – a Cessna C170 model. In fact, it was the same one that many prospective field pilots including myself had exciting experiences with at Ballarat in Victoria. By the time we arrived in PNG, even the Cessna C180s (230 horsepower) which were slightly larger and much more powerful were being phased out in favour of the Cessna C185 Skywagon which had a bigger cabin and a more powerful engine (260 horsepower). It was later changed yet again for an even more powerful one (300 horsepower). This was designated as an A185, as the modification was done by MAF-AIR Services in Ballarat, Australia. While this type had some advantages over models that followed, they were not as passenger friendly or as cargo friendly as the later Utility models (U206 & TU206), but they were certainly pilot friendly as one could go places with them in wet, muddy conditions where nose-wheeled models faltered.

Gradually all the C185s were phased out, in favour of the nose-wheeled model Cessna U206, 'U' being for its Utility designation. While it certainly was great for cargo, it was also great for passengers due to the much easier access to all the seats. During the 1970s when women's miniskirts were fashionable, it was very awkward for a woman wearing one to get into the 185s, especially through the rear cargo door, without it being a tad embarrassing for them. In those times, the pilot needed to look the other way to 'see what the weather was doing'! I remember once, when moving a medical out of Mapoda, the patient was lying on the floor and the accompanying nurse was sitting in the seat beside them. I thought it would make a good deputation photo of a medical, but was thwarted in that attempt by the nurse's miniskirt. What I could see through the lens would not have been acceptable as a deputation shot!

But possibly the greatest and best feature in the U206 was the two large cargo doors on the right-hand rear side of the cabin. While I was not aware of it at the time, we were apparently working under a dispensation which allowed us to fly full 200-litre drums of petrol, diesel, or kerosene on board – without passengers at the same time of course! It was so easy to load and unload the drums on the 206 and as we were able to carry two at a time, it was a lot more economical than the 185. With the 185, while it was possible to carry one, it was infinitely more difficult to load and unload and definitely more dangerous as the drum was normally standing up instead of lying down. This meant the liquid could slop around inside the drum which in any sort of turbulence gave a most alarming 'hunting' or swaying effect! I speak from experience, as I have a distinct memory of this unnerving action once when I went through the Tari Gap.

As mentioned earlier, the normally aspirated U206 had a

300-horsepower engine and performed reasonably well in the lowlands but lacked the power at higher altitudes. The first of the turbo TU206 models were rated at 285 horsepower and didn't perform very well at lower levels. However, a while later, the TU206s were being fitted with 310-horsepower engines, and wow, did they perform! I think that the power was being used more effectively too, because the three-bladed propeller was of a different design. Instead of thinning off towards the tip with rounded ends, they had paddle blades which pretty well maintained the same aerofoil shape until the squared end, much the same as the C130 Hercules. In certain circumstances they were so efficient you could 'feel' the prop coarsen off during takeoff.

Once, when flying back to Mt Hagen from Tari (45 minutes) in the afternoon, I was the only person on board, and typical of the highlands at that time of day, there were a number of big build-ups which, if flying underneath them would have meant flying around in rain and low cloud in hilly terrain. I thought – I have oxygen and a turbocharged engine, let's go home on top – so I wound my way up between the build-ups to 18,500 feet and as soon as I levelled off in cruise, I closed the cowl flaps which is the normal procedure when in the cruise phase of flight. I was really surprised a few minutes later to see that the cylinder head temperatures had started to rise, so I partially opened the cowl flaps again to allow for a greater airflow and it brought the temps down to normal again. I hadn't reckoned on the fact that rarer air, which has less volume at a higher altitude, has less cooling effect than the air at a lower level, even though the higher altitude air is colder. (Cowl flaps are the moveable portion of the outer lower covering of the engine, which allow the pilot to regulate the temperature of the engine by altering the amount of air flowing over it.)

Roughly around 1974, MAF bought a second-hand Beechcraft Baron D55 twin-engine aircraft with a similar capacity to a C206, but oh so much faster. This was achieved through shape, almost double the power of an early C185, and most of all because it didn't have wheels and undercarriage hanging down while flying, but neatly tucked away, making it pretty clean and 'slippery'. To give an idea of just how well balanced the aircraft was, once when I was flying from Telefomin to Wewak in it, I forgot to close the engine cowl flaps when I levelled off and trimmed it for the cruise. When I realised they were open, I closed them as I should have done earlier, but the thing I didn't expect was I had to re-trim the aircraft as they had made such a difference to its forward profile. That's how cleanly balanced it was aerodynamically.

One had to be careful moving from a 206 to the Baron too, because while you could almost get away with thinking as you went with the 206 which travelled at around 3.7 kilometres a minute, the Baron was 50 percent faster again and you really had to think ahead or you could be in some trouble. One place where this was obvious was coming back to Mt Hagen from the west when you went through the Tomba Pass. One had to throttle back to low power; enough to keep the engine warm to reduce speed, put down the undercarriage and trim for that configuration or there was no way you could get down to circuit height in the distance available between the Tomba Pass and the Mt Hagen airfield.

In one way, the Baron was very similar to the old Dominie or DC3 if fully loaded. Should one engine fail for any reason, there was only one way you were going to go and that was down somewhere, even though it would be an extended distance compared with a glide. This was amply demonstrated to me when our chief pilot was checking me out in the Baron at Mt Hagen airport which, admittedly, is at over 5,000 feet elevation. Shortly after takeoff he reduced the power on one engine to simulate just having one engine alive, and with only the two of us on board, it was a struggle to even maintain the height we already had. Fortunately, like the two aforementioned aircraft, the Baron had good faithful engines when well maintained.

As with many mission organisations, MAF always seemed to be short-staffed for the work we were doing. I can only remember a period of about six months when we had a full complement of staff in the 15 years we were on the field. At times, one had to cover for another programme, especially if it was a single pilot base and the normal pilot was away on furlough. In August 1977 I was doing some of the work normally done by the Port Moresby programme, and on 22 August, I ventured into an area I had never been before using the Baron which was normally based at Port Moresby. I was glad that it had two engines as there was quite a bit of over-water flying! This was one of the reasons it was based there, as well as its speed to do longer distance hauls for those arriving at Port Moresby (PNG's main point of entry) from overseas who needed to go to various locations around PNG.

Away off the end of the peninsula that runs eastwards from Port Moresby is Misima Island and I took several people to a mission executive meeting being held there. Two things about that visit I clearly remember. One was the old mission house that we stayed in. I was staggered at the massive size of the pillars holding the house up. They would have been at least as big as my body, if not a bit bigger. It was almost as if they had cut off several trees at the right height and built the house on the top of them. The other thing was the way the original missionaries from England had trained the local people in etiquette when providing hospitality, since by the time we were there it was all being done by the local people. There were starched tablecloths and napkins, and when the waiter came to the table with food, he had a towel draped over his forearm. He could have served at any quality hotel. Brilliant!

The short-staffing was very evident in mid-1976 when I was wearing multiple hats. Fortunately, once again, Elsie was right there, and effectively took over my base manager role, dealing with all the day-to-day stuff relative to the houses, while I coordinated two programmes, did normal flying, check and training, and flew two specialist aircraft – the floatplane and the Baron. This was primarily because others hadn't yet been checked out on them, or they didn't have the experience to do what the particular flying entailed. I was doing a fair proportion of the programming after our evening meal, and I clearly remember the time when Elsie asked me out of kindness and genuine interest, 'How did your day go today dear?' To my shame, I replied, 'Do I really need to spend the time telling you? I have my logbook to write up and the programme for tomorrow to work out yet.' We had started to lose that deep communication with each other where you instinctively know what your other half would do in a particular circumstance. This was sadly demonstrated when Elsie approved a minor purchase relative to the base that I wouldn't have. But as always, the Lord knew our situation and very shortly we were to have a break which enabled us to truly connect again.

In mid-August we had the 1976 annual staff conference at the Lutheran school at Amapyak and it was great to have a couple of days break and a time of great fellowship, but more was to come!

Chapter 23

To the Solomon Islands

Little did we know then, that it was going to mean quite a massive change for our family, as part way through the conference, we were asked to go to the British Solomon Islands and fly the amphibious float plane there, as our good friends Wal and Elizabeth Job and family were due to go on furlough. We were assured that there would be schooling for our girls and after a rather brief time of prayer and reflection, because the 'top brass' wanted an almost immediate answer, we said 'Yes' even though there were a couple of misgivings. The main one as far as I was concerned, was because I was not a licensed engineer, and another air charter company (a subsidiary of the company in Mt Hagen that counted us as 'opposition') was going to have to do the maintenance on the Solomon's aircraft!

At the conference we had been singing that great old chorus: 'He brought me to his banqueting table, his banner over me is love,' and I remember getting up on stage to tell the folk that we'd be heading for Honiara and quoting, 'His banner over us is *love*' while holding my two arms over my head in an arch. Our decision wasn't because those who asked us to move had said they felt the Lord had chosen us to do the job. Afterwards I became aware that they had asked others to make the move before us! However, in retrospect we do believe that God was definitely in the move.

Of course the next thing was to pack up all our stuff. Elsie quite rightly and wisely said she wanted to take a very substantial survival kit with us, as we didn't know how long it would take for our goods to reach us and doing this proved to be a real godsend. While we packed enough into our drums and the wooden boxes we had brought from New Zealand some nine years earlier, we elected to leave some stuff at Mt Hagen. I can remember the general manager's look of utter surprise and bewilderment when I told him we wanted to leave a portion of our stuff left in Mt Hagen 'in case we come back again'. Actually that was prophetic, though I didn't know it at the time!

The only route to Honiara was via Port Moresby and from memory there were only two direct flights per week to Honiara from there at that time. We arrived at the airfield in the afternoon prior to one of these flights and were met by the MAF staff who took us and our large suitcases to 'Mapang', which was a Christian guest house run by a charitable trust. That evening, Elsie said she felt a migraine coming on and was not feeling well. The next day we were due to fly to Honiara. Elsie had been having migraine headaches on and off for a period, quite likely due to the extra pressure and responsibility she had carried on my behalf as acting base manager, and in this case, the stress of packing ready for our move. They often took two or three days to wear off, and naturally, this was a real concern to us both.

I firmly believe in the power of God to heal, and while I don't feel I had (or have) the specific gift of healing, I laid my hands on Elsie's forehead as she was lying there motionless, and pleaded with the Lord to cause the migraine to lift by the morning so we could continue our journey as planned. God abundantly answered that prayer as in the morning, Elsie was fully functional again. Thank you again Lord for answered prayer!

We were met at the Honiara airport by Wal and Elizabeth and it was great to be with them again. We stayed with them initially, as at that stage it hadn't been possible to rent another house and it almost looked as if we were going to need to stay in the workers' quarters. Thankfully, a house became available quite quickly and we were able to move into it and be a family again. I think the only thing I remember about this place was that, like most places there on town water supply, one had to go out near the road and turn the master water valve on. This in itself was no problem, but the hole with the valve in it was already occupied by a number of big brown toads which are similar but quite different to frogs and looked rather gross!

It seemed that just about every other place in Honiara had an outdoor swimming pool which to the uninitiated seemed mighty strange when Honiara is a coastal town with some reasonable beaches. The closest bay is locally called Iron Bottom Bay as there are so many sunken warships there from World War 2. This in itself didn't stop people swimming, but for whatever reason, there were sharks galore in the bay. One tragic story illustrates why people don't swim there. A proud father was out reasonably deep and was in the process of photographing his little child in shallower water when a shark swept in, taking the little one away, never to be seen again.

One weekend, Wal and Elizabeth took us some distance down the coast, past an area that was dedicated to rice production to a river where there was a strong rope for swinging out over the water, which was really great fun enjoyed by us all. I can't remember whether they assured us that the saltwater crocodiles didn't come up the river that far, or whether we just forgot to ask! But the amount of splashing and noise that the happy occasion afforded would probably have scared any off that were around anyway. A little further on, they took us to see, not shipwrecks, but an area where several Bren gun carriers had been driven up off the landing barge and left to rust out. Such is the waste at the end of a war.

One Japanese battleship that didn't go to the bottom of the bay is partially out in the open for everyone to see. When flying from Honiara to Auki (about 35 minutes) on Malaita Island, one flies over a large warship that has about a third of its length out of the water, above high-tide, and with its bow far beyond the beach, extending well into the bush. It is not far from a channel between two islands and, so the story goes, the ship was due to head for the channel at night (possibly with no lights because it was heading away from Honiara in wartime) and mistook a distinctive dip on the horizon for the channel. It must have been going at full speed I would think, for it to have run aground with so much of it out of the water. Of course this was hugely shameful for the Japanese captain and it is said that he took his own life rather than face the humiliation this indiscretion would have brought him.

At that time, the work out of Honiara was mainly transporting personnel, with a high proportion going to Malaita, another large island to the north-northeast of Honiara which is on Guadalcanal. Malaita had a lot of mission activity going on around it and was reasonably heavily populated and the mission we worked for the most was South Seas Evangelical Mission (SSEM). The coast of Malaita closest to Honiara had coral reefs almost all the way up it, while the coast on the other side of the island was called the weather coast, and without the protection of the reefs, one had to land and take off the floatplane either in the lee of another smaller island or once in a small cul-de-sac type inlet.

On the side of Malaita with the reef protection, we would ideally land between the reef and the island but this was not quite as easy as it sounds as the reef wasn't in a nice straight line parallel to the shoreline. When flying overhead, it was very easy to note where the reef was and where the deeper water was so as to be able to land safely, but when taking off, all you had to guide you were red and green markers on poles. For a nautically trained person, this would have been easy to interpret, but sadly, not for someone like me who had done all my water-based flying up to that time in New Zealand and PNG off lakes and rivers.

Most wonderfully for me, I never had any problems but I have to admit I was always grateful to God that I had been able to get a mental picture of the set-up while in the air before landing. I was always very relieved to be off the water and in the air. When we knew that we were manoeuvring close to a reef, we would naturally be taxiing as slowly as we could, but as an added precaution to save the floats, we'd put the wheels of the aircraft down as if on land, so this would give us a buffer if we did get too close to a reef. It would have been highly embarrassing landing on the runway back at Honiara with a punctured front tyre but much less embarrassing than if a float had got punctured while on the water a long way from home! Thankfully God helped me never to hit any reefs!

Our first Sunday church service was both enlightening and somewhat embarrassing for me in conversation afterwards. Can you imagine going to church with your prime minister as the preacher? That was the case for us, as Sir Peter Kenilorea was the first prime minister of the Solomon Islands. He was also a CLTC (PNG Christian Leaders Training College) graduate! It was also great to see that the Solomon Islanders had got to the point where it was possible for married couples to sit together in a block in the middle of the church, with single men on one side and women on the other side. That was the enlightening part. The embarrassing part was after the service when a mission wife asked us how we had managed to get our children into school so quickly as it appeared they had tried to do it unsuccessfully. My unthinking answer was, 'Oh we prayed about it.'

It was never meant to be a poke in the eye or a put-down, but I fear the wife quite likely felt it was. As I thought about it later, I realised I should have assumed that they had prayed about the situation for their children as well. Why they couldn't get theirs into the school baffles me, though I am aware that the administration felt MAF was an essential service which we were to be a part of.

This may have had a bearing on allowing our children into the school when others weren't. But I don't know.

Sir Peter not only took services but Bible studies as well. One that I remember particularly well was the one he led about Jonah. He said that, just because everything seems to fall into place, it doesn't necessarily mean that it is God's will. So often we do take this as a sign of something being His will. God asked Jonah to go and preach to the people of Nineveh but Jonah wasn't going along with that idea, as they were the enemies of Israel and he didn't want to share 'his' God with 'those heathens'. So he went to Joppa and – hurrah – there was a ship all set to sail in exactly the opposite direction, as far away from Nineveh as it was possible to go by sea. But better yet, there was space for Jonah on the boat, so he bought his fare and thought he had won out over God. But while everything had dovetailed together so nicely, in this instance it definitely wasn't God's will.

God always has the last say in a situation like this, and can't be beaten with something as easily as that, as you probably know from the rest of the story. If you aren't familiar with the whole episode, I encourage you to find a Bible, look in the Old Testament, and read the whole of the short book of Jonah. It is quite a tale! Jesus even refers to it in the Gospels.

Before I arrived in the Solomons, Wal had made a couple of long-distance trips but fortunately there was no request for long trips when I was there. One of Wal's was a long way to the north to Ontong Java, but for that he had organised a fuel dump at an island part-way there. The other trip was to Rennell Islands well to the southeast, but there was no possibility of a fuel dump anywhere on the way and it meant that he was going past his point of no return (PNR) without being absolutely sure of what the Rennell weather conditions were like. When I heard about that trip, I decided it was for gannets and albatrosses! This is no way intended to be a criticism of Wal's choice to serve those communities; but rather, it is to say I am obviously not as adventuresome as Wal was! It reminded me of what my brother said to me when he visited us at Wewak much later. 'You must have enough of Dad's caution in you to keep you safe and enough of an adventurous spirit to enable you to do what you are doing.' Sadly, after we left the Solomons, we heard that the local operator had lost a Britain Norman Islander twin on the return from Rennell when it ran out of fuel.

The longest run I made in the limited time we were in the Solomons was on 15 September 1976 when I took a couple of chaps who were the advance party for an evangelistic outreach by the Billy Graham Evangelistic Association to Gizo which is close to the border with PNG on the Solomon's eastern islands. At that time there was no land airport on Nusa Tupe Island as there appears to be now, so the floatplane was the best way to get there. On our way we fuelled at Munda Airport, an old wartime airfield in quite good condition. After the chaps had arranged things at Gizo, we set off again, but by now, the wind had got up and the wave depth had increased markedly.

As I mentioned earlier, Edo floats are great on smooth water but rather poor on rough water. As we pounded and bounced our way forward on takeoff, I was suddenly aware of someone leaning forward from the middle seat behind me and talking in my right ear, warning me that we were headed for a sea marker ahead. I was well aware of it and was heading just to the right of it, but it can't have looked like that from behind me. Having a headwind is normally a good thing as far as a takeoff is concerned, but I assure you that 16 knots or above it is in fact quite detrimental when dealing with open water in a floatplane as a wind like that can easily cause quite heavy water with waves around 40 centimetres or more deep. It is generally reckoned that white caps occur around 15 knots of wind. The headwind doesn't really compensate for the negative effect of all the bouncing and thumping from the crest of one wave to the next until one can coax or jack the aircraft into the air with a little judicious use of extra flap. We had left Honiara in the morning in bright sun, but by the time we were halfway home, we ran into low cloud and drizzle, so you can imagine the joy it was for me to see the shape of an island close to Guadalcanal appear out of the murk! We got home safely and were very thankful for the day's work completed.

One of Wal's wonderful habits, at the end of the day's flying, was to rinse down the whole aircraft and floats with fresh water as we had been flying all day off saltwater, which of course is extremely corrosive of everything about an aircraft even if is well covered in paint. Even minor cracks in the paint allow the corrosive effect of the saltwater in. This was something that we hadn't done in PNG (though possibly we should have), for while we were mainly flying off rivers, even in the Papuan Gulf for Kapuna Hospital, the rivers were tidal and some may have had a salt component. However, the fresh water in Honiara was drawn from an area that must have run over limestone which was plentiful in the area, for when the washdown water eventually dried, it left behind miniature white circles of white lime residue, giving the aircraft a definite measly look! Neither of us wanted that, so Wal suggested that we try different kinds of wax to minimise this effect by encouraging the water to run off faster after we washed the aircraft down. We waxed various easily remembered portions of the aircraft with several different repellents and later counted the number of spots per square foot. Johnson's floor wax came out as by far the best in this situation, so that was used from then on to protect the aircraft.

One of my last flights in the Solomons was to take one person from Onepusu to Auki; both these locations were on the near, or reef side of Malaita Island. For some reason unknown to me, the Solomons programme had been established on a fare-type basis, which meant that MAF had to get sufficient fares tying together to make any trip viable. This day, I was required to move people on the weather coast and so I effectively flew right around Malaita to make the whole flight viable. On the way I had to drop into, and also take off from, a very limited little inlet, a bit like a cul-de-sac on the northern side of the island. Fortunately, as I was flying a floatplane which allows a curved takeoff, I started near the exit point of the inlet and was able to do a curved 330-degree take-off run without any problem. Arriving at Onepusu and being on amphibious floats, I taxied up out of the water onto the mission station area and asked about the passenger whom the whole flight revolved around. The reply? 'Oh, a motorised canoe called in here last night and he went to Auki on that.' I honestly can't remember what I said in reply, but I sure know what I thought and I trust that for the sake of my Christian witness, what I did say didn't accurately reflect what I was thinking!

This indicated the problem with the Solomons programme as it unfolded. After a little while, I formed the opinion that even the primary mission didn't have a sense of dependency on MAF, as there were fast boats operating between Honiara and Malaita. They weren't as dependent on MAF as people were when stuck in the middle of the jungle like many mission folk in PNG were.

We heard an example of how different cultures place priorities on different things when we were in the Solomons. A European saw the possibilities for cashing in on the abundance of crayfish that were around the cost of Guadalcanal, so while his boat was being fitted out with freezers, he went around the coast, dropping in at every coastal village, of which of course there were many. His message was that in a month's time he would call again and buy whatever crayfish over a certain size they had caught. When the month came around, he went back again and was abundantly rewarded with a wonderful response. He said he would be there again in another month's time. But this second time, there were hardly any crays from the first few villages, so he asked them why there weren't so many. The answer was, 'We haven't used all the money you gave us last time yet.'

About a month after we arrived in the Solomon Islands, we heard the sad news that the PNG chief pilot had been involved in an aircraft accident. He had been flying from Porgera to Paiela with a couple of passengers, one of whom was a new pilot being checked out, and he had headed for the low point where we always passed from the Porgera Valley over into the Paiela Valley. Sadly, he mistook some bright cloud for the gap but when he realised his mistake, he made a steep turn away and struck a tree. It was quite remarkable that the aircraft remained reasonably intact and was in fact impaled on top of a tree that pierced the fuselage between the front and middle row of seats. What happened there was bad enough but worse was to come! With at least two pilots out of the system, the Mt Hagen programme was really pressed for capacity but we had a chap there who was a big, energetic, happy guy with a wonderful ability to get the work done. He was also the programme coordinator at the time and had booked himself to do a *lot* of flying to cover the pilot shortage. Apparently even one of his potential missionary customers warned him on the morning radio sched not to overbook himself, but I feel quite sure that factor didn't play a role in this fatal accident – apart perhaps from taking a shortcut because of the amount of work to be done. There had been a women's convention out at the Baptist mission at Yankisa (now called Yenkisa) and he was transporting a full load of these ladies back to their home areas when the accident occurred. Sadly for all, there were no survivors this time.

While he was within the weight limits prescribed by our mission mini manual he was outside the weight that the available civil aviation performance charts allowed and so the Civil Aviation

Authority (CAA) closed MAF operations down until things were sorted out which, after two accidents in quick succession, was quite understandable. So as not to be non-operational for too long, our general manager asked the missions to send messages to CAA explaining how dependent they were on MAF being able to service them. Apparently, the comment from CAA came back to him: 'You have a *lot* of friends out there.'

So what was the difference between our mini manual and the CAA performance charts? And why? In one sense, one could blame the 'old school tie' scenario. Because the United Nations had mandated Australia to administer PNG, the Australian Civil Aviation Authority was controlling the aviation field of work for the Australian administration which was then governing PNG. Earlier, when Max Meyers was chief pilot, he recognised that the Australian aircraft performance charts (normally referred to as P-charts) were very limiting, because they were written with a maximum allowance for a five-degree slope on the airstrip. They also had in mind to keep weekend pilots safe with massive safety margins, and were created for Australia with its wide open spaces with plenty of flat land for airstrips. Many of the airstrips we were working out of were more than double the five percent slope these charts allowed for, e.g. Lapalama's 12.5 percent and Omkalai's 13.4 percent slope. Experience had proven that much more weight than those P-charts allowed could be safely taken off (and into) many airstrips because of the greater slope. So Max went to the Civil Aviation controller in Port Moresby and presented his case. However, the controller was an old RAAF pilot – as was Max – and the response he got was effectively, 'Nah, don't worry about it, I know you and any operation you'll be involved in will be safe,' which in reality wasn't at all helpful.

When we heard about the PNG accidents while in Honiara, we naturally wondered how things were going to work out back in PNG. There was, of course, speculation that a new chief pilot would be needed as, sadly, the current one had been involved in one of the two accidents which had happened in quick succession. There were several great pilots in PNG who had operated there much longer than I had, so when a communication came from Max Meyers (who was, by then, in the headquarters in Melbourne) that MAF wanted me to get back to PNG to take up that role, it came as quite a surprise.

Chapter 24

Back to PNG

Elsie and I went to the airline office and enquired about seats on the very next flight that was in about three days' time. There were only three seats available! It was Elsie who said, 'We'll take them,' as she thought that for some reason that those might be all we would be requiring. The next day Max phoned me from PNG and asked how we were going and I told him what we had booked. He said, 'Ted, we needed you here yesterday, take the float plane and fly it to Kieta and get to Port Moresby as soon as possible.' So you can see Elsie was right – all that was needed were the three seats! God had again made a way in the situation – and Elsie had been in tune with Him enough to recognise it!

So on 29 September 1976 I flew the floatplane the 2.75 hours to Keita from Honiara just 28 days after my first flight in the Solomons. The same day I was able to get a flight through to Port Moresby on which the co-pilot must have been under the hood practising IFR (instrument flight rules) or something, as it was the most 'wandering around the sky' of any commercial flight I have ever been on! They most certainly didn't have the autopilot locked in. I arrived at Port Moresby where Max and Laurie Darrington were waiting for me with that base's TU206 for all of us to fly to Mt Hagen in. Max sat me in the right-hand seat (a pilot normally sits in the left-hand seat and only check pilots sit in the right-hand seat). So there I was, not having flown this type of aircraft type for a month, flying us all up into the highlands late in the afternoon – the latter not being a great scenario!

I remember two things clearly about this flight. As we were starting to climb away and I was re-familiarising myself with things, Laurie leaned forward and asked, 'What are you using as your climb speed, Ted?' I looked at the airspeed Indicator and realised we were going faster than a normal TU206 climb speed so I responded, 'Oh, I am doing a cruise climb.' In fact, it was a 'seat of the pants' climb but saying it was a cruise climb satisfied all on board. And actually, it wasn't a fib, as I would have reckoned on doing a cruise climb in that situation anyway because it was a 2 hour 25 minute flight without the need to get over any high mountains in a hurry on the way. As it was, God had provided a wonderfully clear afternoon in the highlands for the route we took, so we got into Mt Hagen without any trouble.

For non-aviation readers, perhaps my remark about the 'seat of the pants' climb needs some explanation. When I was with Southern Scenic Air Services in Queenstown, one of the pilots there had said to me, 'You have to get to the stage where the aircraft is just an extension of your arms and legs before you can say you are really flying it.' And this is possible. It happens after a lot of experience in different situations; you get the 'feel' of the machine so you instinctively know when things are right. Perhaps another example of this was much, much later when we had returned to New Zealand and were in the home office. We were on a field visit to north Australia, and I was again in the right-hand seat, as the pilot was letting me have a fly.

I hadn't been at the controls of any aircraft for a number of years, and certainly not in a larger twin-engine aircraft like this one, but when we came into the circuit to land (which the pilot did), I had instinctively reduced power and speed to the normal approach speed when on long finals, without knowing it.

Landing an aircraft from the right-hand seat is slightly different, so on our flight from Port Moresby to Mt Hagen, possibly as an incentive, Max said to me, 'Grease it on Ted, and I'll shout you an ice cream.' (Greasing it on, is pilot speak for a really smooth, non-bounced landing.) As good fortune would have it, I did grease it on. After taxiing into the Mt Hagen base, I was introduced to Dave Champion, an Australian aviation inspector who had been detailed by Civil Aviation to come and sort MAF out. I soon got to appreciate Dave and believe he was God's man for MAF at that time – and I still do. Why? At first he naturally went along the official line that the aircraft was overloaded, but unlike many officials he was prepared to listen and was open to reason.

Meanwhile in Honiara, Elsie was packing up the things we had taken with us, plus a bit extra I think because she told me later that Wal Job had to sit on the suitcase lid to get the suitcase shut! She also heard that our drums of luggage had just arrived by boat, so they had them re-directed back to PNG. Elsie and the girls took the three previously booked seats and followed the same route I had, though with a commercial airline all the way. Landing at Kieta, they had to pass through customs because they were leaving the Solomon Islands and entering Papua New Guinea. All the suitcases were duly unloaded and Elsie was horrified to see the way the PNG customs people dealt with passengers' personal goods. They would open up a suitcase, tip everything out on the tarmac, scan through it, and leave the poor individual to do the repacking!

Elsie realised she had no Wal to sit on the suitcase lid and didn't know how she could handle things if they did that to her suitcases. As the customs guy came a little closer, Gwen said, 'Mummy I have to go to the toilet *right now!*' So Elsie had no option; she felt awful doing it, but she left eight-year-old Ann in charge of the suitcases as a lone little white kid amongst all the very dark-skinned Papuans. The customs chap came up and asked Ann if these suitcases were hers, and she said, 'Yes.' What made him leave them alone – apart perhaps from Elsie's prayers – I don't know, but when Elsie came back with Gwen, she was very much relieved to see their suitcases being loaded into the aircraft bound for Port Moresby. Elsie and the girls made it to Mt Hagen the day after I did and as she has always done, Elsie immediately started to make our new house into a home where peace is the norm.

Having been in the Solomons for a month was an advantage in two ways. Firstly, Elsie and I got back onto the same page again as far as communication between us went, which was not only helpful to us personally but also necessary in our new roles. The other major advantage of being elsewhere when the crashes in PNG occurred was that while we knew about them and felt for all those involved, we weren't as deeply emotionally involved as those on location. As far as I was concerned, I could get into doing what needed to be done more rapidly, with a less cluttered mind. Again, thank you Lord for that provision!

On 1 October 1976, Dave Champion the CAA inspector took me up for three circuits at Mt Hagen to assess whether I could take up the responsibility of being the MAF-PNG chief pilot. Things went well, even though I was a tad nervous when he reduced the power and asked me to do a glide approach and land on the 'piano keys'. This term refers to the band of white stripes 30 metres in length across the ends of a tarmac runway starting six metres in from the end of the runway. They are similar to a pedestrian crossing and do look like a set of piano keys from the air. Why was I nervous about him setting this as a goal? Because for both my private pilot's licence as well as my commercial pilot's licence I had failed to execute this exercise to the examiner's standards! You see, all during my training I had been so focused on being able to land exactly where I wanted to, I had almost exclusively practised landings using a powered approach, not a glide approach which is perhaps a bit more skilful. Knowing that this would probably be expected of me, I had already asked some friends to pray that I wouldn't stuff up this exercise. In this instance, the Lord was surely with me and I touched down exactly on the piano keys. Praise the Lord! Apparently Dave considered me good enough for the job and approved me for the role of MAF-PNG chief pilot.

From my logbook, I see that in the days following my approval, I was doing a lot of checking of three new pilots into a good many airstrips. This activity wasn't too new to me, as I had previously been approved to do check and training, so I was back into a reasonably familiar role with this. But, along with others, I wanted to know exactly what had been the underlying cause of the crash near Yankisa. Max Meyers had been to the site and had seen the wreckage and noted one rather strange thing. The ignition switches had been turned off. This, to my mind, indicated that the pilot was aware he wouldn't be able to out-climb the ridge and was going to crash and had the alertness of mind to switch the ignition off to reduce the possibility of fire which, from my understanding, didn't happen.

Early in my role as chief pilot, I contacted the CAA crash investigator in Port Moresby to get some professional input, but sadly he was just departing to go on leave and said he wasn't available. Then the replacement fellow considered he was too busy coming to grips with everything new and so he wouldn't come either. So the underlying cause of that crash has never become officially known, although I have my ideas.

As we walked to the aircraft on the morning of 1 October 1976, he reiterated the official line that the reason for the fatal accident was that the aircraft was overloaded. To which I replied, 'I'm sorry Dave, I can't agree, for if the aircraft was actually overloaded, it would have crashed somewhere just beyond the end of the airstrip, or thereabouts, not about half a kilometre away and approximately

200 to 300 feet higher.' He looked at me and said, 'You're right. Are you willing to prove to me that your mini manual figures are correct?' To which I responded, 'Sure, no problem.'

I presume Dave had to get permission from his superiors to even engage in the idea of seeing if our mini manual figures could be proven, because the next time I flew with him was 55 days later on 24 November. That day I had arranged with the Wapenamanda programme to have some top-up goods at Porgera. The Porgera airstrip was at 7,200 feet altitude, with a 10 percent slope, but when the pressure altitude is taken into account it was the equivalent of doing a takeoff at about 1,000 feet higher than the peak of Mt Egmont/Taranaki (to give New Zealanders some perspective). Dave and I flew out to Porgera, to start a day of flying to various airstrips. We did a shuttle across to Paiela, the 'aircraft carrier' airstrip referred to earlier, then one to Oksapmin on the western side of the Strickland gorge and back again to Porgera.

We loaded the C185 up to maximum takeoff weight according to our mini manual, i.e. an all-up weight minus 54 kilograms, and lined up. Poor Dave – he looked over at me from the right-hand seat and said, 'You're sure of this Ted, aren't you?' I replied, 'Sure, no problem,' and roared off down the sloping airstrip, breaking ground about two-thirds of the way down. I think Dave was rather relieved. The load was to go to a CMML (Brethren) mission station at Auwi which is at about 4,500 feet altitude, on a level strip around 687 metres long. (Sadly it doesn't feature in my old mini manual, hence the approximations.) According to the CAA performance charts that we were supposed to be using, you could perhaps carry one person into this airstrip, but not one person and 227 kilograms of cargo! I had to make a right-hand circuit because the strip is aligned alongside a ridge and I must confess it wasn't the prettiest of circuits, but I got lined up well out and came in safely slow and low, touching down about ten metres from the end and, braking quite heavily, pulled up in around three-quarters of the length of the strip. I think Dave's remark was something like, 'I see.'

Before we took off again, Dave said, 'You chaps must get special training for this type of work,' to which I agreed that we certainly did, but added, 'Dave, we are professional pilots going in and out of these strips almost every day, not weekend pilots who aren't very current.' I think it is the only time I have ever used the word 'professional' in relation to our flying, but I believe all MAF pilots were and still are professional, so felt fully justified in using that term on this occasion. Nor am I slating weekend pilots here, but when you are flying every day in quite challenging conditions, your skills are naturally more finely honed than someone who only flies very occasionally.

The parameters for the Australian P-charts reckoned on the aircraft *gliding* in over the approach threshold of the strip at 50 feet above it and when taking off, achieving 50 feet by the far end of the airstrip. They also included a mass of allowances for poor braking, and even irregularities on the skin covering of the wings so as to make sure that anyone would really have to botch it up to have a landing or takeoff accident.

Again, as I have said previously, I believe Dave was God's man for MAF at that time, because when we got back to Mt Hagen, he said to me something like, 'If I can get one of our performance engineers to come up here, would you be prepared to fly for him so we could make some more realistic P-charts for you?' I replied, 'Yes, sure, I'd be glad to,' because I realised that if we could get something that allowed for slopes and better parameters, it would be helpful not only to MAF but to all the other mission operators in PNG who had their own aviation wing, of which there were a few.

There was an understandable delay in getting everything together for the special flying for the new P-charts as it wasn't until 12 July 1977 – 10 months later – that Dave was back with a performance engineer with a video camera and small marker sticks to get all aspects of the takeoffs and landings recorded precisely for the performance charts. This is normally done under controlled conditions by the aircraft maker's test pilot, but this was very much a field trial with yours truly in the hot seat. We did takeoffs and landings at half a dozen representative airstrips in the highlands at maximum loading or at the loading values that our MAF mini manual allowed in all the aircraft types MAF was using at the time. It was a great exercise to be a part of, and I thought back to how the Lord had prepared me for this. I reflected on the short-field practices I had done in my private pilot stage at Ardmore, then on the exacting venison recovery airstrips in South Westland, as well as the 10 years of flying in PNG. Thank you Lord, because it was in his strength and for his workers that this was being done.

I guess you can imagine our praise and delight when the new 15 percent P-charts arrived. After working out what loads we were allowed to take in and out of a variety of airstrips, we found the allowable totals were all around five kilograms of what our mini manuals said! They were colloquially called 15 percent P-charts because they made allowances for takeoff and landing limits for airstrips with slopes up to a 15 percent.

However, making allowances for the slope on the airstrips wasn't the only parameter they had modified. There were another couple of adjustments, possibly because of the video camera evidence. The landing threshold height was reduced from 50 feet down to 20 feet; the takeoff height over the far end was reduced from 50 feet to 30 feet; and the braking factor was modified, as was the 'skin wrinkle' factor. So the performance people had really taken some notice of Dave and the evidence of the test flying that had been done.

This was truly the Lord's doing, and it was marvellous in our eyes! Initially I thought that the new P-charts were just for the mission aviation groups in PNG but in time they became the charts used by all commercial operators using the single-engine aircraft of those types that the flight tests had been carried out on. It gave us all a new confidence in using P-charts that were workable. So once again, I really do believe that God gave us Dave Champion to investigate us and give us this new legitimacy.

So what sort of things did a chief pilot do back in the 1970s? A major aspect of the job was maintaining a good relationship with the Civil Aviation Authority (CAA), which was the licensing and governing aviation body in relation to work done by aircraft. Thankfully, this wasn't a too onerous task, as all our pilots generally did an excellent job, so there weren't too many 'please explains'. There was a lot of checking and training of all pilots in accordance with what the Australian regulations required at the time. This entailed checking new pilots into airstrips; flying over any given route a certain number of times with them; testing pilot skills annually to maintain pilot standards; acting as a safety officer; and at times opening up new airstrips with a first landing.

It was always interesting to see how different personalities coped with the flying in PNG. I had a 'D' category instructor's licence which only enabled me to give type ratings of new aircraft to people who already had a commercial pilot's licence. I was on the lookout for someone more qualified than me who I felt could probably do a better job than I could. We had a young couple arrive and the husband was an Australian 'A' category instructor and so I was interested to see if he could possibly be my successor. He wasn't afraid to speak up at a pilots' meeting when I referred to a 'powered approach' and corrected me by calling it an 'undershoot approach', which would certainly have been correct if you were making a glide approach. However he didn't take to the PNG type of flying very well at all and was doing some navigational things that one wouldn't expect from even a new commercial pilot.

He was obviously a perfectionist and didn't cope well with

the constant route and loading changes which, for some reason, seemed to be a constant part of our programmes. They were posted to Kawito and sadly for all, didn't last there for very long before wanting to head back to Australia. The wife, who was a nurse, felt there was little she could do to contribute, as there were no nursing opportunities. Sadly, some wives don't adapt to doing whatever needs to be done, because of a number of different factors, such as temperament, background or culture. However, we are forever grateful to her because it was while they were at Mt Hagen that she had a ministry amongst our young people and helped some to a living faith in the Lord Jesus.

On one occasion, a pilot returning to Telefomin had what appeared to be an engine problem. He gave a mayday call, which is the highest priority call when you are in a life and death situation. He possibly thought he was, but in fact the aircraft was still operational and the call should have been a 'pan-pan' call (pronounced 'pahn' or 'parn') which is a distress call, but not as high a priority as mayday ('pan' is short for 'possible assistance needed'). I felt I needed to write to him once everything had been sorted and point out the correct distress call he should have used. At the bottom of the letter, I said something like, 'And how are you and your family getting on?' He told me later that he was a little surprised at my pointing out his incorrect use of the mayday call, but the short personal note made him realise I was still human and interested in them as a family, which made all the difference.

As mentioned, opening new airstrips was also a function of the chief pilot. I will always remember two openings for very different reasons. One was a mission airstrip called Nagri which is in the Sepik Basin, not far from the Sepik River. The inspection from the air, landing and measurements went well and although there wasn't the degree of prancing, whooping and jubilation from the locals which I had witnessed in other places, they were extremely thankful that the strip had been okayed so it could be used. In thanks for this, they presented me with a trussed-up live hen, a gift which it would have been most impolite to refuse. I placed it in the cargo pack under the aircraft with its legs tied together. When I got home, the problem was where to give the poor bird some sort of freedom. Ah!- An empty, open-ended 200-litre drum would give it the space to at least walk around in circles and be kept safe overnight. I always thought that chooks cackled when they laid an egg, but this one did it silently because, here in the morning was an egg for us! The drum couldn't be its permanent home so we gave it to one of our cargo handlers. I don't know whether it lived to lay another egg or whether it was the meat for the evening meal, as I didn't ask for any progress report.

The other time was when I opened another new mission airstrip in the area south of the Fly River after a responsible person had looked at it from the ground. After the normal air inspection, I landed and taxied into the parking bay which was full of warriors all dressed up ready for a celebration – or was it for a kill? I should have known better but – wow! – for just a fraction of time, I felt insecure when they all started dancing and whooping, rattling their bows and arrows. And then it happened. One guy's white teeth showed in a big broad smile! Thank you Lord, I have at least one friend here. In fact, they were all most friendly, so appearances and actions can certainly be deceiving!

Yet another time, it was not an airstrip opening officially, but a mercy flight into an airstrip that had not yet been opened or approved. A Baptist missionary couple had trekked from Tekin into the next valley where a new airstrip was almost finished. As this couple hadn't been able to have children of their own, they had adopted one when home on furlough in Australia and they were all there at Bimin. However, during the night, their daughter had a most severe asthma attack, even though Bimin was roughly at the same elevation as her home base of Tekin. They came up on the morning sched asking if it was possible for an aircraft to come in and take the mother and child out to the Baptist mission hospital at Kumbwaretta (45 minutes). To do this flight, I had to call the Civil Aviation Authority and get approval for a medical mercy flight, which they granted. Declaring a flight a mercy flight while airborne meant that you could just about break any flight rule but had to have a really good reason for doing so, with a major 'please explain' paper submission later. Explaining the situation and asking permission first saved the paper war.

After I landed and got out, I saw the father draped over the rear of the fuselage like an exhausted athlete sobbing with relief as help was at hand. Because of the little girl's condition, I flew her and her mother at low level, following the valley systems to get to their destination, and thankfully she came right and was able to go back home to Tekin a short while later. As it ultimately turned out, this airstrip (Bimin) had been built on a massive landslip which was very slowly moving down the valley floor and some years later had to be closed; but another airstrip was built on the side of the same valley.

During this time when I had chief pilot responsibility, the annual conferences were still being held at Amapyak in the Wapenamanda Valley. The Saturday evenings during these conferences were set apart for a talent quest and fun night, and believe me, there was a lot of diverse talent in MAF back then (and probably still is) which only became obvious on those nights. Who could forget one engineer doing a fantastic impersonation of *Fiddler on the Roof*? Or the chief pilot before me, taking the mickey out of me with regards to my checkout on the floatplane in the Kapuna area?

Some items were artistic and had an international theme. I remember one pilot, who used a marker/paint system that was common at the time, showing a design on the back of a tee shirt of a kiwi bird pecking at the back of a kangaroo – much to the amusement of Kiwis and the Aussies alike who graciously took it all in good part.

In one of the rooms at Kapuna there was a poem 'An Ode to the River'. I surprised myself at the way I was able to use that as the basis to make up a similar poem, 'An Ode to Kapuna'. I read (and performed) it one conference night, much to the mirth of those who weren't even in the know about all things at Kapuna. I take no glory from it as it was a once-only effort, and sadly I never kept what I wrote as I'd love to be able to read it again now. However, later that evening, a new pilot who I had been checking out came up to me and said, 'I really didn't think you had it in you to perform like that!' Such was the honesty of some, but I thanked him for his appreciation of it.

I think it was probably at this conference that those in the kitchen really turned things on for us, and part of the dessert was real whipped cream, which I hadn't seen for some time. As cream was a bit of a rarity, I think I must have indulged quite a bit more than my gallbladder figured was good for me, and that night I had the most excruciating pain in my back. I asked Elsie to warm my back in the hope that her body heat would do some good, which it must have, for by the morning, I felt fine and was able to continue with the flying programme without thinking about it again.

After some time though, I started to experience other symptoms which weren't normal for a healthy person, and our MAF doctor (the daughter of the doctor couple who operated Kapuna Hospital) tried to find out what was going on with my health. After a stool test it was obvious that I had giardia; pathology indicated that they had never seen such a heavy infestation. According to the internet, giardia is 'a common illness caused by a parasite that may result in diarrhoea and stomach cramps. The giardia parasite can spread through contaminated water, food and surfaces and from contact with someone who has it. Antibiotics can treat giardia.'

As a part of my treatment, I was taken with Elsie to Goroka Hospital for further tests etc. On the morning Elsie left to go back to Mt Hagen to resume care of our daughters who were being looked after at a Wesleyan boarding school hostel in our absence, I was given a couple of greasy poached eggs. Not knowing then what I do now about fatty substances and gallbladders, I ate them gladly, while not overly relishing the way they had been cooked. Wow, then it came again, the severe aching pain in my back but this time, there was no Elsie to warm my back and help in the recovery. A few days later, I was transferred back to our home in Mt Hagen where an English doctor at the Mt Hagen hospital said to Elsie something like, 'It is probably better you care for him at home, rather than here in hospital.' Elsie took up the offer, and I was glad she did so.

But while this was a good idea, we did strike a problem. My temperature went off the charts and I well remember sitting one morning in a cold bath in an attempt to cool myself down. What was actually happening, though, was that I was warming up the water, that is, until I pulled the drain plug a little and ran more cold water. This was the turning point in bringing my temperature down.

As a result of the greasy eggs, the medics realised that I not only had giardia but also a gallbladder problem. As a result, it was decided I needed a time of rest away from the programme and any responsibilities before moving back to New Zealand for a gallbladder operation. We were indebted to our friends and colleagues at CLTC (Christian Leaders Training College) who made a house available for us. The whole family moved, and our two daughters went to yet another school, this time at Banz with the other children from CLTC. I am amazed at the resilience of children and how our girls managed to cope with all the changes of location and schools that occurred in their young lives, and I thank God for it.

A strong earthquake happened while we were at CLTC. These

were not uncommon in PNG as I have already related, but a few things struck me this time. Our little car was parked on a driveway quite close to the house we were in, and while the quake was happening, the car bounced around as if two heavyweights were having a fight inside. Another remarkable thing was that one of the CLTC staff members had a couple of wooden music speakers attached to the wall high up near the ceiling; one became detached and fell with its corner hitting the floor at such an angle that it punched a hole in the wooden floor, while the speaker box itself was completely undamaged. One of the student houses was shaken off its stumps and the poor occupant thought the rapture had taken place and they had been left behind!

Chapter 25

Returning to New Zealand for an Operation

After that time of recuperation, it was decided that I should move back to New Zealand and have my gallbladder operated on.

At Port Moresby on the way home, we heard that one of our younger pilots had gone missing in the East Sepik. It is a classic example of the pressure passengers can put a pilot under, and re-emphasises the need for pilots of all ages and experience to set definite boundaries between the desire to help and the need to do it safely. The pilot was based at Anguganak where there had been a CMML (Brethren) mission conference and it was time for the people to disperse. Most families were pretty relaxed as to whether they left that afternoon or not, except one, who rearranged the different aircraft schedules so they could get back to their base that afternoon. The young boy of this family had hoped one day to become an MAF pilot. The night before, his mother had sung the hymn: 'Because he (Jesus) lives, I can face tomorrow.' Little did they know that they would be seeing Jesus face to face the next afternoon. The aircraft was later found burnt out, having apparently been in a turn to get out of a heavy rain storm.

The pilot had seen what appeared to be heavy rain clouds in the direction of his destination and had asked Air Radio if there were any aircraft operating in the area. The answer came back from a pilot based at the destination that there was a heavy rain storm out to sea, but he gave no indication of its movement. By the time the

MAF aircraft was loaded and had set off, the storm had apparently moved in over the land and it seemed that our pilot had tried to penetrate it.

This accident also highlights the need to treat all outside input with respect but also follow a logical path when doing search and rescue. Apparently some very well-meaning people in New Zealand said they had seen a vision of the aircraft hitting the top of a ridge or knoll (not unreasonable, given the terrain and the route taken) and I was told that some time was spent searching those sorts of features. However, the aircraft was eventually found in the foothills on the northern side of the Torricelli ranges.

Arriving back home for my gallbladder operation, we were extremely grateful that the Brethren folk made their special mission flat in Mt Eden available to us for the period we were in New Zealand. Like most people who need to get around, we contacted Doug Mawson in Dargaville who had been helping MAF with vehicles for furloughing staff, and asked if he had anything suitable for us to buy. The answer was, 'Yes, do you have a heavy traffic licence?' to which I replied, 'Yes.' He then said that there was a truck in Auckland that he needed to get up to Dargaville, which could be used to come and pick up the car. Coincidence? I don't think so, as God takes care of the little things as well as the big ones.

We were in contact with an ex-PNG mission doctor who had a surgeon friend 'over the back fence' and it was a case of getting my inflammation settled down before the operation could take place at Greenlane Hospital. The surgeon was a lovely, humble chap and after a Sunday morning visit to me to make sure things were going okay, I thanked him for his services, He replied, 'Oh that's okay. I'm just a plumber with clean hands!' Apparently, my gallstone count was 108. A few stones and a whole lot of pebbles! I forget whether it was the surgeon or a lecturer who rang up a few days after I had returned to the flat and asked if he could borrow the jar of stones as an illustration to go with his lecture. Much to his massive disappointment, I had to tell him that I'd thrown them out as I could see no useful purpose in retaining them! It was a pity that he hadn't asked sooner, as I would have gladly given them to him to illustrate how many a person can accumulate. I thank the Lord that I can now eat pretty well everything that we normally have without any ill-effects. Apparently though, it is not necessarily so with many people who have their gallbladders removed. When I was coming home to have mine out, I was often told, 'I'm okay except for XXX' (usually something such as ice cream). I don't have any of those problems, though we have slightly modified our diet. Thank you Elsie!

I had a number of visitors while in hospital, one of whom was the MAF office secretary who gave me a devotional booklet on Psalm 23. The man in the bed next to mine reminded me so much of my dad, and after I had read the devotional and I was up and around a little, I passed it on to him when he was moved to another ward. As a result of this, the man's wife kept in touch, saying that he really treasured it. Sadly, not too much later, he passed away and we attended his funeral at Waikumete Cemetery. I have the feeling that the Holy Spirit used it to bring that person (and who else?) into a new relationship with Jesus. While I was getting healthy enough for the operation, we had attended the Salvation Army in Auckland City and it was a joy to have some folk from there come one Sunday afternoon and sing by my bedside while I was in hospital.

Our daughters attended yet another school at this time and while they seemed to be doing okay, Elsie went to the school after a couple of weeks and talked to their teacher to make sure they had settled in. The teacher was very impressed that Elsie had done this, as it so rarely happened even when Kiwi families moved location. The teacher assured Elsie that they had settled in better than many New Zealand kids who had to move schools. Perhaps the frequent moves in PNG had been of some help? Yes, I think so, but also the care and encouragement of a loving mother was so vital and valuable.

Once I had almost recovered from the operation, I got a call one afternoon from Max Meyers who was then managing the head office in Melbourne, asking how I would feel about returning to PNG as the area manager at Wewak, rather than the position I had left as chief pilot. I said it was not a problem – we'd be happy to fill whatever space was needed. Max told me later that our willingness to do that was a real blessing to him in the overall planning of personnel positions. Unfortunately, after we got back, not all the other staff were as happy with this change as we were because some felt that it was something of a demotion. Thankfully, it never struck me as being that.

As we prepared to return to PNG, we sold the car back to Doug Mawson, the garage owner and car dealer in Dargaville from whom we had bought it, and he put it on his sales lot. It was a measure of the man that when he sold the car for more than he had paid us for it, he gave us the difference!

Chapter 26

To Wewak for the Second Time

Back in Wewak in what had been familiar surroundings 12 years earlier, it was interesting to see the changes that had taken place, but it was soon evident that the work and the flying were very much the same. The houses up on Wewak Hill that we had lived in previously were no longer being used by MAF, and we settled into the two-storey house that had once been occupied by our customs agent when MAF was doing customs clearances for PNG missions. As there were only two bedrooms upstairs and one below, Ann our eldest daughter took up residence in the room downstairs that had been the customs office. She loved the independence of it, and started to develop a love of reading while she was there.

At this stage, both girls started to learn music from one of the MAF teenagers who had access to a keyboard. There was one limitation – the electricity had to be on for a lesson to happen and unfortunately, there was no guarantee that it would be!

In many places in PNG, electricity is supplied by variously-sized diesel engines driving an electric generator. The size of the unit depended on the number of people likely to be connected to its grid. For an average mission station, a single cylinder Lister was sufficient but for a town like Wewak, several large units were used. Like any other engine, they had to be kept in good order with regular maintenance and oil changes so that they were reliable and kept working continuously. As I have said previously, the PNG fellows had learnt a lot, but at times they didn't quite understand the repercussions of certain actions.

One unit at Wewak had a warning siren when the oil was getting low and/or the engine was starting to overheat. This wonderful warning system was built in but had one severe drawback in its design – the siren had an off switch incorporated in its circuit so the siren could be silenced. Yes, you guessed it, the siren started blowing, and the attendant turned it off because he said 'the noise was so annoying', with the result that the engine seized up through lack of oil and all the lights attached to that circuit went out.

While the MAF customs agency for PNG missions had officially been closed down, it didn't mean that there was no customs work for MAF still to do in Wewak, especially for our friends of MAF-US who were operating over the border in West Papua (then Irian Jaya). To facilitate this customs work, MAF-US had bought a small but useful pickup to transport what came in for them from the wharf to the customs office and then to the airport for them to collect when their Aero Commander or other aircraft came over to get what had accumulated for them.

But there were a couple of memorable things about this Toyota Stout pickup. One was that it had been badly affected by the salty environment it had obviously lived in for some time and had noticeable gaps in the cabin floor and the tray. This of course was a problem with all vehicles on the coast at Wewak; not only was it the effect of the salt air but also the coral which was being used as roading metal. When the coral got wet and thrown up under the vehicle or caked on anywhere, there was effectively a wad of salt having a grand old time with the steel.

The other thing about this MAF-US vehicle was the timing on the motor. When coasting down Wewak Hill, which is quite steep, it would backfire very loudly about every 10 seconds. Once, when

Elsie had a fellow MAF wife with her on the tray at the back. She became so embarrassed about the constant loud explosions emanating from the vehicle that she lay down flat on the deck so no-one would know she was on board!

As with all tar-sealed roads, the substructure gave way in places and left potholes. Normally they would get filled with coral or something similar which would splash away with the constant rain that prevailed. But when the then Prince Charles was about to arrive, they filled the potholes with concrete. This solution admirably suited the purpose during his visit, but in a surprisingly short time the road gave way around the edges, leaving concrete 'pillars' in the middle of even larger potholes. As can be imagined, if you hit one of these, it played havoc with the vehicle tyres.

I have always recognised that Elsie is quite quick when it comes to giving on-the-spot answers in different situations, and she is much better at it than I will ever be. She puts some of it down to when she was in training as a Salvation Army Officer, selling *War Cry* magazines in hotels frequented by university students who wanted to take the mickey out of her. She had to use this skill when she was doing the customs clearance work for the folk across the border too. She said that it was absolutely staggering the number of parcels that came through with *totally* incorrect customs declarations on them. As Elsie was the one doing the clearance work, it was she who had to try and appease the Papuan customs officers when what was on the label bore absolutely no resemblance to what was inside the parcel if they opened it! That was one part of this operation that she really didn't like.

There was another job associated with this operation that could be quite frustrating too! When the chaps came over from Irian Jaya with any of their aircraft, *nine* copies of the customs papers had to be typed up for the goods to enter that Indonesian state. (This was before we had computers and printers.) As Elsie was not a typist, this was a pretty stressful exercise! One pilot once said to her, when she was having a bit of difficulty and getting somewhat stressed, 'I hope you had your spiritual devotions this morning, Elsie!'

However, the goods got through, even when one American pilot used (in my opinion) a most unsafe method of loading very small stuff. He had come over with a C185 which has a tail-wheel and quite a large capacity between the back of the cabin and the rear of the aircraft. He took out the rear cabin wall and started tossing small mail items down the back end amongst all the control cables. He obviously got back home, as we didn't hear of any accident, but I am sure glad I didn't have to fly with him! I have no idea what the mail looked like when it eventually arrived there either.

That reminds me of another true story, once again from the MAF-US chaps from over the border, though it could just as easily happen anywhere in the tropics. A C185 had been sitting on the ground for a few days, and all went well until its first flight when the pilot tried to adjust his elevator trim towards nose-down travel because of the loading. It went so far and then started to feel a bit spongy and soft, rather than the firm feel it would have had if it was at the end of its travel. On investigation after landing, they found the reason. While the aircraft was on the ground, a snake had taken up residence and this was the soft, spongy feel, as the snake had got jammed, limiting the travel of the tail plane!

As everyone is aware, certain mosquitoes carry the malarial disease, but others in Australia can also be responsible for spreading Ross River fever, which thankfully I have never had a brush with. However they can also be carriers of the 4 variants of the dengue virus. In earlier times it was called break-bone fever (because you ache all over) and this I did experience during the last couple of years we were at Wewak. Very fortunately for me, we had a copy of a very early book on tropical diseases and it warned of a couple of things which can be a trap for those new to the disease. The most critical time is when you are starting to feel better, because your heart *really* slows down and it can literally be deadly getting up and going again when you feel like doing so. I remember lying on our couch, feeling okay but taking a regular note of my pulse which went down into the 30s. I waited until it became normal again for a day or two before getting up and about again.

Dengue can also make you have a lapse of concentration when you think you have got fully over it, especially when the local doctor (who obviously wasn't fully aware of all its effects) has given you the all clear to fly. A good Aussie mate of mine who'd had dengue had just swapped aircraft but had not been told there was some heavy cargo in the cargo pack under the U206. As the passengers at Liagam fitted easily into the cabin with all their bags, there was no need to look into the pod, and he took off without realising he had the added weight. Soon he knew he needed to return to the airfield because the aircraft felt so heavy. Sadly, he wasn't able to complete the turn successfully and 'mushed' into a kaukau (sweet potato) patch. However, the Lord undertook in that there was no loss of life, though a couple of the passengers did have back injuries. After he had flown a 'mahogany bomber' (desk) for some time and the effects of the dengue were no longer evident, it was my joy when in my chief pilot role to fly with him again and clear him for operations, which he was so glad to get back into. We have gotten to know and respect each other even more since going back to our home countries as we have had a lot to do with each other internationally in our recruitment roles for MAF.

I think this lack of memory and attention to detail shortly after having dengue may have been a factor in the only real accident I had in Papua New Guinea. At the time, I was area manager, base manager, flight programmer, and check and training and line pilot at Wewak. On this particular day, there was a full programme, but it was raining too heavily to get out flying early in the day. I had quite a bit of area and base work that could be done so I got on with that. At about morning tea time, the rain eased off so the load was readied and put on the aircraft. After I had done a portion of the busy programme that had started late because of the rain, I flew from Ambunti to Brugam (15 minutes) about lunchtime.

Perhaps because I thought I was under time pressure, instead of doing an overfly of the strip as I normally would have done to check its condition, I joined on the downwind leg to land. Very late on the approach, I realised I hadn't put out full flap and was going a little faster than I should have. When I touched down on the wet slippery strip, there was no effective braking at all. I slid the whole length of the airstrip. As I approached the end where there was a low hedge, I initiated a ground loop, only to find that 206s aren't nearly as responsive to this manoeuvre as 185s because of the nose-wheel. The result was I got through about 120 degrees before impacting the low hedge, with my starboard wing dipping down just enough to put a slight upward bend in it. So that was the end of my flying that day. I read in a much later report from another MAF pilot who had had an intimate connection with that hole in the said hedge that it was known locally as 'Crawford's gap'. I somehow wish I had been remembered for a much nobler event!

In my opinion, the accident investigations being carried out by an ex-staff member around this time were 'in depth enough'. Obviously, unless the cause of the accident could be proven to be mechanical failure, all accidents are, to some extent the pilot's error and they were invariably classed as such. The reason the pilot made the error never seemed to be investigated; or if it was, it never came out in any report I read. One could ask in my case – was it a memory failure because of dengue fever, or was my workload too heavy? What was the root cause of all this?

Interestingly, in a much later accident, why did a pilot make at least a couple of attempts (over and under the cloud) to try and get into a particular airstrip that was covered in cloud, when there was another airstrip about three minutes away where he could have landed safely? Yes, it could have meant an extra shuttle to get everything to the destination, but what sort of pressure was he under that caused him to persist in trying to get into the destination strip and so have an accident? I was able to read the report for this accident, which of course put the blame on the pilot. However, the background information I read revealed it was a non-operational person who, in my opinion, asked the right questions. Why did he persist in trying to land? What was going on in the mind of this experienced pilot? What sort of pressure was he under? It felt to me that at times the organisation didn't want to take any responsibility for the accidents that occurred. Thankfully, many things have now changed; and there have been fewer accidents in recent years, and we all rejoice in that fact.

As the area manager, I was responsible for approving new equipment for outstations, both for homes and for the base. I well remember one request that I spent some time thinking through. A new young pilot family had just been based at Anguganak and asked for their own deep freezer. There was already a base deep freezer in which frozen goods for outstations were stored and other pilot families had used that without saying anything. Sure, it was a little way away from the house, but for someone like me who hadn't had a personal deep freezer on any of the MAF stations we had been on, it seemed a bit of a big ask. As I pondered it and tried to put myself in their shoes, I soon realised that they had come from a culture and environment vastly different to mine, an era where everyone had a personal freezer at home, so I approved the purchase. When I told this story at one of our later farewell meetings at Mt Hagen, one of the older engineers came and thanked me and said, 'You are right, those of us who have not had these sorts of things for ourselves need to remember the environments these younger staff are coming from.' Thank you Lord for the right prompting!

It wasn't work all the time. On Saturday afternoons we would frequently head down to the beautiful sandy, palm tree-lined beach and have a swim (or wade around, depending on one's ability) and often we would have dinner there. During this time, we had an Australian pilot with us who could make and fly training boomerangs – the sort that come back to you when you know how to throw them correctly – a skill he taught me. He would often bring one down to the beach and throw it out over the group who were in the water. This was perfectly safe, but always caused us to duck down when we heard the 'swoosh, swoosh, swoosh' overhead! After leaving MAF, Gary became a vicar in an Aboriginal community back home in Australia. (Sadly, since originally writing this, Gary has gone to be with the Lord he so effectively served)

It was Gary who had the discernment to put one of our peers right when that person, who had come from flying heavier aircraft, told him: 'Ted has no ambition, he isn't even thinking of going into airlines.' Apparently, Gary's response was: 'If Ted thought that God wanted him pushing a wheelbarrow, Ted would be pushing a wheelbarrow.'

In much the same way that the fun evening at the conferences showed up the vast and varied talent among the MAF staff, it was also true of the different backgrounds we pilots had come from. In the flying field, there was an ex-RAAF jet-jockey, an RNZAF pilot, a former Qantas Boeing 707 first officer (due for captaincy training) through to all kinds of engineers, tradesmen, teachers, former top-dressing and spraying pilots and at least one or two with a farming background. In our last two years in PNG based at Wewak, we had on the base a person whose wit was so dry, it is a wonder it didn't catch alight! He had an electrical engineering background, having worked previously on the Sydney electric train network. Compared to his electrical background and his mathematical skills, I was a babe in the woods. He was to become the Wewak base manager when we finally left to come back to New Zealand permanently.

Not too long before we were to leave, I saw him up on the tank stand of one of our houses wondering how to fix a problem with a downpipe which was bringing water into the tank. I went over and asked if I could help and he showed me the problem. I simply said, 'Have you got a bit of wire?' The wire was produced, and the problem was fixed without too much trouble and then he came out with it, 'What are we going to do, without an old ex-farmer on the base?' The point of this story is that we need people from a variety of backgrounds, all working together in harmony to get the best results.

Towards the end of our time at Wewak, we had the privilege of hosting the widow of the young Anguganak pilot referred to earlier who crashed while trying to deliver a missionary family back to their home at Aitape. She had their young son with her, who at that stage was about three. Elsie, realising things could be quite boring for him, gave him a little job to do each morning. This was to go down to a nearby hibiscus bush and pick flowers to go on our coffee table. A hibiscus flower closes up overnight, so it was a case of refreshing the simple table arrangement each day and he delighted in doing this.

One afternoon, the mum asked Elsie to take her to the place at the western end of Wewak Hill where her husband had been buried in a small cemetery. At her request, Elsie left her there so she could have time for herself, but was somewhat surprised at how quickly she returned, saying, 'I don't know what I was thinking – Jim isn't there. His remains might be, but his spirit is with Jesus.' This statement showed her deep understanding of the difference between body and spirit. Many years later, it was a thrill to hear that her son had taken up flying with MAF. After he married, he and his wife worked in PNG with MAF, but sadly for only a relatively short time.

During those two years at Wewak my (now late) brother and his new wife came to visit. It was great to host them both and to do some things with them that we hadn't done before ourselves. But the fact he hadn't lived in the tropics came out in two ways. Once when he was uptown he bought some chocolate and when he opened it, he found white weevil tracks showing up as wiggly white lines over the back of the bar. When he told us this, I said, 'What did you do with it?' and he answered, 'I biffed it into a waste bin.' Our reaction: 'What? Perfectly good chocolate into a bin?' For us, signs of weevils in food were perfectly normal in the tropics. Another comment was, 'I don't know how you guys keep going in this heat. I am exhausted with doing virtually nothing!' It was great to have them visit and see for themselves the work we were engaged in.

Chapter 27

Home to New Zealand

After a couple of years back in Wewak, both Elsie and I were feeling the effects of having been in the tropics for nearly 15 years. With a scripture to back the decision, we decided it was time to come back to our home country, New Zealand. I say 'our' home country because it certainly wasn't that for our two daughters who were then aged 13 and 12. They had both been born in PNG and considered PNG to be their home, so we saw their need to get to know New Zealand for themselves. For them, New Zealand was the place they went to every three years to see grandparents, family and cousins and go to schools very different from those they were used to. Such is the life of missionary kids or 'MKs'. After we had been back in New Zealand for a while, we did a deputation meeting in Whangarei and Gwen really 'said it like it is' when she took part. She said that it was embarrassing when well-meaning folk came up to them and said something like, 'I hope things are going well for you now that you are back home.' She pointed out that New Zealand wasn't home for them; in fact, at that stage PNG felt more like their home country than New Zealand did!

After the meeting, one sensitive, dear old lady came up to her and thanked her for telling them what it's like for MKs because she said she was one of those 'old dears' who would say that sort of thing to missionary children back on furlough. Actually there is a term for young folk like ours, as well as children of foreign government appointees, until they settle down in their parents' home country. They're called 'third culture kids' or TCKs because at first they don't belong to their parents' culture, nor to the culture where the parents have been working, but have one of their own which is a mix of the two. The feeling of not being completely at one with the parents' culture can hang around for a long time, sometimes for as long as they were immersed in the culture where their parents worked. This concept is borne out by Ann's comments on her 26th birthday, when she said, 'Now that I have been in New Zealand as long as I was in PNG, I suppose I will have to start calling New Zealand home from now on!'

When we left Wewak for the last time in November 1981, it was great to have all the staff based there say goodbye, have hugs all around and sing, 'We are one in the bond of love'. Mt Hagen as the first stop as we headed to Port Moresby on our way back to New Zealand via western New South Wales in Australia.

Jocelyn, whom we had hosted for a time in Wewak with her small son, had invited us to spend Christmas with her on her parents' farm in Tottenham, NSW. It was a sheep and grain property and we really enjoyed our time with them. Having had a background on the land, I was interested in some of the differences to New Zealand farming. Another new experience for me was to be driven in their Ford Fairlane car to the back of a 400 acre 'paddock' to muster sheep, using the car and dogs to move them towards another 'paddock'! And yet another experience in the same car that I will never forget was when we were out as a family together with Jocelyn and her dad, driving over a recently ploughed paddock that hadn't yet been sown down. We saw about three emus a little distance away and her dad told Jocelyn to head for them. I think she had a bit of feeling for the poor car's suspension which must have been having a real work-out, as we were crossing the furrows at right angles and her dad was egging her on – 'Faster, Joc, faster!' The emus outran us and managed to get into some scrubby bush bordering the paddock, after managing to fight their way through the boundary fence.

I have no doubt that apart from wanting to show our girls the emus, Joc and her dad did this to tell the emus that they weren't welcome in a paddock that was soon going to be sown down in wheat. As it was a wheat growing area, there were *massive* storage facilities near town, which we were taken to see. I used to think of wheat being stored in tall cylindrical vertical silos – but not these ones! They were massively big gable-roofed sheds into which the grain was dropped from the apex of the roof.

A short while after arriving back in New Zealand, we again made contact with our Dargaville car sales friend and bought a new Mitsubishi L300 van from him, similar to those that we had used in PNG. Later it was used in a way we had never imagined. While we were initially staying at my brother Rob and his wife Molly's place, we had a welcome and goodbye afternoon at the farm; welcome home for us and goodbye to another pilot family who were going to PNG. MAF-NZ had asked us if we would lead the work here in New Zealand and our reply was that first of all we needed to get to know New Zealand again. I also didn't want to do deputation meetings for quite a while, as I had already been away from home a lot in my chief pilot role, and we wanted to help our daughters get to know New Zealand. They saw the points and appointed Rod and Cherry Peek to the role, who made an excellent job of it, setting up electronic office systems, which I knew nothing about at that time.

It wasn't long before we went to our house in Palmerston North. It had been well cared for as earlier mentioned by one of Elsie's friends, but was in need of a paint and spruce-up. This took me a couple of months. Fortunately, I had good weather for the job and it was a good period of re-orientation into New Zealand for me. During this period, we had the privilege of hosting the Australian folk with whom we had spent Christmas on the way home, and we took them for a drive up to Hawke's Bay. I well remember the old wheat farmer's remark as we crossed a very small stream on the way: 'Oh how I wish we had one of those back on my farm.' I don't think we realise how blessed we are in New Zealand when it comes to the (normally) good weather and conditions we have for our agriculture sector.

A lot of things had changed while we'd been out of the country and it took us both some time to re-establish ourselves in our new home and city. At that stage there wasn't the same re-orientation assistance that there is today for missionaries coming back home. However, I realised that when I had finished painting the house, I would need to find a paying job to keep us all going. Ann was into high school and Gwen was in her last year at Intermediate. While it was yet another massive change for them both, they managed it well. It was interesting to note that both of them chummed up with other girls who had lived away from New Zealand for a period, so they had that in common and could compare experiences.

Initially I thought of a flying job, but it soon became apparent that the only possibilities were flight instructing, or even less likely, becoming a charter pilot. I wasn't all that interested in the former and the latter would have only perpetuated what had been happening in PNG with being away for undetermined lengths of time. However, for a time, those who were doing the MAF flight training in Auckland would send a pilot on a cross-country exercise to Palmerston North, and we would host them overnight and at times I would go up flying with them. On one occasion, when I was with a trainee doing a pre-flight inspection, I pointed out a couple of things and the guy said, 'It's been worth the trip down here to hear what you have just told me,' which was rather nice to hear.

While painting in the summer, I had blithely said I would take on any sort of job when I'd finished. As the autumn weather started to cool down, that thought changed to any sort of inside job! I saw a position for a bookkeeper at the local Guthrie Bowron store and went to apply. Alan Wilson, the manager said, 'Sorry, that has already been taken, but do you know anything about paint? I need a mature chap behind the counter in the shop.' This was one of those times when my bald head worked in my favour! I replied that I had just painted our house and he said, 'Great, you can help us in the store.' Yes, I had just painted the house, and had installed some double glazing as well, but wow, did I have a lot to learn! Alan was a really good and helpful boss, though, and I was as keen to expand my knowledge as he was to give it.

I became a 'counter jumper', which of course also included tinting paint. This was quite easy when you followed a recipe for a specific colour and it wasn't long before I got a reasonable idea of which coloured tints were needed for a particular result. Colour matching (or eye-matching) to a sample was an interesting exercise, especially when dealing with water based paints because they change colour quite significantly as they dry. The darker the colour, the more significant the change.

Before long I was also mixing automotive paint, which again normally followed a recipe but, unlike the water paints, the colour didn't change when it dried. At times one was asked to eye-match to some rather unusual things, such as a pink carnation that one woman brought in. She wanted her original VW Beetle painted that colour! Alan got me doing a full range of things from the paint and wallpaper counter work to tinting both decorative and automotive paint to being the store-man out the back, all of which I really enjoyed.

As we settled into Palmerston North, we linked up with the Salvation Army where we had been members before leaving the country 15 years earlier. In 1983 they were in the process of building a new citadel and I naively volunteered to help with the fundraising.

The net result was that the van we had purchased came into its own as, each month we transported a one-tonne pallet load of all-sort liquorice from the railway to our garage for further distribution. Fortunately, there were some members in the corps (church) who took a carton at a time to sell to their workmates. Seeing the way these people managed to sell them, I asked Alan if I could put a small carton of liquorice on the counter and join the sales team. His reply? 'It costs me $5 a head in advertising to get people to come through that front door, so if you can get them in with a $2 liquorice all-sorts bag, go right ahead,' which I did, selling many cartons of them over the time we were fundraising.

After a few years, one of the travelling representatives for the company left, and Alan offered that position to me. I took it, selling the whole range of products Guthrie Bowron offered. Alan told me the 3Rs of being a good rep – regular, reliable, respectful. A little while later, I was dealing mainly with automotive paint, and while I had made up automotive paint in the shop, it was quite different answering questions out on the road! Initially, there were quite a few times when I didn't know the answer to a question so I would say, 'As soon as I get back to the shop, I'll ask Alan (who was a walking paint encyclopaedia) and let you know the answer.' I made it a rule to do so, and got back to the customer asap. It wasn't long before this really paid off, tripling the previous rep's sales about four months later.

I learnt a couple of things while out on the road. Human nature determined that whenever there was a problem, it was *always* the fault of the paint! Wrong! For example, we sold some paint to a racehorse breeder who used it to paint their wooden fence railings. It wasn't long before the paint was flaking off and of course it was the paint's fault. No, what had happened was that the treated timber for the fence hadn't been left to weather so that the salts involved in the preserving treatment were still on the surface and hadn't weathered or washed off. The paint had stuck to the salts' residue, not the timber, and so when the salts lost their grip, both came off easily.

At that time, Guthrie Bowron owned 28 shops in New Zealand and was expanding. After I had been about two years travelling as a rep, GB took over what had been the Odlins shop in Rangitikei Street and I was offered (and took) the position of managing it. This was quite a new experience for me and utilised all I had learnt in the Church Street shop and on the road. I was fortunate to still have the most gracious and helpful former Odlins manager working with me. The shop was two-storied, with much of one wall of half the top floor taken up with large pigeon holes as it had been Odlins' main wallpaper store at a previous time. It still had quite a lot of older wallpaper rolls there, and I saw the opportunity to use this space to store old rolls for people who just wanted one roll because their fireplace had been taken out, or the cat had used the wall to sharpen its claws, etc. But I had a problem. How was I going to keep a track of what was there easily and efficiently?

At that time computers were new to me and the public generally; I wasn't even aware whether a computer would do the job, so I did some night classes to find out a computer's capability. I needn't have concerned myself, as it wasn't long before I had bought a computer and tabulated all the stock we had. I then used to buy the tail ends of batches from the other stores and made a nice profit on-selling the old rolls back to them or to our own customers.

The other half of the top storey had other uses too, apart from storing quantities of paint. Elsie had teamed up with the Christian Women Communicating Internationally (CWCI) 'Know Your Bible' section and I used to store much of the material used by that organisation in one tiny corner. As well as that, having been on the road selling mini paper rolls to car painters for masking off areas they didn't want overspray to get on, I saw the opportunity of using the local newspaper's tail-end rolls to manufacture our own mini rolls. The tail-end rolls were stored upstairs in the shop before being taken home where they were cut and rolled. This was done in our home garage with equipment I put together and the profit from selling the rolls to GB helped support MAF-NZ.

In late 1987 I was with my area manageress working out the budget for buying patterns and grades of wallpaper for the next year, as wallpaper comes in various grades with a corresponding range of prices. I had suggested that we purchase about the same quantities of the whole price range, but she had seen the changes that were already happening in society and said, 'No, buy a greater quantity of cheaper lines and dearer lines.' The pay gap in society was getting wider, so we were losing the middle-income range of customers. She saw a pattern which sadly has become the norm. When I was in this management role, the company ran a series of courses for all the branch managers, something that was going to be helpful in my next situation. I hadn't realised this at the time, though Elsie had, but thank you again, Lord, for the preparation!

Chapter 28

Into MAF Again

While I was still at the old Odlins branch, the chairman of the MAF council asked if we would again consider taking up the leadership of MAF in New Zealand as its manager. It worked brilliantly with regards to my work situation, as Guthrie Bowron had by this time bought out another paint shop and the old Odlins branch was going to be closed as GB figured that they didn't need three branches in the same city. By that time, both of our daughters had graduated from high school and were in the workforce, so we accepted the challenge. The girls said they never left home; home left them although it wasn't too long before they also migrated to Auckland and found work here.

Thankfully, selling a house in Palmerston North and buying one in Auckland wasn't nearly as difficult as it would be today, but we still had to cash up all we could and take out a mortgage to buy our new house. I have to honour the real estate person who introduced us to this place where we have been living now (2024) for the past 37 years. She could see how wonderful it would be for us, but we had a limit on what we could spend and the seller said he wanted a certain amount out of the sale. I forget just how much the difference was but after consultation with her boss, the agent adjusted her fees so that the purchase became possible. It is the only time I have heard of that happening. Once again, thank you Lord.

The changeover period when following someone else into a position is often not very easy but Rod and Cherry Peek, who had been in the MAF role for the seven years we had been in Palmerston North, made it easy for us. This was not only on a personal level, but also in setting up office systems and equipment which were far more appropriate than I would have done if we had accepted the position earlier. While they had used an office in Manurewa, the MAF hangar at the Ardmore airfield had just been dedicated a few months earlier, so after a couple of months we moved the office there. This meant we had a close relationship with the newly established Flight Training Centre (FTC) which became quite busy with a number of Christian Air New Zealand staff involved as instructors, as well as an engineer. Later, ex-field staff members became instructors as well.

Here I must mention the amazing contribution David and Robyn Brown made through Christian Aviation to the workings of the training programme from an early stage. It was Dave who put forward the concept of having an aircraft that trainees could learn to fly in and build up their hours of experience. After a period of fundraising by all who were interested, he sourced, bought, and flew the C172 from the United States to New Zealand and it was used for many years in the Flight Training Centre. But this was not all. He also covered the maintenance on the aircraft (often assisted by volunteer engineers) in his appropriately licensed hangar facility. Both the aircraft and the 'free' engineering were an enormous contribution to the whole flight centre training programme. Again, thank you Lord, for the Browns' contribution.'

Although the FTC did do initial training, the main focus was to extend the skills and capabilities of those preparing to go to the field, and in later times to train them in basic instrument flying. Some instrument skills were required in Australia for even an Australian visual flight rules (VFR) licence, as were found when converting a New Zealand VFR licence to an Australian one.

In the MAF office, Elsie once again became my fantastic helper as well as two other part-timers. Apart from taking many meetings in churches, etc. I was involved in writing monthly prayer notes; doing the financial bookwork in a double entry system which was new to me; and keeping an eye on the FTC. Both of us were involved in encouraging, developing and following through with enquirers. We had a monthly MAF Associates group where young and old met together for mutual encouragement, prayer and constant updates about field staff. All staff (either going to the field or coming from the field) were encouraged to come to one of these meetings. When they did so before going out to the field, it meant all interested Aucklanders had quite a personal relationship with them, which made praying for them on the field more meaningful.

Having been on the PNG field ourselves with MAF, we realised how important the wife is to any staff member being able to stay on the field and be successful. Sadly, not all wives can adjust to not pursuing their own career while fully supporting their husbands in a different and sometimes trying environment. We know of one pilot and qualified Kiwi engineer who did not leave home because his wife was not prepared to go into an unknown environment. Because of this, Elsie used to hold an annual women's day to introduce wives and girlfriends to the things they would possibly encounter. Some things of course couldn't be fully understood because they didn't have a relevant base line to work from. As one wife wrote back to Elsie after having been in Arnhem Land for a little while: 'I know you said it would be hot, but you didn't say *how* hot.'

In the time we were in the office, MAF-NZ had 28 staff units on the field with MAF Australasia which had work in PNG as well as in Arnhem Land, the Aboriginal reserve in North Australia. It also had an operation in Alice Springs in central Australia where MAF gave technical support and expertise to a number of small tribal Aboriginal airlines, which often had just one light aircraft each. We also had one couple working in Kenya and one in Tanzania with MAF-UK. The council was most supportive of us taking a trip to Australia every second year and PNG every other year to encourage the staff, as well as to keep up with the inevitable changes that were occurring. We really enjoyed doing this and it was good to hear first-hand how folk were getting on and any issues they wanted to talk about. As the New Zealand manager, I also went to Australia for their council and managers' meetings, which helped me keep up with current thinking and new developments.

One afternoon when Elsie was at home, she had a call from a supporter who asked, 'Have you and Ted ever been to the United Kingdom?' Initially, Elsie thought it was a prank, but when it became obvious that it wasn't, the supporter said, 'No, I didn't think you had been, so my wife and I would like to fund a trip for you there, as your education isn't complete until you've been.' They also thought we were working too hard and this was a way to give us a break. After fully coming to grips with this wonderful offer, we asked if we could incorporate a visit to Africa on the way, with the idea of visiting our Kiwi folk there. The supporter said, 'This sounds a bit like work to me, but if you take in a game park as well, then that's fine.' It took us about 15 months to organise a time slot without other commitments, but we enjoyed visiting peers in Perth and then the staff in Africa on our way to the UK.

It was an overnight flight from Perth to Johannesburg and the South African Airways plane was a very early model Boeing 747, which could easily be identified by the range of toiletries available. Not long after leaving Perth, the captain told us we could be in for a bumpy ride as they were going to have to push through several weather fronts on the way. These were evidenced by the aircraft giving a thump and an almighty shudder as we punched through some tall cloud with severe up and downdrafts. Surprisingly, Elsie seemed less concerned about all this than I was. I wasn't so worried about the movement, but I did keep in mind the age of the aircraft and the number of times it must have experienced this sort of weather. Possibly also fresh in my mind was the tale Ann had told us about when she was flying from China to Mongolia during a short mission trip she had recently done there. She said, 'Dad you wouldn't have liked to see what I saw when doing that trip. Some obviously loose rivets on the top of the wing were twisting around!' No, Ann, you are quite correct, I would *not* have liked seeing that!

The reason for going via Africa was to visit two New Zealand staff families – the Highams in Dodoma, Tanzania, and the Hardings in Nairobi, Kenya. We flew from Jo-burg to Nairobi and were met with enthusiasm by the Hardings. While we were in Africa, two vehicles needed to be transferred from Dodoma to Nairobi and Bill Harding had kindly arranged for us to take part in that transfer. We flew by MAF from Nairobi to Dodoma in a C402 and struck a little turbulence on the way.

Someone had begun pouring a cup of tea out of a Thermos just when the turbulence started and was trying to do it by following the movement of the aircraft up and down with both the cup and Thermos. The pilot noticed this, and called out, 'Put the cup on the floor,' which they did, and that wonderfully solved the problem! After landing at Dodoma which was the administration centre for Tanzania and clearing customs there, we visited the Highams as well as a future MAF New Zealand manager before driving one of the vehicles to Morogoro the next day in convoy with Bill.

We spent a day visiting the game park there and it was an amazing experience. It was just after a wet period and the grass was quite tall, so we didn't see many smaller animals except warthogs, but the bigger ones were out and about and it was great to see them in their natural habitat. While driving from there up to the Kenyan border, we saw what I would estimate to be thousands of hectares of what seemed like good land suitable for any type of farming just growing rank grass. Because of my background, I thought of all that potential apparently going to waste. We also saw hundreds of hectares of what appeared to be neglected sisal plantations, apparently of little worth as a result of the synthetic materials now being used for making rope and the other things which sisal had been used for formerly.

One thing that did remind us of driving in PNG was the way all sorts of things were being sold on the roadside, though in Africa the sellers were a lot more aggressive (or foolish), moving well out onto the road and holding up their wares. We did stop at one wayside place and saw the remarkable articles the local people had made out of empty five-litre cooking oil cans. I bought an unmistakable replica of a Land Rover wagon, which sadly didn't survive the rigours of some baggage handlers on the way home, even though it was well packed.

We learnt something else while driving from Morogoro to Arusha in the north of Tanzania. We were cruising along quite nicely and I noticed that Bill had pulled off to the side of the road a way up front, but didn't know why. Then a police car came barrelling down the road on our side! As I wasn't in the mood for playing chicken I pulled off to the side, and then a second Land Cruiser sped past with Tanzanian flags flying. Bill told us later that apparently a previous Tanzanian president was killed in a car crash so the current one wanted the whole road to himself when he travelled!

I hadn't experienced crossing an international land border in a vehicle before and was interested to see that there were about 50 metres of no man's land between the customs stations for exiting Tanzania and entering Kenya at one particular border point. Bill took the number plates off the vehicles at the Tanzanian border to hand them in, but Kenya wasn't able to issue new plates on their side of the border, so there were our two lone vehicles, not registered anywhere. We all had to pile into a taxi-van to be taken on to

Nairobi. While waiting in this vehicle at the border, we had to close our windows even though it was stinking hot because some very aggressive locals were so sure we needed some of the things they were selling that they were poking them through the open window into our faces!

The environment that MAF and mission staff work in and how it can affect family members became very apparent one morning. We were being driven out to the airport to the hangar that Bill had arranged to be built while he was there, which incorporates some very worthwhile and innovative ideas. As we travelled that morning, there lying off to the side of the road was a person with dark curly hair who appeared to have been hit by a car, with a few people standing around him. One of the Harding boys said, 'That isn't my daddy, because he has curly hair.' Serving the Lord has its costs for the whole family, not just those the Lord has called to do his work. Thankfully the joys outweigh the costs.

When we reached the United Kingdom we had a wonderful time with the MAF-UK people in Folkestone and were enlightened by the response to one of Elsie's words of encouragement. She had said something like, 'It is wonderful seeing how well you are all working together,' meaning for the good of MAF. However the response indicated that the remark had been taken to mean the workers were gelling well together. Even in a Christian organisation, people don't always see things the same way!

We also went on a couple of tours, one up to Glasgow in Scotland, the country from which my ancestors came. The local chap who was explaining things to us all as we went around the city said, 'Don't say that it is me who has an accent, because I am a local and you are not!' The other tour was over into Cornwall where Elsie's mother came from to New Zealand at age three. There were a number of things that impressed us both about the UK, and one was that it didn't matter where you went, you were immersed in history.

Whether it was the chapel in Edinburgh Castle, built around the 11th century, or in Tintagel, Cornwall, where one part of the village church was built in the 5th century, history was just everywhere. I noticed that even the paving stones into one cathedral were worn into shallow hollows because of the number of people who had walked over them.

What really amazed me was the size of the cathedral buildings, considering they were built without all the modern equipment we have now. Take the Salisbury Cathedral for instance. Building started in 1220 AD and it was opened just 38 years later. Its 400-foot tall spire is the tallest in the UK, and was so tall that it was used by pilots in WW2 to home in on for an airfield close by. It has a congregational seating area alone of almost 3000 square feet. Bath Cathedral has windows all around up high making the building much lighter than most Cathedrals, with an organ playing until a midday prayer session which all visitors were invited to be a part of. All visitors receive a leaflet with a brief history of the building, and it included one of the clearest explanations of the way of salvation through Jesus Christ I had ever read. As seemed to be the custom in a number of these cathedrals, there were some crypts in the back of this church. One, in which a British commander in the Spanish War was laid, had on it an inscription that revealed his sincere Christian faith. I remember thinking, 'Wow, I wouldn't mind if people thought that well of me and my faith when I pass on!'

With the airfare scheme we were on, we were able to do a side trip to Switzerland before we headed back to New Zealand. There had been a Swiss chap by the name of Christian Josi who had initially come to New Zealand to improve his English, but when he heard how comparatively cheap it was to fly in New Zealand, he decided to finish off his flying lessons at the MAF-NZ Flight Training Centre at Ardmore. When returning to his homeland, he had said, 'If you are ever in Switzerland, I would love you to come and stay with us,' so this was our opportunity to take him up on his offer. While we couldn't communicate with his mother because of the language difference, Elsie seemed to be able to have a good conversation with her through basic signing.

While we were with them, Christian drove us up into the Alps to a fellow Salvation Army member who was making cheese. It was so high up that the vehicles down in the valley below looked like miniature toys! There were a number of things about his farming operations that were so different to New Zealand! He had nine cows in his herd, five of which were leased, and they produced enough milk for his cheese making. (He also worked in a timber mill down in the valley below.) As the breed of animals had large white patches on them, they were often brought into their stalls during the heat of the day so they didn't get sunburnt. Like most alpine houses, the cattle stalls were on one storey of the house. They often seemed to have a dung heap immediately outside that neither smelt nor attracted flies. I couldn't figure out why that was, unless it was the cooler temperature or the altitude.

We were there in summer, but of course this area was well covered with snow in winter and because there was higher country behind the house from which an avalanche could come, the farmer had built a wedge-like mound on that side, shaped in such a way as to split and divert the avalanche away from the building. He had also built a simple and novel way of getting his hay for the cows down to the stall floor which was below the living area. Once cut and dried, the hay was dropped down a chimney-like chute which took it directly to its destination. This was made possible because of the previously mentioned avalanche mound, which made the top of the chimney chute effectively about ground level.

The type of cheese he was making required him to maintain the milk at 35.5 degrees C, and to do this, he had the milk in a metal container, rather like the 'copper' our parents (or grandparents) used to boil clothes in. It was suspended over an open fire, and he constantly stirred it and took the temperature of the milk. To decrease or increase the milk temperature, the copper container was hung from a swinging arm which allowed him to move it all over or away from the open fire. His store of cheeses was quite extensive. Christian's family, who we were staying with, used cheese in almost every meal. The texture of some of it was so hard and potent and it could be sliced so thin that you could almost see through it, but it was still unmistakably the taste of cheese. To cut it so very thin, they used what looked like an upside-down cabinet-maker's hand plane; you slid the cheese over it, taking a shaving of cheese at a time.

He also took us to see the massive Grande Dixence Dam which, at 285 metres high and almost 700 metres long, is the tallest gravity dam in the world, storing water for hydroelectricity production. One very sad feature of this dam was that during its construction, which was done with a continuous pour method, someone fell into the concrete. The pouring of the concrete didn't stop and so he went literally into a concrete grave. The dam was projected to produce sufficient electricity to be able to export some to France, as well as supply electricity to homes and industries in a wide area. The other lasting memory I have of that area was a line of poplar trees on the side of the road, which Christian said Napoleon had planted. God's trees obviously outlasted him!

On route home from this wonderful experience in Switzerland, we came through Amsterdam and Singapore and noted something at each airport that is vastly different from what we have in Auckland's International terminal. At Amsterdam, the public notice announcements to people were very clear and extremely easy to hear, despite the accent. I tried to figure out why this was and concluded that there were two things that I believe made the difference – the ceilings in the departure lounges were much lower and the audio speakers were spaced at around four-metre intervals. These two factors meant that the volume didn't need to be high and so the announcement was clear because it wasn't echoing around the much higher ceilings from fewer speakers like it does at Auckland.

The overnight flight to Singapore was with KLM, an airline that I understood had a very good record. We might just have caught it on a bad day! When the lights were turned off to encourage people to go to sleep, mine stayed on. I asked about it and the hostess said, 'So sorry, it has been noted but not fixed yet.' Okay, I thought, I will look at some entertainment until I get tired enough to go to sleep. Wrong! That didn't work as it should have either as I couldn't get anything up on the screen. I eventually succumbed to one of those black eye-covers supplied by KLM and thankfully had a reasonable sleep.

Arriving at Singapore Airport I was amazed at the enormous size of the arrivals hall. There was no queuing to get through Immigration formalities; in fact it was a case of which desk will I go to? And that was with at least one jumbo-jet load of passengers having just arrived. Singapore itself is an impressive city with orchids (their national flower) everywhere, and we enjoyed some of the highlights of that place hosted by a friend of Elsie's who had been at Bible Training Institute (now Laidlaw College) when Elsie was leading a prayer group there.

It had been a wonderful trip and we'd seen many new things, but it was great to arrive back home again and get into the office routine once more. Field staff often asked for a vehicle to use while they were home on furlough for, as you are well aware, public transport doesn't always go exactly where you want to go. Initially we loaned them one of our private vehicles but that soon wasn't enough, so I asked the council if we could buy a vehicle for staff to use while on furlough. The council readily approved the purchase of a station wagon and so a diesel Toyota Caldina was bought. When staff on furlough weren't using it, it was taken on long distance deputation trips, like going south to the Wanaka Air Show.

However, this was one time when the law of averages my dad used to speak about didn't seem to work out. We had 28 units (which included both singles and families) on the field at the time on two-yearly contracts, but the car sat in the hangar every second year, so its use was extended to other missions' staff, which was very much appreciated by them.

Towards the end of our time in the office, both the faithful Cessna 172 and the hangar were sold. There were good reasons for these sales. The C172 had been repainted a couple of times previously and on one occasion had been subcontracted to another company who used a system of paint stripping that left a lot of plastic sand-like residue in the wings. This had been managed for some time, though it did add to the empty weight of the plane. On the last repaint, a very effective but corrosive paint stripper had been used and some had got between the lap joints so that many parts needed attention. On top of this, because of the need mentioned earlier to give trainee candidates some realistic experience in instrument flying, it was going to cost almost as much to upgrade and repair the aircraft to the full, modern instrument standard as to purchase another suitable one to carry all this out, so the council decided to sell it.

The sale of the hangar was also for a good reason. On my way to work one morning, I noticed that all the internal fences on a farm at the top of Keri Hill near Ardmore had been pulled down. I went to the local council and found that the area had been rezoned for lifestyle blocks. This was not necessarily a bad thing in itself, but it was right underneath the downwind leg of the southwest duty runway and I figured that it wouldn't be long before a number of restrictions would be placed on the airport's operations. This has turned out to be true, but to be honest, the restrictions haven't been as severe as I thought they would be – at least not yet! Previously, when the airport area was governed by the Manukau District Council, they had a defined zone around the airfield in which they wouldn't allow any residential buildings to be built. Sadly, when the area came under the governance of the Papakura District Council (before the Greater Auckland Council), they gave permission for a dwelling to be built right across the road off the end of one of the runways!

It was about this time that the New Zealand Qualifications Authority (NZQA) came into vogue, which would mean a rather expensive change for the Flight Training Centre. To continue to do the type of training that was most important for us would have meant employing a highly qualified full-time instructor and doing a lot more general flying training to keep the person occupied, let alone pay them. As a result of these new regulations, two of the biggest aero clubs on the Ardmore airfield needed to combine to remain viable, and this supported the decision to close the MAF Flight Training Centre.

Together with all of the above, the airport was sold by the Government's Landcorp to a private group, with the result that landing fee charges rose dramatically, as had the rental for the land the hangar was on, so it was decided it would be best to sell the hangar too.

The money from both of these sales was wisely invested and played a part in the purchase of what has become the Kendon-Strong MAF Centre at Tauranga Airport. As that land is owned by the Tauranga City Council, there should be much greater security of tenure, and with an ex-field Cessna U206 available for trainees to fly, the new situation will be even better than before.

Chapter 29

Retirement

As I had been managing everything relating to the previously mentioned furlough car when the time came for me to retire from MAF, I asked the council if they wanted to be responsible for operating it, as I thought it was something I could do in retirement to benefit others in much the same way as we had been blessed when on furlough. The council was very happy to sell me that car and so it became the first car of my new venture, Tedz-Cars. Initially, we prioritised MAF staff on furlough but as we bought more vehicles and I got the necessary transport services licence, we widened the ministry to any Christian worker or supporter of mission staff.

I had been aware for a number of years prior to retirement that I had angina. I had medication for it but I had also learned to manage it. Just before I was to move out of the office, our doctor realised that I had been on the same dose of medication for quite a long time, so on the first day of my official retirement, I was on a treadmill with ECG monitors attached. I thought I was going quite well until the nurse told me to lie down, and I was surprised that the angina feeling came on when it did. Usually, it came on when I was doing the activity.

The result of this was that I had an appointment on Friday 22 June 2001 at Greenlane Hospital for a technician to put a dye into an artery in my groin and see the results on a monitor. Part-way through, he said, 'Well, that will mean an operation.' I went back to a ward and after a time asked when I could go home. The answer surprised me. 'Knowing what we know, it would be irresponsible for us to let you out of hospital. You will be top of the list for surgery on Monday morning.'

On the Monday morning I had a four-way bypass operation, and I must admit that in one photo Elsie took of me when I got home from hospital, I looked extremely gaunt. During this recovery period, I spotted a car yard having a major sale of diesel vehicles. I couldn't go, but the garage chap who was doing our maintenance at the time offered to go with Elsie and check them out. After briefing her with his backing, expertise and information, he left Elsie to do the negotiations. The result was that we added a van, a station wagon, and a small four-door car to the fleet all at once.

We concentrated on diesel vehicles to start with because, at that time, the price difference between petrol and diesel made it worthwhile, even with the addition of the road user charges. In fact, on a deputation trip in the original MAF car, we went from Auckland to the outskirts of Wellington on one tankful. The price of diesel back then was such that a normal tankful from near empty was less than NZ$20. Later decisions by the oil companies meant that, overnight, the cost of diesel stayed the same while petrol prices fell, so the diesel advantage was lost. We gradually switched to petrol vehicles, including one hybrid.

At the peak, we had eight vehicles but with the closure of borders in 2020 due to Covid-19 we sold a number off. We were thrilled that four of the Tedz-cars we had been operating went to mission staff who were coming home permanently at that time, so it worked out brilliantly for both parties. I am sure that the Lord was in that process, for a number were bought sight unseen! At the time of writing this (October 2024), due to ill health we have closed down the ministry.

Both of our daughters have been involved in short-term mission outreaches, but in different areas of the world, in different capacities.

After she left High School, Ann qualified as a hairdresser, topping NZ in the hairdressing theory exam for that year. Later, she did a discipleship training course while in the YWAM (Youth With A Mission) ship 'Island Mercy', and then another short term mission to Mongolia, which was quite an experience.

Ann then took up floristry and headed off on her OE to the UK, incorporating a European tour. While in London, she joined a short term mission to China, through her church, which was a very brave outreach.

Returning to NZ, she gained her professional floristry certificate and after working for others she managed her own florist shop for fifteen years, qualifying as an Interflora shop. This was a time when Ann enjoyed entering floral competitions and she won Gold at the Ellerslie International flower show.

She is now again working for others as a senior florist, and enjoying her church and small group.

After her school graduation, Gwen spent some time in office work and trained as a travel consultant working initially in Palmerston North (as they both did). After a while she moved to Auckland where she continued for a time in that industry before moving to World Vision. While there, she took a correspondence course in accounting which has been helpful in a number of positions. She heard of the need for a touch typist to work for a mission in Tari, in the Southern Highlands of PNG to type up material in various local languages for the mission's print shop.

It naturally took a few months to get everything together and complete the mission's orientation course, only to find when she arrived at Tari that the print press manager had left due to ill health. As she was no longer needed in the original capacity, she became the field leader's personal assistant. The previous one had just retired after twenty years, so Gwen was moved to that role. This was a very steep learning curve for her. In addition, she was expected to learn the PNG trade language, Tok Pisin alternatively called Melanesian Pidgin. However it wasn't long before her previous travel agent skills became a real asset and was appreciated by all. They were especially helpful when arranging travel for folk going on furlough etc. as she was able to tap in directly to the various airline booking sites. Sadly, because of some unrealistic expectations, after a year she came back to New Zealand due to ill health. When she was almost fully recovered, she worked with Elsie and myself in the MAF-NZ office and kept it going with the part timers while we were away in Africa and Europe. Gwen has worked in several finance roles and is now working in Tauranga for one of New Zealand's biggest finance, investment and share-broking firms.

I trust that you have recognised throughout all these experiences that Jesus our Saviour has been with us by his Holy Spirit, helping, guiding, strengthening and encouraging both Elsie, me, and our daughters.

I freely acknowledge the amazing support that Elsie my wife has been in all circumstances, and in more recent years, that of Ann and Gwen as well.

To God be the glory for everything he has done for and through each one of us!

Glossary

Abbreviations
ABMS: Australian Baptist Missionary Society
ANZAC: Australia and New Zealand Army Corps
ANZ: Air New Zealand
AOG: Assemblies of God
APCM: Asia Pacific Christian Mission
BCNZ: Bible College of NZ
BOAC: British Overseas Airways Corporation
BTI: Bible Training Institute
CAA: Civil Aviation Authority
CLTC: Christian Leaders Training College
CMML: Christian Missions in Many Lands (Brethren)
CPL: Commercial Pilot's Licence
CRMF: Christian Radio Missionary Fellowship (now merged with MAF as MAF Technologies)
CWCI: Christian Women Communicating Internationally
DOC: Department of Conservation
DRC: Democratic Republic of Congo
ECP: Evangelical Church of Papua
ELT: Emergency Locater Transmitter
EPS: Emergency Precautions Scheme
ETA: Estimated Time of Arrival
FTC: Flight Training Centre at Ardmore
G-force: A measure of acceleration. 1G is the acceleration we feel due to the force of gravity that keeps us on the ground.

GB: Guthrie Bowron, paint and wallpaper specialists
GPS: Global Positioning System
HF: High Frequency
LMS: London Missionary Society
MAF: Mission Aviation Fellowship
MAF-A: MAF Associates group.
MAYF: Mission Aviation Youth Fellowship
MIA: Misima Island and United Church mission
MK: Missionary Kid (i.e. a child of missionary parents)
NAC: National Airways Corporation which has become Air New Zealand Domestic
NT: New Testament
NZQA: New Zealand Qualifications Authority
OE: Overseas Experience
OSH: Occupational Safety and Health
PIC: Pilot In Command
PNG: Papua New Guinea
POW: Prisoner of War
RAAF: Royal Australian Air Force
SAR: Search And Rescue
SIL: Summer Institute of Linguistics
SPANZ: South Pacific Airlines New Zealand
SSA: Southern Scenic Air Services
SSEM: South Seas Evangelical Mission
SU: Scripture Union
TCK: Third Culture Kid (can apply equally to any child who has spent time in a country with their Parents
TEAL: Tasman Empire Airways Limited – now Air NZ International
UFM: Unevangelised Fields Mission
UK: United Kingdom
VFR: Visual Flight Rules

VHF: Very High Frequency (radio)
WW1: World War One (1914-1918)
WW2: World War 2 (1939-1945)
YFC: Youth for Christ
YWAM: Youth With A Mission

Airstrip codes
APE: Aitape, a Roman Catholic mission airstrip
AGK: Anguganak, a Brethren (CMML) mission headquarters strip
AMI: Ambunti, a government airstrip
ANA: Amanab, founded by the CMML mission, but became a government strip
ARF: Arufe, an APCM mission strip
AWB: Awaba, another APCM strip serving their high school
BLI: Balimo, a government station airstrip
BRG: Brugam mission, a South Seas Evangelical Church mission strip
BSV: Bosavi mission airstrip
DARU: Daru Island, point of entry government airstrip
DBP: Debepari mission airstrip
ERV: Erave, a government airstrip
FUG: Fugwa, a Wesleyan mission strip and station
GRN: Green River, a government airstrip
KOM: Kompiam, a government airstrip
KWT: Kawito airstrip and base
LMI: Lumi, a government airstrip
LPA: A Baptist Mission airstrip
MIA: Misima Island, a private/government airstrip, and United Church mission
MGU: Mougulu mission airstrip
MH: Mt Hagen airfield and base
MUN: Munduku, a government/Swiss mission airstrip

NDR: Nomad River, a government station and airstrip
PGA: Pangoa on Lake Murray, an APCM mission strip
PY: Port Moresby, the main overseas airport near the capital of the same name
RMG: Rumginae mission airstrip and hospital location
TLF: Telefomin, a government, ex-wartime airfield close to the West Papua border
TSU: Tsumba, a Church of Christ Mission strip
WAA: Wasua airstrip and base
WDA: A government, Enga HQ tar-sealed airfield

Light aircraft types
Auster J5F: A 4-seat tail-wheel type, made from steel tube covered with fabric
Beechcraft Baron: A 6-seat light twin (260hp each) with retractable wheels which made it quite fast
Cessna C172: A 4-seat nose-wheel general light passenger and training all-metal aircraft
Cessna C180: A relatively high performance tail-wheel type with an all-metal airframe (235hp)
Cessna C185 'Skywagon': A 6-seat tail-wheel medium performance all-metal utility aircraft (260hp)
Cessna A185: Same as above, but with a 300hp engine which markedly increased the performance
Cessna C205: A 6-seat nose-wheel general light passenger all-metal aircraft
Cessna U206: A 6-seat nose-wheel general light passenger all-metal aircraft configured more for cargo
Cessna TU206: Same as above, with firstly a 285hp engine, but later a 310hp engine which made a real difference
Cessna C336: A 6-seat nose-wheel general light passenger all-metal twin aircraft (fore and aft engines)

Glossary

De Havilland DH89: A 1930 9-seat tail-wheel biplane short-haul mini airliner made from plywood and fabric

Miles Gemini M.65: A light, 4-seat tail-wheel twin aircraft, powered by two Tiger Moth engines

Mooney Super 21: A 4-seat tricycle nose-wheel aircraft with retractable wheels giving it extra high performance

Piper Cub: A 2-seat (fore and aft) tail-wheel type trainer, made from steel tube covered with fabric (65hp)

Piper Cherokee PA28: A 4-seat nose-wheel general light passenger all-metal aircraft

Piper PA 23 Apache: A 4- to 6-seat light twin nose-wheel general light passenger all-metal aircraft

Comments

The following unsolicited comments were sent to the author from former colleagues during the writing of this book:

Were it not for Ted our time in PNG would have been short lived. Another check pilot pretty well had me convinced that I would never make the grade as a PNG pilot. I was wondering if there had been a terrible mistake somewhere.

Then Ted took me on and helped me to get up to standard. I remember Ted checking me into the Wewak area strips and introducing me to all the missionaries and church workers.

Things improved dramatically, leading to six years service in PNG plus relief flying in later years, time in Arnhem Land and a six year stint in Alice Springs as well as relief flying back in PNG, not to mention a booking system and a stint in Cairns. We never regretted any of it.

You were indeed a hard act to follow in Wewak! We shan't forget your farewell. Hardly a dry eye.

My wife and I would be just two, amongst the many that have been blessed by knowing you both and working with you.

Ted, I would be remiss not to take this opportunity to acknowledge your friendship and operational leadership when I was in PNG. I had the absolute privilege of working beside four heroes during my time in PNG as a youngish pilot, and you were one of those heroes.

However it was your peaceful strength underpinned by Godly wisdom that I remember most.

It often kept me going when things got hard, especially so after being involved with the accident when I was a passenger. I was very much the better from your advice, Godly friendship and operational experience. Thanks is not sufficient, but thanks none the less.

For more copies or to contact Ted,
email tedz-cars@maxnet.co.nz

www.ingramcontent.com/pod-product-compliance
Lightning Source LLC
Chambersburg PA
CBHW051416290426
44109CB00016B/1323